HIGH ALBANIA

Edith Durham was born in London in 1863, the daughter of a distinguished surgeon. She began her career as as artist and illustrator. In 1900 after illness and depression she sailed to Montenegro, and so began her lifelong involvement with the Balkan states: her imagination was at once captured by the peoples and cultures of the region, and by the political upheavals which accompanied the last years of the Ottoman Empire. Further travels in the region led to her first book, *Through The Lands of the Serb*, in 1904, while *The Burden of the Balkans* (1905) describes Durham's relief work in a strife-torn Macedonia, and her first journey through Albania, a country which increasingly came to dominate her interests and sympathies. *High Albania* (1909) describes a demanding and unprecedented journey through the proud and independent tribes of the North Albanian mountains.

In the years of rebellion and war after 1911, Durham's energy in organising relief work won her the lasting love of the Albanian people, and the unofficial title of 'Queen of the Mountain People'. She describes the tumult of the times in *The Struggle for Scutari* (1914).

After the First World War, Durham's travels were restricted by poor health, but she continued to publish extensively on ethnology and politics, and was to the end of her life a tireless polemicist in the cause of Albania. She was active in the work of the Royal Anthropological Institute, and her final book, *Some Tribal Origins, Laws and Customs of the Balkans* (1928) is an authoritative work on the ethnography of Montenegro and North Albania. She died in 1944.

HIGH ALBANIA

Edith Durham

With an Introduction by
John Hodgson

"Oh, we're back to the Balkans again,
Back to the joy and the pain –
What if it burns or it blows or it snows?
We're back to the Balkans again.
Back, where to-morrow the quick may be dead,
With a hole in his heart or a ball in his head –
Back, where the passions are rapid and red –
Oh, we're back to the Balkans again!"

SONG OF THE BALKAN PENINSULA

PHOENIX
PRESS

5 UPPER SAINT MARTIN'S LANE
LONDON
WC2H 9EA

DEDICATED TO
MY SISTER NELLIE

A PHOENIX PRESS PAPERBACK

First published in Great Britain
by Edward Arnold in 1909
This paperback edition published in 2000
by Phoenix Press,
a division of The Orion Publishing Group Ltd,
Orion House, 5 Upper St Martin's Lane,
London WC2H 9EA

Copyright © 1984 Dr. J. C. D. Hickson
Introduction copyright © John Hodgson 1985
Map by John Flower

A CIP catalogue record for this book
is available from the British Library.

Printed and bound in Great Britain by
Clays Ltd, St Ives plc

ISBN 1 84212 207 X

CONTENTS

LIST OF ILLUSTRATIONS

LIST OF ILLUSTRATIONS

INTRODUCTION

MARY EDITH DURHAM stole out of the northern Albanian town of Scutari at five o'clock one morning in May 1908. At that hour the Turkish governor would still be asleep, and his verdict on the expedition, if asked for, might have put paid to the whole trip. Every sober counsel would have warned against it. There was little reliable information about the Albanian highlanders; the mountain tribes had maintained their separate identity for centuries, sullen in their opposition to a Turkish government that had never won more than nominal suzerainty over their wild expanses of inhospitable rock. They were fiercely attached to their own customs and laws, handed down over the centuries in the unwritten 'Canon of Lek Dukagjin'. Their blood feuds were notorious.

The courage of the mountain tribes had preserved their independence and traditional way of life, but their suspicion of alien influences had discouraged every kind of contact with the outside world. Earlier visitors had been few and timid. In 1907 'An Observer in the Near East' had travelled up-country, protected by a large armed escort. Edith Durham took with her one horse-boy and a guide – the inexhaustibly loyal Marko Shantoya, Scutari Albanian, German-speaking, sixty years old and rather stout. For, she announced, 'the Albanian is an old friend of mine.' The journeys described in *High Albania* – there are three major excursions from Scutari – were the culmination of seven years of regular Balkan travel, and Durham's experience of the mountains in 1908 was to serve her well in her famine and war relief work of the years following, when the local cult sprang up of 'Kraljica e Maltsorëvet' – 'The Queen of the Highlanders'.

As with many other women travellers of the time, Edith Durham's journeys began suddenly, relatively late in life, and in response to a crisis in her personal circumstances. She was born in Hanover Square, London, in 1863. The Durhams were a family with a distinguished tradition in medicine. Edith was the eldest of eight brothers and sisters, almost all of whom rose to eminence in their chosen professions. Her first ambitions were as an artist; she was educated at Bedford College (before its days as a university college) and at the Royal Academy of Arts, where her two exhibitions were moderately successful. But by the late 1890s Durham found herself the constant attendant of her invalid mother and in enfeebled health herself: 'The future stretched before me in endless years of grey monotony, and escape seemed hopeless.' Her doctor wisely prescribed for the spirit, and insisted that she take two months holiday each year: 'Get right away, no matter where, so long as the change is complete.'

In April 1900 Durham boarded a boat of the Austrian Lloyd company at Trieste and sailed down the Dalmation coast. Her diary entries lengthened each day, recording her growing enchantment with the peacock-blue sea and 'The Islands of the Blessed' with their polyglot, gorgeously embroidered population.

Her voyage ended at Cattaro, where she hired a horse and climbed high above the port to gain her first sight of the tiny, land-locked princedom of Montenegro – 'one vast desolation of impassable rock, crag over crag, an endless series of bare mountain tops, utterly arid and lonesome'. In the little capital, Cetinje, Montenegrin national pride ran high. Talk was all of heroism and of Montenegro's national calling – the centuries-old struggle against the Turks. Durham did not know whether to be impressed or appalled by Montenegro's 'impossibly feudal views'. There was dreadful poverty, and the mundane labours of house and field fell to the cruelly burdened women while the men lounged and swaggered, dazzling in crimson braid and gold embroidery, waist sash and revolver. Durham's imagination was immediately caught by the superficial picturesqueness of Balkan life; as yet she could have no idea how deep her Balkan involvement was to become.

On her return to London, she immersed herself in Balkan history and the Serbian language. Her first journey had extended to the limits of the reasonable bounds suggested by Baedeker – but not beyond. In the following years, her travels grew more adventurous, bringing to the surface buried resources in her character for physical endurance and, what she at first found most difficult, the necessary tolerance of a degree of dirt. In 1904 she published *Through The Lands of the Serb*, the result of four trips to Montenegro, an extended tour through the Kingdom of Serbia, and a sortie into the province of Kosovo, then still part of the Ottoman Empire.

Her travels had acquired a serious ethnographic purpose. 'It occurred to me,' she wrote on her eightieth birthday, 'that the vexed question of Balkan politics might be solved by studying the manners and customs of each district, and so learning to whom each place should really belong. I cheerfully started on this vast programme' – a project which, she knew, ignored military realities and the diplomatic intrigues of the Great Powers which for decades had been poised for the dismemberment of the endlessly dying Turkish Empire.

By the end of the nineteenth century the Balkan provinces of the Ottoman Empire had reached a state of utmost misery. An exhausted peasantry coaxed a mean subsistence from the land, plundered by tax farmers, harried by half-starved regular soldiers months in arrears in their pay. Schools – nurseries of sedition – were few, and doctors even rarer. For centuries the Turks had exploited the differences between their subject peoples of Europe – Serbs, Bulgars, Greeks, Albanians, Macedonians – on a principle of 'divide and rule'. Ottoman officials, who considered a Balkan posting an exile almost as barbaric as the Yemen, languished in their crumbling *konaks*, dispensing corrupt or whimsical justice. At times Turkish misgovernment attained surreal proportions. The impressive 'Carte des Communications Postales de l'Empire Ottoman' showed roads and bridges where none existed. Commissions of Enquiry toured devastated regions and returned to Constantinople with *bakshish* and enthusiastic reports of the unparalleled prosperity of the Sublime Dominions. It was, in Rebecca West's phrase, 'the dusty, fly-blown, waking-dream of Turkey in Europe'.

In 1903, Macedonia rose in revolt. The rebellion was

quelled with exceptional brutality, and wretched villagers –
whether they had supported the rebels or not – were burnt
out of their houses. Their crops were destroyed by wandering
bands of Turkish soldiery. A Macedonian Relief Committee
was set up in London; Edith Durham, claiming extra leave
from her family obligations, hurried to Macedonia, where she
travelled on horseback through the villages, distributing flour
and blankets and vaccinating against smallpox. She was
without medical qualifications, but the condition of the people
was so desperate that the most elementary hygienic and
dietary precautions and the simplest antiseptics and bandages
could save many lives. She was delegated to co-operate with
qualified local staff in organizing a hospital at Ohrid, which
she did for two months, tending gunshot wounds and, in the
teeth of patients' opposition, substituting a 'clean, carbolicky,
sunny and bright' atmosphere in place of the previous foetid
air. Her hospital work completed, she toured Albania from
south to north in the company of an Albanian colporteur of
the British and Foreign Bible Society.

In England, the 'Balkan Question' was commonly imagined,
on Gladstonian lines, as the struggle of the European Christian
to throw off the Moslem yoke. In Albania, Edith Durham
found striking evidence for her belief that the conflict was of
national, not religious character. Of all the peoples of the
Balkans, the Albanians were the least known. They were also
the only people without a sponsor in a Great Power beyond
the Ottoman Empire. The very national existence of the
Albanians had been concealed from the eyes of the outside
world. A majority of the population was Moslem, which led
the world to believe they were Turks. A large Orthodox
minority in the south was claimed by the Greeks to be Greek.
The Catholic tribespeople of the north were the poorest and
least accessible of all, and their lands were coveted by
Montenegro. As Edith Durham travelled the length of the
country she became aware of the strong and growing feeling
of national unity among the Albanians, despite their differences
of religion, dialect, economy and culture. She recognized that
any answer to the Balkan Question that failed to consider
Albanian national aspirations would be inadequate. She

described her Macedonian and Albanian experiences in *The Burden of the Balkans* (1905), and reviewers recognized in her 'a successor to Mrs Bishop and Miss Kingsley'.

The following year, after the death of her mother, Edith Durham continued her systematic study of the Balkans with a journey through Bosnia and Herzegovina. Her base remained in Montenegro, and her work caught the attention of Prince Nikola, who entrusted her with the task of arranging the Montenegrin contribution to the Balkan States Exhibition in London in 1907. The exhibition did little to promote Montenegrin industry, then in a most rudimentary state, but it did bring Edith Durham into anthropological circles. London ethnologists visited Earl's Court to study, and acquire for the Horniman Museum, examples of Montenegrin workmanship. Durham was elected a fellow of the Royal Anthropological Institute.

Edith Durham's 1908 tour of the Albanian mountains was the fulfilment of a long-held ambition. She knew something of the tribespeople's world from the highlanders who came down to market in Scutari, and from her visit to Orosh, capital of the large Mirdite tribe, on her journey north in 1904. But there was simply no precedent of a foreign woman travelling through the mountains. The very amateur nature of her expedition may well have contributed to its success. Certainly Edith Durham must have cut a disarmingly unusual figure in her 'waterproof Burberry skirt' and 'Scotch plaid golf cape'. But there is no doubt that her absolute and well-placed trust in her highland hosts was rewarded with insights into north Albanian life denied to all previous travellers which enabled her to write, in *High Albania*, her most spirited and exultant book. For one reviewer, too spirited:

> It is perhaps not too much to say that she has even acquired some of the savagery which is to her the most attractive quality of the Albanians. The blood feud seems to make an especial appeal to her. The book literally reeks of blood.

Edith Durham did discover the delights of firing ball cartridge in the streets; otherwise the criticism is not fair. She admired not the feud, but the steadfastness of the tribesman in following the strict code he had laid down for himself, and the incorruptibility of the *besa* or 'trust' which ensured safe-conduct through the bitterest quarrel and protected the guest against all harm. In the Albanian tribesman's distinctive kind of discipline, Durham perceived qualities which, enlisted in the service of a sound government, could lead to a peaceful and just state of society. She also hoped that the material and social advancement of the Balkans would not be imported from abroad, but would grow from the virtues inherent in local traditions.

In 1908 such optimism for a while seemed justifiable. The travel narratives of *High Albania* are interrupted by two heady scenes of celebration – the welcome of the Turkish Constitution in Scutari, and the return from exile of Prenk Pasha, hereditary prince of the Mirdites. Both celebrations are false dawns. The 'Young Turk' turns out to be no better than the old. We sense that Prenk will disappoint his people – as indeed he did – and Durham perceptively notices that he has become a stranger to his own country when he flinches at the welcoming volleys of gunfire. But Durham, with the highlanders, leaps to share these momentary glimpses of hope, although the disillusionment of the following years was to be a painful one.

In 1911 the highlanders at last revolted against Ottoman rule. Edith Durham was in Scutari with flour, money and roofing-felt for burnt-out houses. It was at this time that the legend of the 'Queen of the Highlanders' began. Up-country tribesmen would travel for days to Scutari to visit her. It was a fame Durham found alarming: 'It is an awful responsibility – to be fallen in love with by a whole nation.' Incurable cases of suffering were brought for her attention, to which almost miraculous powers were ascribed. But Durham's popularity was earned less through kindliness than courage and honesty. The journalist H. W. Nevinson wrote of her at this time:

> But there was little of the sentimental nurse or philanthropist about Edith Durham. Her manner towards strangers and people whom she distrusted was abrupt to rudeness, and she would contradict her best friends with a sharpness that silenced dispute if not opinion. Her language in conversation was even more racy

than the style of her books, and she had a way of hitting off
affectation or absurdity with a slashing phrase that was not
exactly coarse, but made the cultured jump. I have never known
a woman to express facts or opinions with such startling vigour,
especially in disagreement.

Edith Durham remained in Montenegro and Scutari during
the two Balkan Wars of 1912 and 1913, describing her
experiences and the conduct of the wars in *The Struggle for
Scutari* (1914). Teresa Buxton, a nurse who worked alongside
Durham during the campaign of the Second Balkan War in
1913, conceived a warm admiration for her colleague, but
noted in her diary a vivid description of her when relief work
was at its hardest: 'short hair, no stays, very plain and stout –
old filthy tam o'shanter and dirty dark-green flannel blouse.'

The outbreak of the First World War drove Durham back
to England. As a close and cynical observer of Great Power
diplomacy, she was less surprised than many at the arrival of
the war, and exceptionally conscious of its futility and waste.
Her experiences at the Balkan fronts had bred in her a
forthright pacifism. She was heartbroken at the plight of the
Balkans. In 1918, Woodrow Wilson's principle of self-
determination for small nations appeared to offer hope for
Albania. In London, Durham became secretary of the Anglo-
Albanian Society, a small caucus of Members of Parliament
and others concerned with the promotion of Albanian interests.

Her last visit was half-triumph, half-disaster. In 1921 she
arrived in Tirana, and was welcomed by processions and
singing crowds. Streets were named after her. She attended
sessions of the Albanian Parliament, and dined with politicians
– but immediately fell desperately ill. The Albanians refused
to be denied their festivities. In Scutari the town band turned
out, and deputations of tribesmen arrived to greet her. Reeling
with fatigue, Durham replied to their speeches of welcome.
'I must get away,' she confided to her diary, in unsteady
handwriting. A few days later she left for Rome, too weak to
record her departure.

In her last years in London Durham was active on the
council of the Royal Anthropological Institute, and a frequent
contributor to its magazine, *Man*. There were further books.

Twenty Years of Balkan Tangle (1920) is a summary of her travels, with a mainly political commentary. *The Serajevo Crime* (1925) is purely political, while *Some Tribal Origins, Laws, and Customs of the Balkans* (1928) is a systematic collation of her ethnological researches in Albania, Montenegro and Bosnia. King Zog (whom Durham sharply disliked) awarded her the Order of Skenderbeg, and the Albanian government offered her a home in Albania. She chose however to remain in London, where she died in 1944.

The mountains of northern Albania are today even less accessible to the individual traveller than they were in 1908. But ironically the regions that to Durham seemed the most remote – Vuthaj, Gusinje and the Plain of Kosovo – are now in Yugoslavia and open to the visitor.

It is worth noting that the Albanians have held on to many of the traditions described in *High Albania*. The tribal system still survives to the extent that a Kosovo Albanian will be aware of a tribal identity, and will not marry within the tribe. The blood feud is almost extinct, its loss unlamented – but a village wedding or the birth of a child will still be marked by celebratory bursts of gunfire. Above all, the laws of hospitality are very much alive, and the guest at the *sofra* is still welcomed, as Edith Durham was welcomed by the tribesman of Kastrati, with 'bread, salt, and our hearts'.

John Hodgson, Sussex, 1985

PREFACE

If a book cannot speak for itself, it is idle to speak for it. I will waste but few words on a Preface. In my two previous Balkan books I strove to give the national points of view, the aims and aspirations, the manners and customs, of the Serbs and of the mixed population of Macedonia.

I would now do the same for the people of High Albania.

From the mass of material accumulated in an eight months' tour, together with that collected on previous visits to Albania, it is hard to know what to select, and want of space has forced me to omit almost as much as I have put in, of folklore, custom, and tradition.

The land is one so little known to English travellers that I have given rather a comprehensive view of it as a whole than details of any special branch of study, and have reported what the people themselves said rather than put forward views of my own—which are but those of an outsider. Of outsiders' views on Balkan problems we are, most of us, tired.

For any success I may have obtained, I am indebted entirely to the kind and most generous help I met on the way from all and sundry—more especially to the Franciscans and Mission priests of the mountains, and to my guide Marko; but also to my hosts and guides of all races and religions. Faithful, courageous, and hospitable, it is perhaps written in the Book of Fate that I shall see many of them no more, but " if a Man be Gracious and

PREFACE

Courteous to Strangers, it shewes he is a Citizen of the Worlde; and that his Hearte is no Island, cut off from other Lands, but is a Continent that joynes them." And they will not have passed across my life in vain, if from this brief record some few readers learn a truer insight into the character of the mountain tribesman.

Lastly, I would say that, though I made very careful inquiry in many places before recording any custom, errors must have crept in, and for them I alone am responsible.

M. E. D.

September 1909.

HIGH ALBANIA

CHAPTER I

THE LAND OF THE LIVING PAST

"Of old sat Freedom on the heights"

THE great river of life flows not evenly for all peoples. In places it crawls sluggishly through dull flats, and the monuments of a dim past moulder upon the banks that it has no force to overflow; in others it dashes forward torrentially, carving new beds, sweeping away old landmarks; or it breaks into backwaters apart from the main stream, and sags to and fro, choked with the flotsam and jetsam of all the ages.

Such backwaters of life exist in many corners of Europe—but most of all in the Near East. For folk in such lands time has almost stood still. The wanderer from the West stands awestruck amongst them, filled with vague memories of the cradle of his race, saying, "This did I do some thousands of years ago; thus did I lie in wait for mine enemy; so thought I and so acted I in the beginning of Time."

High Albania is one of these corners. I say High Albania advisedly, for the conditions that prevail in it are very different from those in South Albania, and it is with the wildest parts of High Albania alone that this book deals.

The history of Albania, a complicated tale of extreme

interest, remains to be written—strange that it should be so. The claims of Greek, Bulgar, and Serb in the Balkan peninsula are well known; so are the desires of Austria, Russia, and Italy. But it has been the fashion always to ignore the rights and claims of the oldest inhabitant of the land, the Albanian, and every plan for the reformation or reconstruction of the Near East that has done so has failed.

"Constantinople," says the Albanian, "is the key of the Near East, and Albania is the key of Constantinople."

The history of every people is a great epic, the writing of which is beyond me. The following brief sketch shows only the passing of the peoples that have swayed the fortunes of North Albania, but never yet subdued its stubborn individuality.

Illyrian Period (*from about* 700 B.C. *to* 230 B.C.).—A fierce tribal people, known as Illyrians, are recorded as dwelling in the lands now known as Montenegro, High Albania, the Herzegovina, and Bosnia. About 300 B.C. they were invaded by the Celts, who have probably left a deep mark on the people of to-day by the infusion of Celtic blood.

Roman Period.—Fierce fighters and inveterate pirates, the Illyrians brought down upon themselves a Roman punitive expedition in 230 B.C., and, after a long struggle, Illyria became a Roman province. Gentius, last king of Illyria, was defeated and captured at Scodra in 169 B.C. The land must have been thickly populated, for the Romans were long in subduing it. Thousands of prehistoric graves exist in vast cemeteries throughout Bosnia and the Herzegovina—similar ones are found in Servia, Montenegro, and High Albania. They yield many bronze and iron objects of the highest interest, for the patterns are still worn, or have been till recently, by the peasants of Bosnia, Servia, Albania, even of Bulgaria. The rayed ball or circle is not only a common pattern in silver, but is also a traditional tattoo pattern (see illustration).

Rome found some of her best soldiers among the fighting tribesmen, and more than one Emperor—Diocletian and Constantine the Great, and many of lesser note, were of native blood.

In the mountains, it would seem the natives retained their own speech throughout. In the fat plain lands of the peninsula the Romans left Latin dialects. The Roumanian language still survives. The Latin dialect of Illyria, spoken universally in the coast towns in the

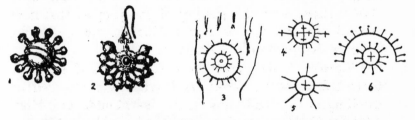

1. Prehistoric Bronze Ornament, Bosnia (Sarajevo Museum, Sjeversko, T. 2).
2. Modern Silver Earring, of type common to Bosnia, Servia, Bulgaria, and Kosovo Vilayet.
3, 4, 5, 6. Common Catholic Bosnian Tattoos.

Middle Ages, died out at the end of the nineteenth century, on the island of Veglio.

Christianity reached the Dalmatian coast as early as the first century. In the interior it made little progress till the fourth.

The transference of the capital of the Roman Empire to Byzantium had but little effect on Illyria, which remained part of the Patriarchate of Rome. And to Rome the descendants of the Illyrians have to a large extent remained faithful.

Servian Period (*Seventh Century to Fourteenth Century*).—The next event of importance was the Slavonic invasion. The ancestors of the modern Servians poured into the peninsula in irresistible numbers, overpowered the inhabitants, and reached the Dalmatian coast, burning the Roman town of Salona, 609 A.D. Serb influence grew stronger and stronger. At first as tribes suzerain to Byzantium, and then as an independent kingdom, they dominated the west side of the peninsula, and finally, under the Nemanja kings in the thirteenth and fourteenth centuries, almost the whole of it. The Venetians came in as protectors of the remaining Latin coast population in the eleventh century, and crept by degrees along Dalmatia.

The inrushing Slav appears not so much to have displaced the native population of old Illyria as to have absorbed it. There is no record of when the native Illyrian language died out in Bosnia, nor to what extent it had been replaced by a Latin speech by the time the Slavs arrived. In Albania it never died out, but survives to-day as modern Albanian. And with the language has survived the fierce racial instinct, which to this day makes the Albanian regard the Slav as his first and worst foe.

Empires came and went, and passed over the Albanian as does water off a duck's back. In the fastnesses, which he held, he was never more than nominally conquered, and retained his marked individuality and customs. He was probably one of the causes of the instability of the successive mediæval kingdoms, which were all, indeed, but loosely strung collections of temporarily suzerain tribes.

To race hatred was added religious hatred. The Slavs, converted to Christianity by missionaries from Salonika in the ninth century, decided eventually for the Eastern Church. The Albanian remained faithful to Rome.

A certain Frère Brochard in 1332—the palmy days of the Great Servian Empire—gives a vivid picture of the hatred of the Albanian for Serb rule.

"There is among other things, one that makes it much easier to take this kingdom (Servia). . . . There are two people, the Abbanois and the Latins, who belong both to the Church of Rome. . . . The Latins have six cities and as many bishops. Anthibaire (Antivari), Cathare (Cattaro), Dulcedine (Dulcigno), Suacinense (?), Scutari, and Drivasto. In these only Latins live. Outside the walls of them are Abbanois, who have four cities, Polat major and Polat minor (the tribal districts of Upper and Lower Pulati), Sabbate (diocese of Sappa), and Albanie (diocese of Durazzo). These, with the six above, are under the Archbishop of Antivari. These Abbanois have a language quite other than Latin, but use in their books Latin letters. Both these people are oppressed under the very hard servitude of the most hateful and abominable lordship of the Slavs. If they saw a Prince of France coming towards them, they would make him Duke against the accursed Slavs, the enemies of the truth and of our faith. A thousand cavaliers and five or six battalions, with the aforesaid Abbanois and Latins, would with ease conquer this kingdom, great and such as it is."

And no sooner did the Servian Empire break up after the death of Tsar Dushan in 1356, than the Albanians arose, and powerful chiefs ruled soon in lands that had been his.

The Servian kingdom shrank northward. The Balshas, a line of chieftains of Serb origin, formed a principality which in time included a large part of Albania and the Zeta (modern Montenegro). Though of Serb origin they were probably of mixed blood. Their sympathies were Albanian, for they made alliance with the Albanian chieftains, and fought against Marko Kraljevich, the best beloved of Serb heroes, wresting from him Ipek and Prizren (1373).

Down on the struggling mass of little principalities

came the Turks. Greek, Bulgar, and Serb were shattered. The final great victory of the Turks at Kosovo estabblished them in Europe to this day.

The Albanians were the last to fall. Led by their great hero Skenderbeg, they offered a magnificent resistance. But they had not outgrown the tribal system, and on his death (1467) broke up under rival chiefs and were overpowered. And after this the ancestors of many of the modern tribes fled from Bosnia and Rashia, and refuged in High Albania.

As for the very large population that must have been of mixed Serbo-Illyrian blood, whether they eventually called themselves Serb or Albanian seems to have largely depended upon whether they decided in favour of Rome or the Orthodox Church.

There are certain old Roman Catholic communities in Bosnia that have preserved to this day the ancient Illyrian custom of tattooing. This is never practised by the Orthodox or Moslem Slavs, but is common among both Catholic and Moslem Albanians. It is therefore possible that these tattooed Bosnians, though now Serbophone, descend from the pre-Slavonic inhabitants, and have not yet lost the custom of putting on a distingushing mark. It is of special interest to note that, of the present tribes in North Albania, the most tattooed are those that relate that they fled from Bosnia to avoid the Turks.

Forced to accept Turkish suzerainty, the position of the Albanians was yet different from that of the other conquered peoples. They retained very many privileges, and remained semi-independent under their own chiefs.

Their race instinct—the unreasoning, blind instinct of self-preservation—drove them ever against their old foe, the Slav. They did not hate the Turk less, but they hated the Slav more. Turning Moslem in numbers, and thereby gaining great influence under Turkish rule,

Moslem and Christian Albanian alike supported Turk against Slav.

Already in the sixteenth century the Albanians began to go over to Islam. To-day two-thirds of the Ghegs (North Albanians) are Moslem. The reasons are not far to seek. School for native priests there seems to have been none. Foreign priests were often ignorant of native language and custom. The bishops, largely foreigners, strove only each to obtain power for himself. "The hungry sheep looked up and were not fed."

As early as 1684 the quarrels of the bishops for territory had become so bitter that a commission was appointed to delimit the bishoprics of Sappa, Durazzo, and Alessio, and the three bishops were solemnly adjured to observe these limits. "For it is not meet that your lordships should contend further, because of the scandal that may be caused, not only among the faithful, but also because of the grave inconveniences that arise from quarrels in those parts that are under the Turks."

Yet in 1702 it was again necessary to call the bishops to order. Pope Clement XI., of Albanian blood on his mother's side, wishful to save his Albanian brethren, sent Vicentius Zmajevich, Archbishop of Antivari, as Visitator Apostolicus, to Albania. After traversing the mountains and visiting all the tribes, he makes a most lamentable report. The vineyards of the Lord are corrupt, desolate, given over to pagan and Turkish practices; the bishops are quarrelling with one another for various villages. The worst case he gives is that of Postripa, for which three bishops at once contended, while the people were left "without leader or shepherd, like a scattered flock subject to persecution and oppression." To-day a very large part of Postripa is Moslem, which is not surprising. That any Catholics now remain in North Albania is mainly due to the efforts of the Franciscans, of whose courage there can be no question, and who, through the three darkest centuries, took Albania under their special care.

During the years dating from the Turkish conquest to the end of the eighteenth century, the Albanians continued to press the Slavs back and to reoccupy territory. More than once, especially under the powerful Pashas of Scutari — the Bushatlis — they were on the point of gaining complete independence ; and, had they possessed organising power, would have done so.

But though they were a serious danger to the power of the Turk in Europe, their successive efforts were doomed to failure, owing to the want of unity caused by the tribal system. And before they were ready to stand alone the tide of Turkish affairs turned. The Serb arose ; the Slav again appeared as invader. Russia proclaimed a Holy War to free the Serbs after four centuries of oppression.

The details of the Serb resurrection, and of the successive Russian campaigns, are too well known and too recent to need re-telling.

The Albanians had, and have, no allied power to come thus to their aid. They threw aside plans of independence, and again made common cause with the Turk against their old enemy the Slav, in the struggle for existence. This time they played a losing game. They had not merely military force to contend with, but also the forces of education and civilisation. Between the campaigns, Russia spared neither effort nor money to raise the condition of both Serb and Bulgar. More especially between the Crimea and the war of 1876–77, money was poured into Macedonia and Bulgaria lavishly. Schools and churches were built, teachers sent to preach the Panslavonic idea and fit the people for freedom.

The Slav triumphed. Turkey, utterly crushed, had to accept such terms as Europe chose to dictate. And

with the Turks fell the Albanians. They were in fact
the greatest sufferers. As valiantly as any others they
had fought for their fatherland, but they were classed
as Turks and their claims ignored.

Europe, too, was now afraid of the Slav. To check
Slavonic advance, the wholly Slavonic lands were handed
over to Austria to be " administered " (have their Slavism
crushed out of them), and lands wholly Albanian were
awarded to Montenegro.

The Albanians flew to arms and saved their towns of
Gusinje and Tuzhi, but were ordered instead to cede Dulcigno, one of their best ports. Never has there been a more
mistaken piece of bullying than the naval demonstration,
instigated by Gladstone, to force the cession of this wholly
Albanian town. The large maritime population left it, and
has never been replaced. Trade has decreased, and Dulcigno remains a monument of diplomatic blunder. The
Montenegrins have been unable to develop it ; it is a
constant reminder to the Albanians that they may expect
no justice from Europe, and it has enhanced their hatred
of the Slav. Austria has taken advantage of this, and
works upon it. Only last winter, when war between
Montenegro and Austria was imminent, the Albanians were
advised to attack simultaneously with Austria and redeem
Dulcigno, and were offered rifles.

North Albania is a hotbed of Austrian intrigue. The
Austrian Consul-general even takes it on himself to spy
the actions of tourists, as though the land were already
under Austrian jurisdiction.

Scutari swarms with foreign consuls, and the Albanian
has acquired the bad habit of crying to one and the other
for help. Austria, by lavish expenditure, strives to buy
up the tribes. Italy offers counter attractions. The
Albanian has learnt by long practice how to play off
one against the other. He accepts money upon occasion
from each and all that offer it, and uses it for his private

ends. This annoys the consuls. They hate to be outwitted at their own game, to find that when they mean
to use him as a pawn he cries, "Check to your king!"
They call him bad names—but it is only the "pot calling
the kettle black"—and they offer bigger bribes.

"'Will you walk into my parlour?' said the spider
to the fly." And should he ever rashly walk into either,
he will rue the day.

One must live in Scutari to realise the amount of
spying and wire-pulling carried on by the Powers under
pretence of spreading sweetness and light.

The Alphabet question will suffice as a sample. In
early days an alphabet was made by Bishop Bogdan, and
used by the Jesuits for all Albanian printed matter
required by the church. Briefly, it is the Latin alphabet
with four additional fancy letters. The spelling used is
otherwise as in Italian. Help from without had enabled
Greek, Serb, and Bulgar under Turkish rule to have
schools in their own tongues. The natural result has
been that each in turn has revolted, and, so far as possible,
won freedom from Turkish rule. And those that have
not yet done so look forward, in spite of the Young
Turk, to ultimate union with their kin.

Albania awoke late to the value of education as a
means of obtaining national freedom, and demanded
national schools. But the Turks, too, had then learnt
by experience. They replied, "We have had quite
enough of schools in national languages. No, you
don't!" and prohibited, under heavy penalty, not only
schools, but the printing of the language.

The only possible schools were those founded by
Austria and Italy, ostensibly to give religious instruction.
These used the Jesuits' alphabet. Ten years ago some
patriotic Albanians, headed by the Abbot of the Mirdites,
decided that the simple Latin alphabet was far more
practical. They reconstructed the orthography of the

language, using only Latin letters, and offered their simple and practical system to the Austrian schools, volunteering to translate and prepare the necessary books if Austria would print them—neither side to be paid. A whole set of books was made ready and put in use. Education was at last firmly started; it remained only to go forward. But a united and educated Albania was the last thing Austria wished to see. Faced with a patriotic native clergy and a committee striving for national development, Austria recoiled. Three years ago the simple Latin alphabet was thrown out of the Austrian schools and a brand-new system adopted, swarming with accents, with several fancy letters, and with innumerable mute " ee's " printed upside down—a startling effect, as of pages of uncorrected proofs!

It was invented by an influential priest. Its adoption enabled Austria to split the native priesthood into two rival camps, and—as it was not adopted by the Italian schools—to emphasise the difference between the pro-Italian and pro-Austrian parties; and that it was expressly introduced for these purposes no one who has heard all sides can doubt.

Nor can Albanian education make any progress till it has schools in which no foreign Power is allowed to intrigue. Such are now being started.

But enough of Scutari. I was bound for up-country.

Travel in Turkey is generally complicated by the fact that the political situation is strained. It was exceptionally so in the beginning of May 1908. An Englishman who, six weeks before, had applied for a *teskereh* to travel inland, had been flatly refused, and had had to give up his tour.

To ask, I was told, was to court refusal. I must "take my blood on my own head" and slip off quietly—or give up.

" It is my duty to show you this," said our Vice-consul; "but, as I know you, I do not suppose it will make any difference." It was an official letter from our Embassy in Constantinople, warning all persons travelling in the Turkish Empire merely for pleasure, that the British Government would neither be responsible for their safety nor pay ransom. The palmy days of *civis Romanus sum* are over.

As I knew there was no case on record of a stranger being "held up" in North Albania, and, moreover, the Albanian is an old friend of mine, it "made no difference." Meanwhile, it remained only to find a suitable dragoman.

Meanwhile I explored the environs of Scutari. They are strewn with the wreckage of dead Empires—past Powers—only the Albanian "goes on for ever."

In the fourth century the district was a Roman province called Prevalitana—its chief towns were Scodra, Dioclea, and Drivasto. Scodra was very early a bishopric, and, according to a Bull of Pius IX., was raised to an archbishopric from 307 to 601. The Archbishop was then transferred to Dioclea, and thence at the end of the tenth century to Antivari. Antivari is still an archbishopric—the remains of Dioclea have been recently excavated. Drivasto was a bishopric till 877, and is now a heap of ruins. Scutari alone survives as the capital, and was raised again to an archbishopric in 1867. So turns the world.

I left Scutari at 5 A.M., piloted by a native who " knew all about guiding foreigners," and regarded it as running contraband. " The Vali," he said, " at that hour would still be asleep." Going over the plain, we followed the Kiri and crossed it on the fine stone bridge, the Ura Mesit, said to be Venetian.

High on a hill that guards the entrance of the Kiri valley stood Drivasto—Drishti as it is now called. Half-way up, the modern village is built among the ruins of little houses. A rude gateway in the remains of an old wall leads to it. The people have been Moslem just two centuries—that is, since the bishops quarrelled over them. On the summit are the ruins of the citadel that in the thirteenth, fourteenth, and fifteenth centuries was of some importance. From the thirteenth century the Comneni—Despots of Epirus, and descendants of a side branch of the Byzantine Imperial family—were lords of Drivasto. It was part of the Balsha Principality, and in 1396 the Balsha prince, unable to withstand the oncoming Turk, sold Drivasto with the consent of its last lord, Angelo (Andrea?) Flavio Comneno, along with Scutari, to the Venetians. But in vain.

The Turks took it, after a most bloody struggle, in 1478, hewed off the heads of the conquered leaders, and set them on pikes round beleaguered Scutari to strike terror into its defenders. Scutari too fell. The survivors from both Scutari and Drivasto fled to Venice—in the records of which the names of many well-known Albanian families occur—and Drivasto was wiped out of existence.

Naught remains now of these " old, unhappy, far-off things " but the outer wall of the citadel, of rough, unmortared stone, and a few fragments of buildings. Coins and other relics are found from time to time, but the Drishti folk keep jealous watch that no stranger shall search in what they regard as their own Tom Tiddler's ground.

The Moslem village people, reputed fanatical, were most friendly. We were asked into the wide balcony of a house where the women—unveiled, and wearing a big tuft of black-dyed hair on either side of the face—were busy weaving red and white striped cotton. Men and women sat round and amused themselves hugely, teaching me Albanian. Then the women boiled milk for me, and the men inveighed against the Turkish Government. Had to pay tax, could not avoid it, the town is so near—

and it all goes into the Vali's pocket. Nothing is done for the land. By God the men of the mountains are better off! Nothing is done for them, but they do not have to pay for it.

Drishti folk are thrifty and industrious. All the river bank is made into neat market-gardens, full of little ponds, from which the water is scattered with huge wooden ladles, and the produce is taken weekly to Scutari. When I left the elder lady rubbed cheeks with me, and all begged me to come again.

My next walk was to the villages Guri Zi and Jubani, with a lad of twenty. Over the plain we went, east of Scutari to the Kiri, which was deep and full, and bridgeless, and found a wadeable shallow where it spread in four wide streams. The water was cold from the mountain snows, and the bottom slippery shingle. It was one of the occasions upon which I wonder why I have come. Nor was the other side much better. All the fields were flooded. We dodged ditches and paddled in liquid mud. But the frogs kept us happy by hollaing and shouting " Brek-kek-kek-kek " all the time. Their Albanian name, *bretkots*, must come from that classic chant. It should be noted that they pronounce " koax " as " koach," with a gutteral German " ch." Perhaps they are the only people who remember the correct pronunciation. And the mudflats were beauteous with tall white flowers like bunches of snowdrops on one stalk.

Christian Jubani was hospitable as Moslem Drishti. The men were out ploughing, but the women, sewing and weaving at home, welcomed me to their little red-tiled, white-washed houses. These, quite unfurnished within, were very fairly clean, and the children bonny and newly washed. Most of the boys had a cross tattooed on the back of the right hand. Two came with us,: and dashed into the hedge to hunt a large grass snake (*Pseudopus*), excellent eating they said, only you must cut off its head, for it is poisonous (it is not, but can bite sharply); also because you must always cut off a snake's head. If you leave it as dead, and other snakes find it before sundown, they will cure it even though its back be broken to pieces. The grass snake escaped. A few tortoises came out grazing. These too are very nice to eat, I was told, but later in the year—now "they had been eating earth all the winter, so were not good."

From Jubani we went to Guri Zi ("Black Stone") which takes its name from a huge isolated rock. The village is largely Moslem, but friendly. There is indeed no danger in visiting the villages near Scutari, save from the dogs, which are trained to fly at all strangers. They are great grey or white wolfish beasts, often with wolf blood in them (the hybrid is fertile). "Without dogs we cannot live," say the people. And when each house has three or four loose at night, no enemy can approach unnoticed.

Even when puppies—mere fluffy balls—they are extraordinarily ferocious, and before they can run or bark will roll over and choke in their efforts to scare you. Had it not been for the English laws about imported dogs, I felt tempted to buy fifty for Ireland. The drivers of other folk's cattle would find it a case of "the biter bit."

The priest of Guri Zi entertained me with the tale of how his large moustaches caused him to be arrested in Italy on the charge of masquerading as a priest. "A man may be a very good priest," said the old gentleman, "fit for Paradise, but he won't do for Albania unless he has a moustache. If they've made him shave it off abroad, he must just sit in his room in Scutari till it has grown again."

To be without a moustache, both in Montenegro and Albania, is held to be peculiarly disgraceful. The wicked man of Albanian fairy stories is a *chosé* (a hairless man). When I mentioned, in Montenegro, that my brother was clean shaven, I was told not to repeat such disgraceful facts about him.

My youthful guide objected to going more walks without a rifle. I had been specially advised to go unarmed. "If your boy wants a gun he probably owes blood. Don't go with him."

We were to go to Vraka next day, and, contrary to orders, he turned up with a Martini and a belt full of cartridges — borrowed — and persisted in taking them; and, thus weighted, objected to carrying my lunch-bag.

Vraka, the only Orthodox Serb village in the district, lies an hour and a half north of Scutari on the plain.

The people were highly delighted that I could speak with them, and at once started cooking me a meal. It would be a disgrace, they said, for me to eat my own food in their village.

The stone houses are good and large—some great one-roomed structures, others with stable below and dwelling-room above.

The people complained greatly of Moslem persecution. The houses were full of rifles. "Vraka," said my host, "is made up of various families that had fled, because they owed blood, from Bosnia and Montenegro about two hundred years ago." They number now some one thousand souls. His family had six houses, much land, grew maize and vines, and made plenty of wine and *rakia*. Being near the lake, they had enough fish for Wednesdays and Fridays. (A woman was stringing little fish on a long wire, and hanging them in loops to a great wooden frame over the open hearth, to be smoke-dried.) Were it not for the Moslems they could live very well, but not one of the Vraka men could now go into Scutari. They would be shot on the way. The women had to do all bazaar business.

He added philosophically, "The Moslems have killed

a great many of us, but, thanks to God, we have shot plenty of them."

At Scutari I was told it was quite true that the Vraka men lived at the end of a gun—both ends—and had no protection from the Vali. The Vraka women wear their hair looped in two plaits on each side of the face and fastened with a cowrie-shell. It is rare to find the cowrie so far west in Europe. A child had a cowrie and blue beads on its forehead. The women would not say why. The man laughed and said it was against the Evil Eye—the women had put it there.

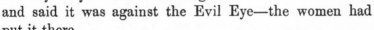

Woman of Vraka.

I began to draw the room. The woman snatched up the baby and drove other children away. "You may write the house," she said, "but not the children."

The head of the family slept in a cubby-house of hurdle, hung from a tie-beam of the roof and supported on a pole below. A long row of chests held clothing, and food was stored in baskets hung out of reach of rats and cats. All houses were marked with many crosses.

The church had been built with Russian help. My youth, a Catholic, disapproved of it, and whispered, "These people are not Christians, they are only Greeks!" I said that the Albanians in the south had churches like this. He replied, "They are not Christians, but Tosks."

We returned to Scutari without meeting any "blood foes," but the youth lost one of the borrowed cartridges, and had to pay threepence for it, which depressed him.

Then there turned up the man for whom I had been waiting, one Marko. He had been in his young days servant to a war correspondent, and knew all about rough travelling. He had friends in all the Christian tribes.

And to his resourcefulness and intelligence I owe whatever success I may have attained on my travels.

His patience was unfailing, nor would he ever allow mine to break down. "We must remember," he would say, "the Wolf and the Fox. The Wolf and the Fox heard that Man was coming to take their kingdom and kill them. One day, when out together in the forest, the Wolf put his foot in an iron trap and began to howl loudly. 'What is the matter?' cried the Fox. 'Oh, my foot! my foot!' screamed the Wolf. 'Is that all?' said the Fox. 'If you make such a noise about a foot, whatever will you do to-morrow when Man comes to hammer you on the head till you are dead?'"

Moral. However bad things are, they might be worse. It is as well to remember this in the Albanian mountains—and elsewhere.

CHAPTER II

THE LAND AND THE LAW

"But natheles, while I have tyme and space,
  Or that I forther in this Talé pace
  Me thinketh it accordant to resoun',
  To telle yow al the condicioun
  Of eche of hem śo as it semede me
  And whiche they weren, and of what degre."

THE land north of Scutari, called Maltsia e madhe, the
Great Mountain Land, is the home of five large tribes—
Hoti, Gruda, Kastrati, Skreli, and Kilmeni. It is part
of the same group of mountains that form the bulk of
Montenegro—the grey wilderness of barren rock, called
Karst, that glares dazzling in the midsummer sun and
beats back the heat with cruel force, takes wondrous
blue and mauve shadows at dawn and even, and, when
wet, is the heavy purple-black of a thunder-cloud. Very
little of it is cultivable. Great tracts are waterless, de-
pending solely on rainfall—aching wildernesses, the bare
bones of a half-created world.

The whole district consists, mainly, of two long deep
valleys and the high ranges that form their watersheds.

The one is the valley of the Tsem, a swift stream,
never dry, that runs parallel with and near to the
Montenegrin frontier and into the Lake of Scutari.
The other is that of the Proni Thaat (dry torrent),
which but seldom has water in it, but in olden days
must have been of great force, for it has carved a deep
canyon below, and has above a wide bed of water-worn
boulders. The summits of the mountain range that
rises on its left bank form, roughly speaking, the

19

frontiers of Maltsia e madhe, with its neighbours, the Lower Pulati group and Shala.

On its other sides, Maltsia e madhe is bounded by the lake and by the Montenegrin frontier (a purely political and in no way ethnographic line). In the north the mountain range called the Prokletija ("accursed," a name often erroneously applied by travellers to all the North Albanian mountains) divides it from the lands of Gusinje.

To Maltsia e madhe I first turned my steps—not to see the mountains, but to see life, history, the world, and the great unknown, as it looks to the mountain man. One race has never yet seen with the eyes of another, perhaps never will. Universal peace is a far cry. But the perspective of everything, life and modern politics included, depends entirely upon the point from which it is viewed.

To attain this standpoint one must live the life of the people, and know not merely the past, but the present facts of their life. And the main fact is the tribe (*fis*). It has been both their strength and their weakness. Each tribe has a definite tale of origin. Descent is traced strictly through the male line, and the tradition handed from father to son through memories undebauched by print.

The head of each *fis* is its hereditary standard-bearer, the *Bariaktar*. The office passes from father to son, or in default of son to the next heir male. The standard is now a Turkish one. Only the Mirdites have a distinctive flag with a rayed-sun upon it.

Some large tribes are divided into groups, each with its own Bariaktar. A division thus marching under one standard (*bariak*) is called a bariak. Such a bariak may be descended from a different stock from the rest of the tribe, or the division may have been made for convenience when the tribe grew large.

The men and women descending from a common

male ancestor, though very remote, regard one another as brother and sister, and marriage between them is forbidden as incestuous. Though the relationship be such that the Catholic Church permits marriage, it is regarded with such genuine horror that I have heard of but one instance where it was attempted or desired, when against tribe law. Even a native priest told me that a marriage between cousins separated by twelve generations was to him a horrible idea, though the Church permitted it, " for really they are brothers and sisters."

The mountain men have professed Christianity for some fifteen centuries, but tribe usage is still stronger than Church law. A man marries and gives his daughter in marriage outside his tribe, except when that tribe contains members of a different stock, or when it has been divided into bariaks considered distant enough for intermarriage. But in spite of this exogamy, it would appear that, through the female line, the race may have been fairly closely in-bred. For a man does not go far for a wife, but usually takes one from the next tribe, unless that tribe be consanguineous. If not so debarred, he takes a wife thence and marries his daughter there. Kastrati, for example, usually marries Hoti, and Hoti Kastrati. The bulk of the married women in one were born in the other. A perpetual interchange of women has gone on for some centuries.

Even educated Scutarenes reckon relations on the mother's side but vaguely.

A man said to me, " She is a sort of relation of mine. Her mother and mine were sisters."

" Then she is very near. She is your first cousin."

He considered and said doubtfully, " Yes. _Like_ a first cousin certainly, but on my mother's side."

His third cousins on his father's side he reckoned as brothers. One very near and dear cousin was so remote I never quite placed him.

The Catholic Church prohibits marriage to the sixth degree, and the law is now enforced. But among the Moslem tribes, I am told, female cousinship is not recognised. Male blood only counts. That male blood only counted under old tribe law seems fairly certain. In Montenegro, where the tribal system is not yet extinct—under the "old law," which prevailed till the middle of the nineteenth century, though marriage was prohibited so long as any drop of blood of male descent was known of—I am told relationship through the female was but slightly, if at all, recognised.

Church law in Albania has only recently had power to restrain illegal unions. Archbishop Zmajevich, in his report on Albania in 1703, laments: "Among the execrable customs of the mountain people, the wretched parents are in the habit of buying for a price young girls for their sons, who are of tender age, and keeping them in their house till they are of age to cohabit, and of omitting to contract matrimony unless a male child be born, even after fifteen years or more of sinful cohabitation. This pollution is spread throughout the mountains."

The custom exists still among the Catholics along the Dalmatian frontier of Bosnia, who, in spite of the efforts of the priests, refuse to legalise a union till sure that the woman is capable of child-bearing.

The *fis* is divided into the *mehala*, a group of closely related houses, and the *shpi*, or house. The head of a *mehala* is called the *kryé* (head). The head of a house is *xoti i shpis* (lord of the house). The house, among the outlying tribes of Pulati and Dukaghini, is a communal house, including as many as seventy individuals, all under the absolute sway of their lord. The "house" may overflow into two or three houses, all holding goods and flocks in common under one *xoti*.

Forbidden degrees of marriage include not only blood relations on the male side, but spiritual relationships.

According to Church law, those related by having the same godfather are not intermarriagable to the sixth degree, but the Albanians consider not only those related through their *kumarii i pakzimit* (godfather of baptism) to be not intermarriageable, but also those related through their *kumarii i floksh* (godfather of hair).

It is recorded that in very early days the Illyrians shaved their heads. Head shaving was still practised by Greeks, Slavs, and Hungarians in the seventeenth century. The custom prevails to this day throughout Albania and Bosnia, and has only recently died out among the Orthodox Montenegrins. It is practised by Moslems, Catholics, and Orthodox.

Among the North Albanian tribes a patch of hair, called *perchin*, is usually left, varying in shape and position according to district.

Among the Catholic tribes the first shaving of the head is thought even more important than baptism. When the child is about two years old, a friend is invited to be *kumarii i floksh*. (In Montenegro the relationship was called *Shishano Kumstvo*, and prevailed till fifty years ago.) The child's hair must have never before been cut. In the case of a Catholic Albanian, the *kumarii*, sitting on the ground, takes first another child on his knees (to ensure that his godchild be not the last that its parents have), then takes his godchild and cuts from its head four locks of hair, one to each of the points of the compass—north, south, east, and west—thus marking a cross. The Moslems, I am told, cut three locks—a triangle is a favourite Moslem tattoo pattern. Girls as well as boys are shaven, but girls have a fringe left over the forehead.

Handsome gifts are exchanged, according to the means of the family. The *kumarii* gives the child several napoleons, and receives some fine garments or fancy knitted socks. Some tribes have limited the value that may be given, as the gifts became so excessive as to be a severe burden. The relationship thus acquired ranks as blood relationship, and the descendants of children who have the same *kumarii*, though not otherwise related, are not intermarriageable till after the sixth degree—some have told me, never.

Another forbidden degree is created by sworn brotherhood. The custom is old and widely spread. But as the North Albanians almost always call a sworn brother *probo* or *probotin*, an obvious corruption of the Servian *probratim* (*brat*=brother), they have possibly derived the custom, too, from the Serbs. There is an Albanian word, though, *vlam*.

In Montenegro the custom is almost dead. In Albania it flourishes. The procedure was told me by a Catholic Albanian, thus: " I travelled through a dangerous part with a young Moslem. We became great friends. He asked me to be. his brother. I asked leave of my father (the head of the house). He said it was a very good family to be allied with. We waited a short time. Then, as we still both wished it, we met, and each tied a string round his little finger tightly till it swelled, pricked the finger, and let the blood drop on to a lump of sugar. I ate his lump, he ate mine. We swore brotherhood. We were of the same blood. We gave each other beautiful socks in patterns, and I went to dinner at his house. He is dead now, but his brothers are my brothers, and our children are cousins. Of course they cannot marry, they are of the same blood. They cannot marry for more than a hundred years."

In the case of two Christians, three drops of blood in a glass of *rakia* or wine is customary. The Church, of course, takes no notice of this relationship, but I am told that persons so related never marry unless the relationship has become remote.

There is, I believe, another relationship acquired by

the woman who cuts the umbilical cord at the birth of an infant. But of this I have learnt no details as yet.

For all their habits, laws, and customs, the people, as a rule, have but one explanation: "It is in the Canon of Lek,"—the law that is said to have been laid down by the chieftain Lek Dukaghin. Lek is fabled to have legislated minutely on all subjects. For example, a man told me that Lek had ordered that men should walk the length of one gun-barrel apart, lest in turning the barrel should accidentally strike the next man, for a blow even by chance must be avenged. And this law was to keep peace. Similarly women must walk the length of one distaff apart—they always spin on the march.

Of Lek himself little is known. His fame among the tribes that still bear his name far exceeds that of Skenderbeg, and the fog of mythology is thick round him. He has left no mark on European history—is a purely local celebrity,—but must have been of insistent individuality to have so influenced the people that "Lek said so" obtains far more obedience than the Ten Commandments. The teachings of Islam and of Christianity, the Sheriat and Church law, all have to yield to the Canon of Lek.

The Dukaghini (Duke John Duka, dux in the Latin sense) were a ruling family in the fifteenth century. (Hopf *Chroniques Greco-romains inédits*) gives an old pedigree of Dukaghini, Lords of Zadrima, the Black Mountains (probably Mal i zion the Drin), of Pulati and Shati, as early as the end of the thirteenth century. Later come Lords of Guri kuch, Fandi and Salita, and the "last Lord of Zadrima and Dagno was dispossessed by the Turks in 1479."

Some of the Dukaghini seem then to have fled to Venice along with the Venetians when they evacuated Scutari, and a "Luca Ducagini Duca di Pulato e dell stato Ducagino" is recorded in Venice in 1506.

The pedigree contains numerous names, and is possibly inaccurate in detail, though true in its main lines—for all the districts above named still quote Lek, keep his law, and call themselves Dukaghini. When not making common cause against the Turks, there was much quarrelling between Skenderbeg and the Dukaghini Princes. They were allies of Venice, and he was friend of the king of Naples. Within the widespread Dukaghini lands there is no local tradition of Skenderbeg, no "castles" or "rocks" of Skenderbeg, but plenty of Lek—which shows that the Dukaghini were the old established hereditary rulers, for their mark on the land is deeper than that of Skenderbeg, whose victories gained European fame. There is, it is true, a tale that Skenderbeg was related to the Dukaghini, but it is vague.

It appears that there were several Dukaghini of the name of Lek (Alexander—I have been told, too, Lek was related to Alexander the Great), and they have become entangled. Tradition tells that the Ljuma tribe had a chief in the fourteenth century called Lek Kapetan.

An Albanian once gave me a message to European politicians in general : "If a man tells you that he knows about the Near East, ask him what is the difference between Lek Dukaghin and Lek Kapetan? If he cannot tell, he should let the Near East alone. We suffer from people who interfere and know nothing." The question, I fancy, would "plough" many a Foreign Office.

Lek of the Canon, says tradition, fled from Rashia when the Turks overpowered it, came with the ancestors of the Mirdites, and is of the same blood as the bariak of Oroshi. The present hereditary prince, Prenk Bib Doda of Oroshi, claims to be descended from the Dukaghins. Nor is it historically improbable that one of the Dukaghins (a chieftain family, widely influential) should have fought the Turks on the plains, and been forced to retire with his men to the mountains.

As for the laws and customs ascribed to him, the greater part are obviously far earlier than the fifteenth century, when he is said to have lived. They probably were obeyed by the unknown warriors of the bronze weapons in the prehistoric graves.

Lek possibly put together the then existing tribe law, but his own laws are probably those only that are designed to check or reform old usage by enforcing punishment. It is impossible to believe, for example, that—as the people declare—Lek both ordered blood-vengeance to be taken, and condemned the taker of it to be severely punished. Rather, that he devised a heavy penalty to check blood feud. But it has signally failed.

He gave his sanction, it would appear, to much barbarous custom—nor with such a conservative people could he well have done otherwise. It is said that Pope Paul II. (1464) excommunicated him for his most un-Christian code. Some have suggested that, as Lek came from Rashia, he must have been of Slavonic blood. This is improbable, as the Canon does not resemble the famous Servian Code of Tsar Stefan Dushan (1349), which we may fairly presume was founded on old Slavonic usage. On the other hand, the "old law" that prevailed in Montenegro and the Herzegovina till the middle of the nineteenth century resembles very strongly that of the Albanian mountains. The chief differences seem, so far as I have learnt, to have been in the punishments. These therefore I take to be Lek's, and the rest, old tribe law common to this Serbo-Illyrian group of people.

The law in the Albanian mountains is administered by a council of Elders. Each tribe is self-governing. Custom varies with the district.

In the Maltsia e madhe group (Hoti, Gruda, Kastrati, Skreli, Kilmeni) a full council, *i.e.* one that can deal with matters affecting the whole tribe, must consist of the Bariaktar, four Voyvodas, twelve Elders (specially chosen for their intelligence and knowledge of law), and seventy-two heads of houses.

For small local affairs—quarrels, robbery—the Bariaktar and nine Elders suffice. The title Voyvoda (head of a *mehala*) is Slavonic, and does not occur in any other district of Albania.

The council meets near the church (or mosque). I had difficulty in unravelling the procedure, which is complicated. I believe it to be as follows:—

A man accuses another, say of theft. He lays the case before the Bariaktar. The point to be determined is whether a sufficient number of con-jurors can be found before whom the accused may swear his innocence, and who are willing to swear to it with him. The Bariaktar can decide how many to summon. The plaintiff has the right to nominate them. They must belong to the tribe. The accused may object to a certain number—it depends, I believe, on how many are called—and have them replaced. All meet before the council. The accused and plaintiff are heard. Should the con-jurors agree that the accused is innocent, the Elders acquit him. (It must be remembered that in these tribes every one knows all about every one else's doings.) Should all con-jurors but one agree to his innocence, that one can be dismissed, but two must replace him.

The plaintiff, if not satisfied, has the right to demand more con-jurors up to a fixed number according to the crime. Twenty-four may be demanded for murder, and from two to ten for stealing, according to the value of the thing stolen. Eight for a horse. If it cannot be otherwise decided, the defendant may put in witnesses from among his own family.

If the verdict be "guilty," the Elders decide the punishment. For theft, twice the value of the thing stolen must be given to its owner, and half the value to be divided among the Elders. It may, when possible, be paid in kind—for one sheep, two.

For anything stolen off church land as much as ten times the value may be exacted. In olden times a fancy value was set on a stolen cock. Probably because the cock was held of great power against evil spirits, so of much value to its possessor.

If the accused be found innocent, the whole party goes into the church. The candles are lighted on the altar, and, in the presence of the priest, the accused first swears his innocence on the gospel. Next in order swear those of his family who may have been summoned, then all the other con-jurors. Whether innocent or guilty, the accused has to pay each con-juror 20 piastres (about 3s. 4d.). The plaintiff can therefore annoy by insisting on the full number the law allows. A priest counts as twelve con-jurors. Men of importance in the tribe are sometimes also reckoned as more than one. Among Moslems the oath is sworn in a mosque.

In the case of wounding accidentally, or with intent to kill, the damage is estimated by the Elders. For example, a man playing with a rifle shot a woman through the foot, and had to pay her husband 15 napoleons, and must pay 15 more if she ever die from the resultant lameness.

Cases of compounding blood feuds or murder have to be referred (when they take place in Maltsia c madhe) to the Djibal in Scutari. This is said to have been started because on one occasion the tribes could not agree on some point and asked Turkish advice (Kastrati has another tradition about it).

The Djibal is a mixed council. Each of the five above-mentioned tribes has a representative in it (called *krye t malit*), and there is a Moslem representative of each (called a *bylykbasha*), appointed by the Turkish Government. One Bylykbasha can represent more than one tribe. The president of council is the Sergherdé, a

Government-appointed Moslem. The penalty for murder
is about £24 paid to the Sergherdé and £12 to the
Bylykbasha of the tribe. Twenty-four pounds is payable
also to the Church if the murder be on Church land.
Twenty-four pounds also to the *xoti i ghakut* (lord of
blood = that one of the deceased's family who has the
right to demand blood, or its equivalent). Should he
accept it the feud ceases. But he usually prefers to shoot
the offender himself, and the blood feud thus started is not
compounded till several on either side have been killed.

To compound it the guilty party must send emissaries
to the *xoti i ghakut*. If he be willing to compound, a
council is called. It is usual, when the blood-gelt is
accepted, for the two chief parties to swear brotherhood.
If the feud is with a member of another tribe, and the
parties are not consanguineous, it is usual also to give a
daughter in marriage to some member of the offended
family, and thus establish peace.

The Sergherdé and Bylykbashas have no other pay
than the fees they can collect for " blood," so are reported
not to wish to stop the practice. They are called on
sometimes for an opinion in other cases, and are said to
require bribing.

The Canon also punishes the taker of blood by
burning down his house. And, except in cases where the
slaying is thought justified, the penalty is inflicted by
order of the Elders, who can also forbid him to work his
ground for a year or even two.

Neither Sergherdé nor Bylykbashas venture into the
mountains save on rare occasions under promise of safe-
conduct. If their fees are in arrears they arrest any
man of the same tribe that comes down to market, and
imprison him as hostage till paid. As a rule in Maltsia
e madhe it is paid punctually, and all shooting cases are
notified to Scutari by the tribes with surprising speed.
They say Lek ordered a fine to be paid, and that they

themselves accepted the Djibal—" It is the law, so must be obeyed." What the tribesman resents to the uttermost is not the administration of law, but the attempt to force on him laws to which he has never assented.

An occasional paragraph in the English newspapers tells of an outbreak of "Albanian lawlessness,"—that troops have been sent to Ljuma, for example, to enforce the payment of cattle tax, or order the disarming of the population—an expedition that always fails. In these cases the lawbreakers are not the Albanians, but the force sent against them. The Albanians originally agreed with the Turks that they should retain their own law, and give in return voluntary military service. They have kept their part of the contract, and have quite justly resisted Turkish attempts to forcibly break the other part.

The Young Turks have broken the Turkish covenant with Albania, and fighting has in consequence taken place near Ipek.

Among the tribes called Dukaghini, customs are found in more primitive form than in Maltsia e madhe.

Dukaghini—the tribes who accept the Canon, though a more restricted district is now called Dukaghini—includes Pulati proper—that is, Kiri, Plani, Mgula, and Ghoanni; Upper Pulati—that is, Shala, Shoshi, Nikaj, Berisha, Merturi, and Toplana; and Postripa—that is, Ura Strengit, Mazreku, Drishti, Shlaku, Suma, and Dushmani. Also all Puka. The Canon is, however, much more widely spread. It is the law also in Mirdita, and Kthela, and Luria. It has been carried by branches of many of the above-named tribes into the plains of Metoja and Kosovo. It prevails also, I believe, in all the large Moslem tribes, but details of the usages among them I have not yet obtained.

The most important fact in North Albania is blood-vengeance, which is indeed the old, old idea of purification by blood. It is spread throughout the land. All else is subservient to it.

"What profit is life to a man if his honour be not clean?" To cleanse his honour no price is too great. And in the mountains the individual is submerged tribe. He is answerable, too, for the honour of his *mehala*, sometimes indeed of his whole *fis*.

Blood can be wiped out only with blood. A blow also demands blood, so do insulting words. One of the worst insults is the marrying of a girl betrothed to one man, to another. Nothing but blood can cleanse it.

Abduction of a girl demands blood, as does of course adultery. This does not appear to be common. It entails so much blood that "the game is not worth the candle." The blood taken need not be that of the actual offender. It must be male blood of his house or tribe. The usage differs in various districts, and will be noted in the accounts of them.

A man is answerable, too, for his guest, and must avenge a stranger that has passed but one night beneath his roof, if on his journey next day he be attacked. The sacredness of the guest is far-reaching. A man who brought me water from his house, that I might drink by the way, said that I now ranked as his guest, and that he should be bound by his honour to avenge me should anything happen to me before I had received hospitality from another.

Blood-vengeance, slaying a man according to the laws of honour, must not be confounded with murder. Murder starts a blood feud. In blood-vengeance the rules of the game are strictly observed. A man may not be shot for vengeance when he is with a woman nor with a child, nor when he is met in company, nor when *besa* (oath of peace) has been given. The two parties may swear such an oath for a few weeks if they choose, for business purposes. There are men who, on account of blood, have never been out alone for years.

When the avenger has slain his victim, he first

reaches a place of safety, and then proclaims that he has done the deed. He wishes all to know his honour is clean. That he is now liable to be shot, and, if the blood be taken within the tribe, to heavy punishment also, is of minor moment to him.

In the Dukaghini tribes the council has power not merely to burn his house, but to destroy his crops, fell his trees, slaughter his beasts, and condemn him to leave his land unworked. An incredible amount of food-stuff is yearly wasted, and land made desolate.

The house is perhaps not merely the home of himself, his wife and children, but that of a whole family community, forty or fifty people. The law is carried out to the last letter. It crushes the innocent along with the guilty; it is remorseless, relentless. But "it is the Canon and must be obeyed."

A man can save his house only if he can return to it and defend it successfully for three days, so that no one can approach near enough to set fire to it. A "very brave man" was pointed out to me in Berisha, who has three times been condemned to have his house burnt, and each time saved it thus. A man can also save his property by inviting to the house the head of another *mehala*, who must then declare himself house lord and take command. The house is then, for the time being, his; he summons his own men to defend it, a regular battle may take place, and the house be saved. But it is usual at once to call a council of Elders to stop the warfare. In such a case it is usual to burn only the house, and spare the crop and other property (Berisha).

The Canon of Lek has but two punishments, fine and burning of property. Neither death nor imprisonment can be inflicted. Prison there is none. Death would but start a new feud. And Lek's object appears to have been to check feud.

In the case of a man accused of murder, and arraigned before the Elders, should it occur that they cannot come to any agreement as to whether he be guilty or not, a new trial can be made. But the Lord of Blood rarely waits for this. He prefers to shoot the man that he accuses, and by so doing renders himself liable to house-burning, and to being shot in his turn. Sometimes the Ghaksur (taker of blood) flies and shelters with another tribe, leaving his burnt-out family to shift for themselves. Or his relations take him in, help pay his fine —for the honour of them all is cleaned by the blood-taking—give him, one a sheep, another an ox, and he helps work their land till free to work his own again, and so he makes a fresh start. I have met men burnt clean out three times, but now in fairly flourishing condition.

Any house to which a Ghaksur flies for shelter is bound to give him food and protection; he is a guest, and as such sacred. The Law of Blood has thus had great influence in mixing the population of all the western side (at least) of the Balkan peninsula, Montenegrins have for centuries fled from "blood" into Albania, and Albanians into Montenegro. A large proportion of the Serbophone Moslems of Podgoritza are said to derive from Montenegrins, who refuged there from blood in the days when it was Turkish territory. According to the Canon a man is absolute master in his own house, and, in the unmodified form of the law, has the right to kill his wife, and any of his children. My informants doubted whether the killing of the wife would be tolerated now. She would be avenged by her own family. A man may, however, kill his wife with the consent of her family. A case in point took place, I was told, recently. The wife of a mountain man left him and went down to Scutari, where she lived immorally with the soldiers, thereby blackening the honour of her husband, and of her own family.

Her husband appealed to her brother (head of the family), who gave him the cartridge with which he shot her and cleaned the honour of them all. Had she eloped with a man, he would have been held guilty and shot. She would not be punished, as the man would be held to have led her astray. But in the above case her guilt was undoubted. It is very rare that a woman is killed. To kill a married woman entails two bloods—blood with her husband's and with her own family.

A woman is never liable for blood-vengeance, except in the rare case of her taking it herself. But even then there seems to be a feeling that it would be very bad form to shoot her. I could not hear of a recent case. I roused the greatest horror by saying that a woman who commits a murder in England is by law liable to the same punishment as a man. Shala is a wild tribe; it shoots freely. But a Shala man said, "It is impossible. Where could a man be found who would hang a woman? No mountain man would do it. It is a bad law. You must be bad people." He was as genuinely shocked as is a suburban mission meeting over the sacrifices of Dahomey. The tribe cannot punish bloodshed within the family group, *e.g.* if one cousin in a communal house kill another. The head of the house is arbiter. A man said naïvely on this subject, "How can such a case be punished? A family cannot owe itself blood?" To him the "family" was the entity; the individual had no separate existence. Marriage is arranged entirely by the head of the house. The children are betrothed in infancy or *in utero.* Even earlier. A man will say to another with whom he wishes to be allied, "When your wife has a daughter I want her for my son." A wife is always bought. The infant comes into the world irrevocably affianced, and part of the purchase-money is at once paid. She can marry no other man, is sent to her unknown husband when old enough, and the balance of the price handed over. The husband is bound to take her, no matter what she is like, or fall into blood with her family. The girl may—but it requires much courage on her part—refuse to marry the man. In that case she must swear before witnesses to remain virgin all her life. Should she break this vow, endless bloodshed is caused. If her father sell her to another it entails two bloods—blood between her family and her first betrothed's, and blood between her husband's and her betrothed's. Should she make a runaway match there is triple blood, as her family is at blood also with her husband's. In such cases the woman is furiously blamed. " She knew the laws, and the amount of blood that must be shed."

The most singular part of the business is the readiness with which most youths accept the girl bought for them. I never heard of one refusing, though I met several " Albanian virgins," girls who had sworn virginity to escape their betrothed.

The Catholic Church is making strenuous efforts to suppress infant betrothal by refusing to recognise it under the age of fourteen, and trying then to be sure that the girl consents, but as yet little progress has been made. By the Canon a man could divorce his wife by cutting off a piece of her dress and sending her home thus disfigured. The Church has not quite suppressed this among the Christian tribes. It is said to be a common practice among the Moslems. A man though married may take his brother's widow as concubine one month after his brother's death, also his uncle's or cousin's widow. Children of such unions are reckoned legitimate by the people, and may even be considered to be those of the first husband. In Maltsia e madhe this custom is now extinct; but in Dukaghini and Pulati, in spite of all the priests, it is quite common. Throughout the Moslem tribes this practice prevails; otherwise it is said to be rare for a Moslem tribesman to have more than one wife at a time.

(I was told in Montenegro that a hundred years ago it was not uncommon for a man to have two wives. Possibly it was this same custom.) Should a woman bear her husband only daughters, the family on his death have the right to turn her out penniless, though they have sold all the daughters at good prices. A woman believed capable of producing only daughters is valueless, and cannot hope to marry again. Should her own people be too poor to take her in, her lot is most miserable. On this point humaner feelings are beginning to prevail. The birth of a daughter is still considered a misfortune. Yet I was assured everywhere that there were more men than women in the land, and young marriageable widows when for sale are snapped up at once, often fetching more than maidens.

The rule as to whom a childless widow belongs seems to vary in different parts. In Kastrati and in Vukli (Maltsia e madhe) I was told she was the property of her father or, in case of his decease, his next heir male. Should she have children, she must remain with her husband's family to bring them up. The children belong to the family—not to her.

In Dukaghini, should she not be taken on as concubine by a member of her husband's family, his family and her family share the price for which they sell her again.

No man may strike a woman but her husband— or, if she be unmarried, her father. To do so entails blood.

A woman in the mountains, in spite of the severe work she is forced to do, is in many ways freer than the women of Scutari. She speaks freely to the men; is often very bright and intelligent, and her opinion may be asked and taken. I have seen a man bring his wife to give evidence in some case under dispute. I have also seen the women interfere to stop a quarrel, but where the family honour is concerned they are as anxious that blood should be taken as are the men.

The fact that a wife cannot be obtained without paying for her among the mountain tribes is one of the frequent causes of abduction.

In Maltsia e madhe a girl who has sworn virginity—"an Albanian virgin"—can, if her father leave no son, inherit land and work it. At her death it goes to her father's nearest heir male. These women as a rule wear male dress and may carry arms.

The practice of women wearing male dress existed also in that part of Montenegro known as the Brda, which includes those tribes that are according to tradition allied by blood to those of Albania. Medakovich, a Russian traveller, records meeting one at Rovac in 1855. She had sworn virginity and ranked as her father's son, he having none.

In Dukaghini, though I met several Albanian Virgins, I neither saw nor heard of an instance of a maiden in male dress.

Space does not permit further details. I have given sufficient only to make the following travels comprehensible.

CHAPTER III

KASTRATI, SKRELI, GRUDA, AND HOTI

"In a Somer Sesun whan softe was the Sonne
Went I widen in the Worlde, Wonders to here."

IT was Friday, May 8, 1908, and Scutari was asleep—
even the dogs were still curled up tight in the gutters—
when we started on foot and purposely oozed out of
the town by the wrong road in the grey dawning. The
kirijee and the two horses met us in the open. It was
not until we had mounted that I felt the journey had
really begun at last.

There is a peculiar pleasure in riding out into the
unknown—a pleasure which no second journey on the
same trail ever affords.

The great mountains towered mauve in the beyond
across the plain. We turned our horses off the rough
track, and, following the *kirijee*, plunged them breast-
deep into pink asphodel, hoary with dew, forcing a
passage through it in a wide circuit over Fusha Stojit
till we struck the Serb village of Vraka and were well
beyond the gendarmerie outposts. Whether this elaborate
precaution were necessary I doubt. To me it was un-
pleasing, but I had been assured by all the consulates
I consulted that it was the only way. It lost us an hour
and a half but afforded great satisfaction to the *kirijee*
and certainly added a Near Eastern flavour to the
expedition.

Vraka greeted me cheerfully, but we left the cowrie-
decked women behind us and pushed on. Beyond
Kopliku—a small Moslem tribe—the plain rises and

is rocky in parts. Its name, Pustopoj, an obvious corruption of the Servian *pustopolje* (desert land), tells of Servian days.

The *kirijee* here lost the track. We wandered fruitlessly for an hour and a half till we struck the dry bed of the Proni Thaat, and following it up, came to the bridge that spans it—Ura Zais—and to the *han*.

What with dodging Ezzad Bey's gendarmerie and losing the way, we had made little progress, but it was noon and past, so we halted for a midday meal.

A *han* is usually a ramshackle shanty that in England would not be thought fit for a cow of good family. Its window is iron-barred, and the wooden flap that shuts it by night lets down by day, and forms a shelf on which folk sit cross-legged. Within, rows of bottles and a barrel or two loom through the darkness. Furniture it has none, and its floor is mother earth.

A friend in need is a friend indeed. Travellers make a point of abusing "the miserable Turkish *han*." I forget all its shortcomings and only remember the many times I have stumbled in storm-drenched and exhausted, and it has warmed and dried me and revived me with coffee and *rakia*. It has done all it could for me—which is more than can be said for any hotel starred by Baedeker.

We sat beneath a rude pergola of branches with other wayfarers, Skreli men. We were now in the lands of Skreli. The lively *hanjee* rattled away in Albanian and Servian. His predecessor had been shot for blood, thirteen years ago—there was his grave by the path. Talk ran on *ghak* (blood). They treated it from all points of view, from the serious to the humorous, but most of all from the point of view of the man that is born to it.

And from this point of view must it be seen to be understood. It is the fashion among journalists and others to talk of the "lawless Albanians"; but there is perhaps no other people in Europe so much under the tyranny of laws.

The unwritten law of blood is to the Albanian as is the Fury of Greek tragedy. It drives him inexorably to his doom. The curse of blood is upon him when he is born, and it sends him to an early grave. So much accustomed is he to the knowledge that he must shoot or be shot, that it affects his spirits no more than does the fact that "Man is mortal" spoil the dinner of a plump tradesman in West Europe.

The man whose honour has been soiled must cleanse it. Until he has done so he is degraded in the eyes of all—an outcast from his fellows, treated contemptuously at all gatherings. When finally folk pass him the glass of *rakia* behind their backs, he can show his face no more among them — and to clean his honour he kills.

And lest you that read this book should cry out at the "customs of savages," I would remind you that we play the same game on a much larger scale and call it war. And neither is "blood" or war sweepingly to be condemned.

The *hanjee* told how a few days ago two men (whom he named), blood foes, had accidentally met at his *han*. Being with friends and meeting under one roof, it was not etiquette to shoot. They drank coffee together and became so friendly they swore peace for six weeks. The company thought this an excellent joke and laughed heartily.

Having finished our scrambled eggs and fried slices of sheep cheese, we set out again for Bratoshi in Kastrati Sypermi (Upper Kastrati) and soon entered Kastrati land.

The track wound up a mountain-side of bare grey rocks. The horses, sorry beasts at best, were wearied out and the rest of the way had to be tramped. Down below lay, like a garden, the fertile plain of Lower Kas-trati, and Scutari Lake blazed silver in the afternoon light.   It was aksham, past—we had been thirteen hours on the way—when we finally came to the church of Bratoshi.

The young Franciscan in charge made us very wel-come, and his charming old mother bustled round to make ready supper.

The name Kastrati is said to derive from the Latin *castrum*, which is not impossible, for the main road from Scodra to Dioclea must have passed through Lower Kastrati and have needed guards to protect it.

The tribesmen, however, relate that their name comes from their hero, George Kastrioti, the great Skenderbeg.   "When Skenderbeg died we sat by the wayside and wept.   The Turk came by and said, ' Why weep ye?' and we said, ' We weep because we have lost our sword !'   And he said, ' I will be your chief sword '" (Sergherdé).

" Then he read us the Sheriat (Turkish Law) and said, ' You must cease your grief.   Take off your black Ghurdi '" (the black, short jacket which, according to tradition, is mourning for George Skenderbeg and named after him) " ' and put on the Turkish Ghiubé.'

" But we answered, ' Christians are we, and Christians have we ever been !   We cannot take Turkish law. Neither can we wear Turkish garb.   We are ruled by the Canon of Lek Dukaghin.'   Then he offered us the waistcoat that we still call Jelek, saying, ' Je Lek '" (Thou art Lek.)   " So came we under the Turk."

This curious little tale with its fantastic etymology is of great interest, inasmuch as it definitely connects Skenderbeg with a northern tribe.   For it is more pro-bable that he should have taken his name from the place than the place from him.

Kastrati consists of one bariak of five hundred houses

and, as do all tribes, has a definite tale of origin. It traces descent from the famous fighting stock, Drekalovich of Kuchi, which in turn derives from Berisha, by tradition one of the oldest of all Albanian tribes. Kuchi, since the war of '76–'77, has been included politically within the Montenegrin frontier. Actually, it first threw in its lot with Montenegro in 1835, but—together with Piperi, another tribe of at any rate partially Albanian blood —revolted in 1845 when Prince Danilo tried to make them pay taxes. The rising was suppressed, but Kuchi revolted again later. Montenegro owes the subsequent acquisition of the territory to the heroism and military skill of Marko Drekalovich, who with his tribe, after harrying the Turks of Podgoritza for many years, sick of Turkish rule, joined forces with Prince Nikola when war against the Turks was proclaimed. He lies buried on the heights of Medun, the Turkish stronghold which he captured after a heavy siege, and his name is famous alike in Albania and Monteuegro.

The Kuchi are now largely (entirely?) Serbophone and Orthodox. When they became so I do not know.

From Drekalovich, then, "a long while ago" came one Delti with his seven sons to the land of Kastrati. They fought the people they found there, said to be Serbs, beat them, took land and settled. And from Delti and his seven sons descend three hundred houses of Kastrati. The remaining two hundred are of mixed origin ; some, doubtless with truth, are said to derive from the conquered Serbs. They are all now Catholic or Moslem, and Albanophone but Serb names, notably Popovich, show they have not always been so.

The nearest approach to a date that I obtained was that the Church of Gruda was the oldest in Maltsia e madhe, and was 380 years old, and that the Church of Bratoshi Kastrati—third oldest—was built soon after the Delti settled. This definite statement, that the Delti arrived less than 380 years ago, is of much interest, as in spite of the Skenderbeg story in the land, it makes their arrival subsequent to Skenderbeg's death (1467).

Skenderbeg's place of origin is wrapped in mystery. Many places claim him. According to the most recent research (see Pastor's *Lives of the Popes*, and Hertzburg's *Byzantiner und Osmanen*), Skenderbeg was of Slav origin, passed his life in his native mountains, and first leapt to fame when he beat the Turks at Debra in 1444, and inaugurated Albanian independence; and the tale of his captivity among the Turks is mythical. Dufresne du Cange, quoting Flavius Comnenus, gives as Skenderbeg's great-grandfather, one "Constantinus Castriotus, cognomento Meserechus, Æmathiæ et Castoriæ Princeps."

Meserechus must be surely the modern Mazreku, now a parish of Pulati; and if Æmathiæ may be taken as Matija, it would account entirely for Skenderbeg's father being Lord of Kroja, since Matija lies just behind Kroja. These two names, and the fact that he was a Catholic, connect him entirely with the North, and make the popular tale that he derived from Castoria, in the southeast, highly improbable.

Whereas, if the family originated from Kastrati, the tradition that the Slav inhabitants there were overwhelmed and displaced by the Albanian Kuchi, would account for the fact that no more definite tale of Skenderbeg, than the one quoted, exists there.

It is an interesting fact that most of the celebrated leaders of North Albania and Montenegro seem to have been of mixed Serbo-Albanian blood.

I found Kastrati ruing the day when it had accepted the mixed rule of tribe and Djibal.

Already at the *han* I had learned why Scutari was refusing permission to travel in the mountains. The tribes of Maltsia e madhe, exasperated against Schahir

Bey, the then Sergherdé, were in open defiance. Their charges against him were many and bitter, and they swore they would have no more of him.

I had planned to stay some days at Bratoshi, but was urged to go at once to Skreli to the Feast of the Translation of St. Nikolas, the tribal saint, where the tribes would gather in their best array. So, as all the world was going to Skreli, to Skreli I went. Among our company was a Kastrati man from Podgoritza in Montenegro, whither he had fled from blood some years ago. He spoke Serb well, and was in the highest spirits, for the fact that by coming to the feast he risked his life, added much spice to the outing.

"How many have you killed?" I asked. "Eight— up till to-day," said he cheerfully. A Moslem had shot one of his sons, whereon he had shot four of that Moslem's near relatives, and flitted over the border. It pleased him much. The Moslem would mind it far more than being shot himself. He joked about his fellow-tribesmen: "Wild people," said he.

"Art thou wild, too?" I asked. "No, no," said he, adding with a beaming smile: "I've killed many men though, Christians and Moslems, and God willing, I will shoot some more. Now I am going to pray to St. Nikola."

He had a son in training as a Montenegrin officer, and was loud in praise of Prince Nikola. His grand-children will probably be Orthodox and Serbophone, and his great-grandchildren swear they have been Serb from the beginning of time. And thus for centuries have the Balkan races been made.

The track to Brzheta led up over stones to the ridge of the mountain, where a rough wall marked the frontier of Kastrati and Skreli, and then down a stony zigzag, too steep for the horses, which were led round. The church and church-house stand in the valley of the Proni

Thaat. The priest of Skreli, whose own bishop describes him as "tiny but terrible," brimming with energy and hospitality, was making great preparations for guests. On a feast-day, he declared, two or three more or less made no difference, he could find room for me somewhere.

Beyond the green bed of the valley rose, snow-capped, the wall of mountain that parts Skreli from the Pulati tribes. Skreli tells a tale of origin from Bosnia.

I paid visits. The people, most friendly, were delighted to let me "write" their houses. They are of stone with tiled roof. The ground floor is stable. The dwelling-room above is approached by an outside staircase of stone or wood, which leads often to a large covered balcony. The windows are few and small. The fire is lit on an open hearth at one end, the smoke escaping through the unceiled roof. Behind the hearth is a recess in the wall to contain cooking utensils. Many houses have a wattled larder standing on posts in the yard, especially to keep milk in. Every house expected guests.

In the evening the priest's guests began arriving— two Franciscans, two priests, and last not least, the deputy Archbishop of Scutari—and the fun began. As each and his retainers got within howling distance they yelled aloud, hailing their host.

The priest of Skreli then dashed wildly to the window, leaned perilously far out, and hurled his voice back, at the same time emptying a revolver. The visitor replied with a volley, rode up full clatter, rushed upstairs and helped to yell and fire greetings at the next comer. They were all young, and were in the highest spirits—for a mountain mission priest gets very little fun in his life— when the Archbishop turned up. Finding them there, he pretended at first to be severe, for the feast-day to-morrow was a Sunday, and without his permission none were supposed to absent themselves from their own parishes

Fireplace of a House
at Shreli   McDurham 1908

on a Sunday. However, they all vowed that all their own parishioners were coming to the feast, and that it was their duty to come and look after them, and the Archbishop was soon as festive as every one else. Meantime guests were arriving at all the other houses, and a continuous rifle-fire swished and tore down the valley. We sat down to supper, a most ecclesiastical party. I found myself on the right hand of the Archbishop, the solitary female among six churchmen. But they all spoke some language I did, were immensely kind, and all invited me to visit their tribes.

After supper was a sing-song, the typical Albanian songs that are like nothing else. The Albanian scale is not as the modern European scale, but is all semi-tones and fractional tones. Nor has the music regular time. Its rhythm is hurried or slackened according to the singer's dramatic instinct, and the words are incredibly drawn out over long minor turns and ups and downs that few English throats could imitate. To the uninitiated it seems to begin nowhere and leave off anywhere, until, after a few weeks, the ear, accustomed as it were to a new language, recognises both tune and rhythm, and airs that at first seemed all alike become distinct. They are national and original and not without charm, and are sung always at the top of the voice, and that an artificial one, high for men, low for women. The two sexes sing so much alike that I once mistook the voice of a little girl of thirteen singing in the next room for that of a man. Her delighted parents said, " She has indeed a very beautiful voice."

Marko and the churchmen all had huge voices and the roof rang. One song was of a widow who had two sons. The elder went to the mountain and turned robber. His mother believed him dead. The younger stayed with her, but having to cross the mountains for business was shot at from behind a rock and mortally wounded. As he lay dying the two brothers recognised one another. Horrified, the elder was about to shoot himself, when the younger cried, " Do not kill both our mother's sons. Go to her and tell her I have gone to a far country, and that you will stay with her." He died, and the robber returned home.

Another was of a youth who had gone to visit a friend. He rapped on the door with the butt of his revolver. It went off and killed him, and the song mourned his fate.

The feast really fell on the Saturday. It was kept on Sunday because Saturday is a fast-day, and you cannot feast without roast mutton. Early Sunday morning the guests poured down the zig-zag in a living cataract on the one side, and flocked from the valleys on the other— from Hoti, from Kastrati and Boga, all in their best— men first, their women following. As each batch came in sight of the church they yelled for the priest; bang, bang went fifty rifles at once; swish-ish-ish flew the bullets; pop, pop, pop, pop, pop, pop replied the priest's old six-shooter. Before midday the meeting-ground round the church was packed with magnificent specimens of humanity. The visitor to Scutari rarely sees the really fine mountain man—he is either at feud with the Government or owes blood, and sends his women to the town when business is necessary.

Etiquette demanded that the Skreli people, being the hosts, should not wear their best clothes, it is for the guests to do all the peacocking. And peacock they did. Many carried splendid silver-mounted weapons, and even though wearing revolvers, thrust great silver ramrods in their belts, for "swagger." Snow-white headwraps dazzled in the sun—crimson and gold *djemadans* and *jeleks*, the short black *ghurdi*, and the splendidly decorative black braiding of the tight-fitting *chakshir* (trousers), and the heavy silver watch and pistol chains—

set lavishly with the false rubies and turquoise loved of the mountain man—set off the lean supple figures to the greatest advantage. The majority belonged to the long-faced, aquiline-nosed type, with long, well-cut jawbone, eyebrows that slope downwards, and either hazel eyes and brown hair, or grey-blue eyes and fair hair. All had shaven heads, the unshaven patch varying in shape and position. To study head-tufts one must go to

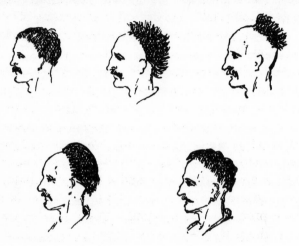

Notes of Variety of Head-shaves in Kastrati and Skreli.

church festivals. Only then are a number seen un-covered.

Of the headwrap the Scutari Christians always say, "They took it from the Turks." But Henry Blunt, writing in 1650, gives a curious legend to the effect that it originated at the battle of Thermopylæ, had been worn ever since, and was adopted by the Turks. This, though the Thermopylæ part is doubtless fabulous, is of interest as showing so early as 1650 a belief that the headwrap was long pre-Turkish, in Europe.

The women, who trooped after their men, also wrap the head. They too are shaven all round the temples and their faces look extraordinarily large and blank. Some are also shaven in a strip along th e top of the forehead, but the shaven strip is often covered by a fringe brought down over it. This is all the hair that shows, and is darkened by dye or oil. Unmarried girls have often quite fair hair.

Girls and women are differently dressed. The girls' dress is of thick, stiff, white wool with horizontal black stripes. The skirt and bodice are joined, and the bodice is open at the sides. The outer garments of both men and women are commonly open under the armpits for ventilation.

Under the dress the girls and women of these parts wear a shirt with long sleeves, and no other garment save the long stockings knitted in fancy patterns of red and black or black and white. Married women wear a black bell-shaped skirt of stiff, heavy wool, striped with dull crimson (native dyed) or purple (bought in Scutari). The bodice is open at the side, and a thick epaulette, heavily fringed, covers the shoulder. Over the skirt is a heavy striped apron of the same stuff. And round the waist is a great leathern belt five or six inches wide, studded thickly with small nails. More inappropriate wear for a married woman could hardly be invented. On the head is a flat black cap on the crown of which is sewn a crescent, or a double crescent, of silver-gilt filagree. Or a similar design is worked in gold thread. This crescent the Christian women say they have always worn, and that it is not Turkish. In this they are probably correct. The crescent and sun are very commonly tattooed together with the cross on all these Christian tribes-folk, men and women. This seems to be the remnant of some old pre-Christian belief not connected with Mahomedanism at all. The Moslems do not tattoo the crescent but a double triangle.

The church-bell rang, the church was packed, Place

was given to visitors, and most of the Skreli tribe knelt on the ground outside.

A week's *besa* had been sworn for the festival, so that all blood foes could meet as friends.

After church there was a rush for the rifles, stacked outside; a shooting competition began, accompanied by a general fusillade. And all were so gay and friendly it was hard to believe that they nearly all owed, or were owed, blood.

About three o'clock the whole gathering broke up with amazing speed, to dine with their Skreli hosts. Firing continued light-heartedly till late at night, but no accident marred the *festa*. *Festas* do not always pass off so well among the wilder tribes. The Archbishop told how, when he was parish priest in a Pulati tribe, he once had seven shot dead just outside his church on the feast of the patron saint.

There being no hay or corn, the horses of the entire party had been turned loose to browse in the copses. Consequently we awoke to a horseless dawn. The sturdy ecclesiastical steeds, not seeing the fun of fasting on a feast-day, had all bolted in search of richer fare, the Archbishop's along with the rest.

My humble *kirijee* horses, having no superfluous energy, were found after an hour's search. Leaving the horseless churchmen disconsolate on the balcony, we started for Lower Kastrati with a Kastrati man—brother of the one who had brought us—a lively fellow, with shaven temples and hair plastered down in a straight fringe over his shaven forehead.

He had enjoyed the *festa* vastly, and fired off his whole belt of cartridges—forty. This is all that most men possess. They buy caps and powder, cast their own bullets, and perpetually refill their empty cartridge-cases. The ease with which a Martini cartridge is filled is the main reason of that weapon's popularity. As a quick firer it cannot of course compare with the Mauser. But it wounds far more severely, and drops its man when the Mauser fails to stop him, and, as there is always plenty of cover from which to get a near shot, it has many admirers. Many people told me that for a real good old-fashioned wound the good old flintlock with a dram of powder well rammed down, carrying a huge bullet, nails, and other fancy articles, was a sure thing at close range.

We walked all down the valley of the Proni Thaat, a strip of cultivated land sown with maize and tobacco, flanked by grey, grim Karst, which nought but centuries of foresting can hope to tame. By the track side we passed a Christian grave, adorned with a cross and a rude relief of a saddle-horse. Both guide and *kirijee* said it was customary to carve a man's favourite horse on his grave. Does it tell of the days when a warrior's horse was buried with him?

I saw other examples.

We turned off Proni Thaat at Ura Zais, and struck over the flat plain to Baitza, past rich fields where the crops were guarded from the Evil Eye by horses' skulls set on poles, or their modern substitutes, twisted petroleum cans whitewashed. A cross gave yet further protection.

The church and priest's house of Baitza stand on a fair plain that lies but little above the lake level, and smiles with crops, cherries, figs, and almonds, but is malarious in summer.

The church-tower is marked by the builder's name, Selim, Debra.

The best builders in North Albania are Moslems from Debra: dark, short men—Albanophone, but wearing the *dolama* (long coat) of the Slav, belted with an orange sash,

Though possibly of mixed blood, the Moslems of

Debra are some of the Slavs' worst persecutors, and are mainly responsible for the Albanian's sinister reputation in England.

In the graveyard is a cross of a type common in many parts of the country. Three rudely carved birds are perched, one on either arm, and one on the top. The natives say the bird is *pllum* (dove), and that it is *per bukur* (for beauty). It is, however, only another way of keeping off *Syy kec* (Evil Eye). The cock, throughout the Balkan Peninsula, is the bird famed for this. A grotesque cockyolybird adorned the headbands of the Herzegovinian women. It is possible

(A) Cock on Herzegovinian (B) Bronze Amulets, (C) Dove on Grave-cross,
Head-dress.   Sarajevo Museum.   North Albania.

that on Christian graves the dove—the conventional emblem of the Holy Ghost—is a substitute for the former bird of magic. But dove-like bronze annulets occur in early Bosnian graves.

Christians and Moslems, of which there are a good many in Lower Kastrati, live together on perfectly friendly terms. Religious persecution never takes place *within* a tribe. It is intertribal when it occurs.

We strolled round. Folk were as eager to see me as I, them. We entered the first house that asked us, and climbed up to the dark dwelling-room.

It was full of people whose talk was bitter lament. All the five large tribes having refused further obedience to the Sergherdé, the men could no longer go to the bazar. They were fierce, hopeless, sullen. Last year the Sultan had wished to cede part of Kilmeni's best grazing land to Montenegro, to please the Powers. What right had the Sultan to cede their territory? If he wanted to give land, let him give Stamboul that belonged to him, not land that had belonged to Albania before ever the Turks came. What has the Turkish Government ever done for us? There is not a road in the country. Give us a just government. We are poor and ignorant. The Turks will do nothing except for bribes. We shall never have justice from them. They vowed they would be loyal to any foreign prince that would lead them. Twenty-five years ago, they had believed that salvation was in sight, but Austria had betrayed them. Now they knew not to whom to turn nor whence to obtain ammunition with which to fight free.

Two of the melancholy household were guests, flying from blood, the burden of their maintenance falling on their hosts. One was but fifteen, from Skreli, and had just killed his first man. He was a big, dark boy, who did not look his age. I think his first blood lay heavy on him—not as a crime, but as a momentous act that had brought him up suddenly against the raw facts of life. He sat silent. The first flush of victory had worn off. We spoke with him. He had been to school in Scutari, and could read and write a little. Now he could return there no more. An outcast, dependent on charity for his bread, his steps were dogged by the avenger of blood. The situation dazed him. Why did he kill his man? He was obliged to by the law. His hosts added that the Turkish authorities had ordered his parents' house (as he had not one of his own) to be burnt down, but, as the tribe was at feud with Scutari they would not obey.

The second guest was a weary-looking man of about forty. He too said he "had been obliged to kill.

is no government, God help us! You must kill the man that injures you yourself by the Old Law or he will treat you worse and worse." The family sheltering the two, was also at blood, and only the women could go out and about. They discussed which Power could save them. The Austrian consul, they said, was no use. He had lately visited them and was a coward. "We made coffee for him and he let his wife take it first. He was afraid of a woman!"

"That," said Marko, "is the custom *alla franga*."

"I would never let my wife eat with me," said the man that owed blood. "She must stand and wait till I have finished. Consul indeed!" And he roared with laughter—a momentary flash in the general gloom.

We left the dreary, blood-stricken house and went on, to be stopped very shortly by a party of men and women, whom the appearance of a total stranger greatly alarmed. They stopped me to learn what I was about. We sat down obediently, and made a solemn declaration that I had not come to seek treasure, and did not propose to remove untold sums of gold in the night. Their minds relieved on this point, an old man at once asked us to his house, a miserable one-roomed hut with a mud floor, and windowless. The loom, with a strip of cotton half-woven, stood in the doorway, where alone there was light enough to work by. The ragged lean old man led us in with a courtly grace, gave us the only two stools, and set his son to make coffee. I meanwhile drew the loom. They were delighted. They had never before seen a woman who could write, and never any one that could "write" a loom. In the mountains folk never differentiate between writing and drawing, I am not sure if they realise they are different processes. One suggested that a "writing woman" would be a good sort to marry, but Marko said that kind would not fetch wood and water, which damped the enthusiasm.

When I rose to go the old man asked if we had a roof for the night. "We are poor. Bread, salt, and our hearts is all we can offer, but you are welcome to stay as long as you wish."

It gave me joy to know that even in the bitterest corners of the earth there is so much of human kindness.

At even I sat with my three men on the grass before the church and watched the stars come out in the cloudless sky. Then there came a woman whom they called in jest a "nun"; one of those sworn to virginity because she has refused to marry the man to whom she was betrothed as a child. This "nun" sat along with us and chaffed the men in a very worldly style. The *kirijee*, roaring with laughter, told how such a nun had been servant to a priest in the neighbourhood. So spotless was her character, and so devout was she, that all said she would be taken straight to Paradise when she died. On the priest's death she shocked the whole tribe by marrying a Moslem from Gusinje! Now she could never come back with her husband, for it meant blood.

I asked her age when she married. She was forty, and her first betrothed had married another long ago. I said it was most unjust that a woman of forty should be bound by a promise made for her before she was born. She had been driven to the sin—if sin it were—of marrying a Moslem because no Christian had been brave enough to marry her. They replied indignantly that she had blackened the honour of her first betrothed, and also that of the twelve witnesses before whom she had sworn virginity, and they hoped, most uncharitably, that by this time she was miserable and repentant. But she was away on the other side of the Prokletija (Accursed Mountains), and I never learnt how the tale of the woman that married a Moslem ended.

Our Kastrati guide offered to lead us on to Bridzha in Hoti, whither we were bound. We started in the early

morning. The track over the lower Kastrati plain is good
—the red earth, well cleansed of pebbles, is sown where
there is enough of it. Wych elm and scrub oak grow in
the rocky parts. We struck inland, riding parallel with
Licheni Hotit (Lake of Hoti), a long swampy arm of the
lake that runs into the plain, and here divides Kastrati
from Hoti. Along it, on the Kastrati side, are the low
hills, the scene of the hapless rising of May 1883, to which
the people refer when they declare that " Austria betrayed
them." Thus runs the tale. An " Hungarian," calling
himself Delmotzi or Lemass in various places, journeyed
through the Great Mountains and spoke everywhere of
freedom. A commission was then on foot to determine
the Albano-Montenegrin frontier. He told them more
land would be torn from them. If they would rise and
save it they should have the support of the Austro-
Hungarian Government, which did not wish Slav borders
extended.

" I believed him," said an old man who had guided
the stranger. " O God, I believed him! I believed we
were to win freedom from the Turks. He asked how
long our ammunition would hold out, and we said,
' Two weeks.' ' Help will come in four days,' he
told us."

Then Kastrati and Hoti rose and took the Turkish
authorities unawares. Had all the tribes risen at once
there is little doubt that, for a time at any rate, they
could have swept all before them. But either the
" Hungarian's " promises were unauthorised or Austria's
plans changed. Most of the priests then were foreigners
under Austrian influence. They held back their flocks,
who were eager to fly to the rescue, and said the orders
had not yet come. Meanwhile the Turkish troops
hastened to the spot. The luckless insurgents held
the low range of hills, defending themselves with the
ferocity born of despair. When their ammunition was

all but exhausted they hurled themselves in a final frenzy on the soldiers, dragged in dead bodies and tore cartridges from the belts of the living and the dead. The Austrian consul, Lippich, and the French consul intervened to stay the final massacre. An armistice was proclaimed, and the survivors, under promise of safe-conduct, were persuaded to go to their homes. Then the Turks fell on them separately, slaughtered many, and burnt their houses. " May God slay him that putteth his trust in a Turk," says the Balkan proverb.

What was behind it all we shall never know. That Austria was implicated the people say is proved. For one of the leaders—furious at betrayal—went straight to Vienna to demand compensation. A card given him by the "Hungarian" obtained him an immediate interview with Baron Kallay, who offered him a post in the Bosnian gendarmerie (which he indignantly refused, for he would not leave his native land), and gave him a small sum of money. The "Hungarian" has never been heard of since, but the people still talk much of the railways and roads that he promised them.

We crossed the border of Kastrati and Hoti. The church of Bridzha showed a solitary speck of white high up at the end of the valley. It seemed miles from anywhere. I asked if any house of those clustered at the mountain's foot would give us a midday meal. To the Bariaktar's house, said the Kastrati guide decidedly, we would not go, because he was a Moslem. But he knew a large Christian house where we should be well entertained.

It was a mass of planks and poles, for the owner and the men of his house were busy enlarging it. We entered up a crazy ladder, through a hole in the wall, and plunged into a huge cavernous blackness, lighted only through broken roof-tiles, by three Jacob's ladders of sunlight, up which smoke-angels twirled and twisted. The two tiny loopholes at the further end showed only as stars in the gloom.

Our welcome was warm. Cushions and sheepskins were strewn for us, and a woman cast a great faggot on to the fire that glowed red under a huge hood at the far end of the room. Slowly, as my eyes grew used to the plunge from dazzle to darkness, I took in the wonderful scene in detail.

It was a vast room—so vast that, though stacked with goods, the twenty-seven persons in it only made a tiny group at either end. Far away at the great hooded fire the women, silhouetted black against the blaze, were making ready the midday meal.

The red flare danced on the smoke-blackened rafters of the roof. Rudely painted chests, twenty or more, containing the belongings of the family, were piled and ranged everywhere. Arms and field tools hung on the walls and from the tie-beams on wooden hooks. Flour and much of the food-stuffs were in large hollow tree-trunks—dug-out barrels. An indescribable jumble of old clothes, saddles, bridles, cartridge-belts, was strewn over all in wild confusion.

The bedding—thick sheets of white home-woven felt, pillows of red cotton, and plaited reed-mats—was stacked on the chests.

The floor was of thick, short, axe-hewn planks; the mighty walls, against which nothing less than artillery would be of any use, were of bare, rough stone. Dried meat hung from above, and long festoons of little dried fish for fast-days.

It was more like a cave than a house. There was something even majestic and primeval in its size, its gloom and chaos. Nor did even cavemen live with much less luxury.

At midday the men trooped in from building. Coffee and *rakia* flowed. The *sofra* (low round table) was brought and a large salt sheep-cheese, cut in chunks, put in the middle, to help down the *rakia*.

The Kastrati man was specially pressed to drink; his presence caused great mirth. The "joke" was a peculiarly Albanian one. Not only was Kastrati at blood with Hoti, but Kastrati had blackened the honour of the very house in which we were sitting, so bitterly, that the whole of both tribes was involved. Except with safe-conduct of a Hoti man—or under the protection of a stranger, as was the case—my gay young Kastrati could not have crossed the border-line save at the peril of his life. But he had chosen to come right into the lion's jaws, and the "cheek" of him pleased every one immensely. All drank healths with him, he was the honoured guest, and they discussed pleasantly how many bloods would be required before peace could be made. The house-master was quite frank; five was the number he thought necessary. And the Kastrati thought that five would satisfy them too. He was told, however, that this visit was all very fine, but that, though he might carry out his bargain and take me as far as Bridzha, he was to go no farther. I asked rather anxiously how he was to get back, as I did not want to have to return in order to shelter him. They laughed and promised him safe-conduct. It was "all in the game."

Our host was lavish in his hospitality—proud of being a Hoti man, proud of his large house, and delighted to tell all about it.

Thank God, he had not only enough for his family but for all his friends. I was welcome to stay as long as I liked. Flocks had he in plenty. His fields, when rain fell, yielded eight horse-loads of maize. (A *tovar*—horse-load—is 100 *okes*. An *oke* is nearly 2½ pounds). If there were only a decent government and a man could be sure of his own, they would be very well off. The Turks?—he hated them. No justice to be hoped there.

He deplored the blood system, but with no government a man must protect his honour and his goods according to the usage of the mountains. His house contained eight men-at-arms, six women, and eight children, also eight brand-new Mausers which had cost twelve napoleons a piece. (The amount spent on arms and ammunition is out of all proportion to other expenses). The Mausers and the new belts, full of glittering cartridges, were exhibited with pride—mainly, I believe, to properly impress the Kastrati and show him Hoti was ready. As he possessed nothing more modern than a Martini, he was deeply interested.

Four of the eight armed men were young and unmarried. Of the six women, one, an active and wiry old lady, was the family's grandmother; another, the widow of our host's brother, who had been shot a few months ago.

Our host was house-master, and had the fates of all in his hands. I asked him the price of a wife in these parts. "Twenty napoleons for one from my house," he said; "some will take as low as sixteen. I call that giving a girl away. You don't get one from me at that price. This one here," he pointed to an infant of eight months tightly swaddled in a large wooden cradle, "is already sold. I've had fifty florins down, the balance to follow when I send her to her husband."

At what age did he send a girl?

"Never under sixteen. It isn't healthy. Many people give them younger, I don't."

"And when do you give a boy a wife?"

"Never under eighteen. I would only marry a boy at sixteen if there were not enough women to do the work of the house, and I had to take another. But it is better not."

Nor would he admit that there was anything wrong in the system of infant betrothal, though Marko pointed out that the Church had recently forbidden it. He regarded his women as chattels, and would allow them no opinion.

Only if a woman were sworn to virginity did he allow her equal rights with a man. He knew one who was forty now. Her only brother had been shot when she was ten. Since that she had always worn male garb. She had a house and a good deal of land. I asked if the men ate with her. He slapped his thigh and said: "Of course! she has breeches on just like mine and a revolver."

Of the strength of the mountain women he boasted greatly. Any one of them, he declared, could start from here with a heavy load of wood to sell in the bazar of Scutari, be delivered of a child without any help by the wayside, take child and wood to the bazar, sell the wood, make purchases, and return home all right.

Some one told the tale of a Pasha of Scutari. Having met upon the road a heavily-laden woman carrying the child she had just borne, he questioned her, and at once returned to his wife, who was expecting a child shortly. "Look here," said the Pasha, "I know all about it this time ; I'll have no more fuss! The mountain women can shift for themselves, and you must too." His wife, a wise woman, said nothing, but waited till the Pasha had gone out. Then she bade the servant saddle the Pasha's Arab steed with a wooden *samar* and take it to the mountains to fetch firewood. When the Pasha came home he found his beautiful Arab raw-backed, broken-kneed, and exhausted. Furious, he asked his wife how she had dared treat it so.

"My dear lord," she replied, "you said I must do as the mountain women, so I thought of course your horse could do as the mountain horses."

Every one laughed. The women brought warm water in an *ibrik* and soap, and a clean towel for each. We washed our hands, the *sofra* was spread with the men's dinner. We squatted round (I am always classed with the buck-herd) and the women withdrew to a respectful distance.

The soup, fowl, eggs, and milk were excellent. We ate with wooden ladles from a common platter. The Kastrati took the breast-bone of the fowl and held it against the light, scrutinised its markings, and declared it foretold no evil to this house—which was very polite of him.

The Hoti took this stiffly and made no comment.

We washed our hands and rose from the *sofra*. The women hurried up and carried the remains to the other end of the room, where they devoured them.

The grandmother superintended the women's work, and was giving orders all the time. Two women of the household were kept all day and every day bread-making. The slap, slap as they whacked the heavy maize dough was ceaseless. It was kneaded in a great dug-out trough, beaten into a thin slab on a circular wooden shovel, and slipped on to the hot hearthstone (or into a dried clay dish made tough with chopped pig's bristles), and baked under an iron cover, piled with hot wood-ash. Baked all unleavened and eaten hot and steaming. Four loaves were made while I was there.

Maize bread is eaten throughout the mountains—not because corn is lacking, but because the people infinitely prefer maize. They will even buy maize when it is double the price of corn. The maize is very coarsely ground, and the bread incredibly heavy. The people eat very large quantities; it is their staple food. They are so used to its weight that they declare corn bread is no good—you never feel full.

When well made it is fairly palatable and very nourishing; but when badly made is a deadly compound and, I believe, the cause of the distended abdomens of the more weakly children. The hot, half-cooked stuff is washed down with quantities of cold water.

Women's work in such a house is extremely heavy. They have scarce an idle minute save when sleeping. They fetch the firewood and all the water; and as they tramp to and from the spring with the heavy water-barrel bound by woollen cords to their shoulders, they spin or knit incessantly. They weave and make all the elaborate garments, doing the wonderful black braiding of the men's trousers according to traditional pattern. Even the braid itself is hand-plaited in eight threads over a half-cylinder of basket-work, which the plaiter holds on her knee, tossing the clicking bobbins from one side to the other, and pinning up the finished braid with swift dexterity. Dozens of yards are needed for one costume; but it is a work of art when finished.

The black wool is mostly natural wool of black sheep. The dull crimson used to stripe the dresses of the married women is home-dyed in all outlying parts. Near Scutari imported dyed wool is beginning to be used. The leathern *opanke* (sandals) worn by all, and made of dried raw hide, are all home-made. Only the heavy, nail-studded belts of the married women are bought in Shkodra. These form part of the bride's costume, are some five or six inches wide, and heavy as cart-harness. The sight of one resting upon the abdomen of a woman in an advanced state of pregnancy is painful in the extreme, but it appears to cause no inconvenience to the wearer.

We crawled out again into the sunlight. Our host and his seven armed men wished us, "*Tun giat tjeter*" (Long life to you), and we passed out of his domain by the row of bleached ox, sheep, and horse skulls, that were to guard him from the grim unseen.

The climb to Bridzha was in the full glare of the sun, over rocks far too rough for riding. My men faced it reluctantly. We crowded, half-way up, into a patch of shade that lay like spilt ink over the white stones, and the Kastrati told us the tale of blood.

A maiden, daughter of the very house where we had dined, had been married into Kastrati but a few years ago. Her husband died a year later, leaving her child-less. She was therefore returned to her father to whom she belonged, and he wished to marry (*i.e.* sell) her again. This she violently opposed, threatening to escape to the Moslems and turn Turk if it were done. She wished to return to her parents-in-law at Kastrati, and to this both families consented.

When she had been there a year, news came to her father in Hoti that she was with child by her brother-in-law. The men of her house were furious at the stain, as they considered it, upon their honour, and flew to avenge it. One of the men with whom we had just dined went hot-foot to Kastrati, found the brother-in-law alone, shot him dead in his own house, and got safely away. This was but a few months ago, and both tribes were furiously at blood. Hoti's honour was not yet sufficiently cleansed—Kastrati had blood to wipe out. But such is the fidelity with which the laws of blood are observed, that our man had dared enter the house that was the centre of the feud.

The child was as yet unborn, and, whether girl or boy, it and its mother must be kept at the expense of Kastrati.

I asked if blame or punishment were given to the woman, which surprised every one. They considered her as a chattel, and in no way responsible.

This Kastrati-Hoti tragedy shows that in Maltsia e madhe the practice of taking a brother's or cousin's widow as concubine—if it ever existed here—has been extinct long enough to be held shameful, at any rate by Hoti.

We finished a weary crawl in the sun to the church

house of Bridzha, on a shelf 380 metres above sea-level, overlooking all the plains of Kastrati and Hoti, the Liceni Hotit, and the Lake of Shkodra, to Rumia, the great mountain over the Montenegrin border.

The Padre was away, but had hospitably left orders that I was to treat his house as mine.

We parted with our Kastrati guide, who lamented loudly that blood forbade him to guide me further. Hoti was polite, but very firm on this point; and supplied a new guide, a tall, lean old man, with keen grey eyes, a heavy fair moustache, and a kindly smile. Wiry and active, he said he was sixty-five, though he looked younger, but he added, with a laugh, that sixty-five was nothing. His uncle had lived to be ninety-six, his grandfather to an hundred and thirty. If folk were not shot, they lived to a great age here in the mountains.

He was a mine of traditional law. And I found his information corroborated everywhere.

Hoti, he said, was one bariak, made up of 500 houses, of which three only, those of the Bariaktar's family, are Moslem. Seven generations ago they were all Christian; then there was a great fight—he believed at Dulcigno, but was not quite sure. The Vezir of Shkodra was commanding, and summoned the mountain tribes to the fray. The town was impregnable till Hoti and Gruda charged. Ulk Lutzi of Hoti was first in. All Hoti and Gruda followed, and the town was taken.

" Said the Vezir of Shkodra to Ulk (*i.e.* the wolf), 'Thou art a hero! Thou shalt be a Moslem as we are, and choose what reward thou wilt.' Then," said the old man, laughing, "Ulk said he would like the right to let his horse stand at the entrance of the bazar without paying tax for it. The Vezir granted it, and made him first Bariaktar of the mountains. Kilmeni used to lead, but that day Hoti was made first and Gruda second of all the tribes of these mountains when they go to war in the north. And so it is to-day. Going south Mirdita leads; but as Ulk turned Moslem, God has not blessed him, and his line has increased but to three houses in seven generations."

This tale tallies fairly with history. About the middle of the eighteenth century Mehemed Bushatli, Vezir of Scutari, with the aid of the mountain tribes, captured Dulcigno, which had become an independent city of pirates, and burnt its flotilla of pirate vessels. Early marriages make generations rather shorter in Albania than in West Europe.

"The tribe of Hoti," said the old man, "has many relations. Thirteen generations ago, one Gheg Lazar came to this land with his four sons, and it is from these that we of Hoti descend. I cannot tell the year in which they came. It was soon after the building of the church of Gruda, and that is now 380 years ago. Gruda came before we did. Gheg was one of four brothers. The other three were Piper, Vaso, and Krasni. From these descend the Piperi and Vasojevichi of Monte-negro and the Krasnichi of North Albania. So we are four—all related—the Lazakechi (we of Hoti), the Piper-kechi, the Vasokechi, and the Kraskechi. They all came from Bosnia to escape the Turks, but from what part I do not know. Yes, they were all Christians. Kras-nichi only turned Moslem much later."

Of these four large tribes, of common origin, Piperi and Vasojevich are now Serbophone and Orthodox. Piperi threw in its lot with Montenegro in 1790, but whether or not it was then Serbophone I have failed to learn. Half of Vasojevich was given to Montenegro after the Treaty of Berlin, the other portion still remains under Turkish rule. Vasojevich considers itself wholly Serb, and is bitter foe to the Albanophone tribes on its borders. Krasnich is Albanophone and fanatically Mos-lem; Hoti is Albanophone and Roman Catholic.

What turned two tribes into Serbs and two into
Albanians, and which was their original tongue, I cannot say; but probably they were of mixed Serbo-Illyrian
blood, and their language was influenced by the Church
to which either chose to adhere. It is said that the
Albanophone Krasnichi were Catholic before turning
Turk.

The date three hundred and eighty years ago gives
us 1528. In 1463 the Turks conquered and killed the
last king of Bosnia; but the whole land was not [finally
incorporated in the Turkish Empire till 1590 (about).
The traditional date of emigration falls well within the
period when the Turkish occupation was spreading, so
is probably approximately correct. A large communal
family, with flocks, would be some time on the way.

The old man said modestly that if I were really
interested in his family, he would like to give me his
family tree, and did so,—from Gheg Laz, through his
second son, Djun Gheg, down to his own great-grandson,
a strapping child, the apple of his great-grandsire's eye.

- "I have been told," said I, "that Nikaj is also a
brother of Hoti ? "

"No, no," said the old man, "not brother. But part
of Nikaj is related to Krasnichi by a later generation,
and so to us also, and we cannot marry them. They
come from the houses of Bijeli-Krasnich and Mulo-
Smaint. Shaban Benaku, the celebrated chief of Krasnich, is straight from Krasni, brother of Gheg Laz, my
forefather. And half the tribe of Triepshi, the stem
of Bakechi, is of Hoti blood. We cannot marry them.
The other half—the Bekaj—we can. They are not our
blood; they come from Kopliku. Triepshi belongs to
Montenegro now, but is all Catholic. When Gheg
Laz and his sons came here, there were already people
here."

Some one suggested they were Shkyar (Slavs), but the

old man was positive they were not. "They were a very old people. No one knew whence they came. Some said they were like Tartars. My grandfather said they were very strong and active, and could leap over six horses at once, and that they ate acorns and horse-flesh. Twelve houses in Hoti are descended from them, and with these we can marry. They are other blood. They are called Anas." (Anas, in the Albanian dictionary of the Bashkimi society, means "indigenous.") Nor could the old man see that, after thirteen generations of intermarriage, the stocks of Gheg Laz and the Anas must be very considerably related. There was none of the same blood, he declared. Female blood does not count.

But the idea of marrying within the stock Gheg Laz seemed to him so impossible, he would not admit that even in the remote future it could ever take place. "We are brothers and sisters. It would be a great sin."

This detailed story of tribal origin and relationship, straight from native lips, is of much interest. Most of the Albanian, also most of the Montenegrin, tribes have a similar tale—the flight of their ancestor to escape Turkish persecution.

We left Bridzha for Gruda at 5.30 A.M., with the old man as guide. The track went over loose rocks and stones along a steep mountain side. Then came a descent over the other side, into a wooded, cultivated hollow, where stood Hoti's second church, that of the men of Treboina, who trace their descent from Pyetar Gheg, fourth son of Gheg Laz.

The priest was away, his man down with fever and parched with thirst. We gave him of our few lemons, for which he was pathetically grateful, as were we too for some bread to eat, for—as is the custom of the land—we had started on two thimblefuls of black coffee.

Further riding was impossible. We left the *kirijee* and the horses behind us, and started on foot.

There was no breath of air. The cloudless sky—a hard metallic blue—shut down on us like a lid. The sun blazed and beat back off the white rocks in a blinding dazzle. The track was all loose stone broken in sharp angles, or boulders, with scrub oak in the crevices. We toiled on to the edge of a mighty cleft, the valley of the Tsem, and saw below us the green torrent. Far away on the left—quivering white in the heat—on a plain at the mouth of the valley was what looked like a large village. The sun caught a white minaret, needle-pointing to the sky.

" Podgoritza ! " said the old man briefly.

Podgoritza ! I thought of the Hotel Europa—it seemed a little heaven below.

I was drenched with sweat, dizzy with heat, had had six days crowded with new events, new knowledge—severe and incessant physical and mental labour and very little sleep. Why suffer torture in an aching wilderness when Podgoritza would receive me joyfully ?

I had only to descend the valley, the plain would be easy going. But I could not show my face in England and say the North Albanian mountains had beaten me in six days.

I dared not look at the map, nor ask how much further we had to go, lest I should " funk " it, but followed the old man dumbly, zigzagging down the steep, shadeless, stony descent to the banks of the Tsem. I was nearly dead beat when I got to the bottom.

There was one tree. A girl was sitting under it plaiting braid on a basket frame. Other shade there was none. The heights had been breathless—the valley was a bakehouse. I imagined we had almost arrived and that the worst was over, till Marko, who is stout, gasped, " And now we have to go up the other side, O God ! "

We tried to get water from the torrent, but its banks were steep rock and we could not reach it. Necessity is

the mother of invention. I lowered my open umbrella
into the stream and baled up a quantity. We drank, and
I poured an umbrellaful over my head and shoulders,
which pulled me together.

We crossed the torrent on a balk of timber. It was
impossible to stay below, as there was neither shelter nor
food, and it was the very hottest time of the day when we
started again. The track zigzagged over loose stone up
a slope so steep that in England we should call it a cliff,
and the rocks were burning hot to touch. The old man
was going strongly. Marko and I crawled and staggered.
He had no protection for his head but a fez, and suffered
horribly from heat. Half-way up he was so bad that
I feared lest he should be sunstruck before we could
get up. A hole in the cliff gave shade. We crowded
into it. I opened Marko's shirt and fanned him with
my hat. The old man spurred us on with the news that
another half-hour would take us to the church. A final
struggle, and we came out on a plain cultivated and
wooded—but no church was to be seen. The next twenty
minutes were the hardest I ever did. I was barely conscious, but the path, luckily, was good, and the church
soon came in sight.

When we arrived there was no house—a new one in
course of erection some way off was all that could be seen
—and no human being!

At the back of the church was a hovel with the door
shut. The old man hammered. I leaned against the
wall, quite done. A long parley from above took place.
Then a Franciscan opened the door. He spoke German,
and said he was very sorry, but could not take us in. He
had only camped here while his house was building.

But Albanian hospitality is unfailing. He was a son
of the soil, and as soon as he realised my plight he took
pity and asked us to share what he had.

It was pitch dark inside. We crossed a filthy stable

on a plank, climbed a crazy ladder, and came into a room
—crowded with workmen at dinner—squalid and airless.

The Padre put a rickety stool by a rickety table. I
sat down. An icy sweat broke out on me, and, as all my
surroundings disappeared in blue and black circles, I
dropped my head on the table with just enough sense
left to say : " Give me drink. Open the window."

" You will catch cold," said the Franciscan.

" Open the window," said I. He kindly did so, and
brought me a glass of very strong *rakia*. I gulped it
down. It burned holes in my empty stomach, but it
brought back life. I knew where I was again, and
asked for food.

The poor Franciscan was horrified at my greed. He
said patience was a beautiful thing. I knew it was, but
thought bread better. He pressed *rakia* upon me. One
dose was very well, but I knew a little more would make
me as sick as a dog. I begged for bread. He was a
kind man and gave me a piece. I dipped it in the *rakia*,
and by the time the fried eggs were ready was fit to eat
a good meal. I do not think I ever felt so grateful to
any one as to that Franciscan—more especially as I must
have been a great nuisance to him.

He offered me his own bedroom—the only other room
in the house—and I slept for three hours. Marko slept
on a plank in the church, and the old man somewhere
else. We had all had enough.

When I awoke I went out, as in duty bound, to see
the neighbourhood. But I had no energy to interview
the many natives who came to see me, save one, a cheery
fellow who had won much popularity by shooting several
Turkish soldiers from the nearest frontier blockhouse.
All the tribesmen hate having Turkish blockhouses
planted among them.

Supper, as is native custom, was not till nearly ten
o'clock, by which time I was dropping with sleep. The

Franciscan was particularly pleased to see the old man, and bade him sup with us. At his own request he sat on the floor at a *sofra*—chairs and tables not being his wont—ate hugely and enjoyed himself vastly. Was delighted to yarn about the tribes.

Gruda is reckoned at five hundred families. About half of them are Moslem. But there is no difficulty between them and the Christians.

I asked how long these of Gruda had been Moslem.

"They have stunk for seven generations," said the Franciscan.

"Stunk?" said I.

He explained, and the rest of the company agreed, that all Moslems stink. You could tell by the smell as soon as a Moslem entered the room. He was amazed I had not remarked it. I ventured that in some districts Moslems washed more than Christians, but was told that washing has nothing to do with it. It is the Islamism that stinks. And this is the common belief of the mountain Christians.

About eighty houses of Gruda spring from Berisha, reputed one of the oldest, if not the very oldest, Albanian tribe—a tribe that does not tell of immigration but claims to have been always in its present home. The rest of Gruda came from the Herzegovina between three and four hundred years ago. The church of Gruda, Prifti, is said to be the oldest in Maltsia e madhe, founded by the Herzegovinian branch, which is called Djell, and claims to have been Catholic when it came.

The house-building men corroborated the old man's tale. He had heard it all as a boy from his grandfather.

"It is true that we cannot write in a book," he said, but we have it all written here." He tapped his forehead. "We are an old people. The Romans were in this land a long time ago. They fought the Mirdite tribe on the plain of Podgoritza." The Franciscan laughed at him, but the old man stuck to his tale. "I had it from my grandfather, and he from his. And the ruins of the Roman town are there now."

As I jotted down all the talk in the cover of my sketchbook, I had hanging over me, like a Damocles' sword, that I must start next day and retramp that weary way back to where we had left the horses. I could not trespass longer on the Franciscan's hospitality.

It was near midnight when we turned in, and we turned out in the grey dawn. We descended the cliff, and were up the other side before the sun's rays penetrated the vale, and reached Treboina in less than half the time we had taken the day before.

Poor Marko never forgot the climb to Gruda, and referred to it as the "road to Calvary," for which he was severely taken to task by the Franciscans.

Treboina welcomed and fed us. The old man, who had been much distressed at my collapse the day before, wrapped me in a coat as soon as I arrived to prevent my being chilled, sat me by the window, gave me black coffee, and withheld cold water till he thought me cool enough.

Treboina asked how we had slept at Prifti. I said my sleep had been only a horrible dream of cliff-climbing in which I had grabbed at burning rocks, waking every time with spasmodic clutches. Nothing could be better, said the company. The dream of climbing-up was one of the very luckiest, even better than dreaming of fishing.

The return to Bridzha was largely uphill, and the horses were rested, so riding was possible. A thin film of cloud tempered the sun. A great glass-snake (*Pseudopus pallasi*) hurried out of our way, and to my surprise the old man correctly said that it was not a real snake but only like one. There was a smaller kind, he added (*i.e.* the Blindworm)—quite harmless and blind, but it was said that on Fridays it could see for a few hours. The old man and Marko agreed that the common land-tortoise, boiled in oil, was not only good eating but very efficacious in cases of lung disease.

The Catholics of Dalmatia also eat land-tortoises. The Orthodox peasants, on the other hand, I have found regard them as most unclean.

We arrived early at Bridzha, and all my desire was for a night's rest.

The Albanians have a custom, cruel to those that are not to the manner born. No matter what is the time of year, they eat rather before midday and again one hour after sunset, or even later. This means that in the summer it is rarely before ten, and one goes eleven or even twelve hours between meals.

Sunset in Turkish time is twelve o'clock. They therefore maintain, nor could I ever convince them to the contrary, that supper is always at the same hour all the year round. As soon as they have eaten they lie down to sleep, and they get up with or rather before the sun. In the summer you get no food till too tired to eat it—and almost no sleep. Whereas in the winter your supper is ready at 5.30 or 6, and your host, dropping with sleep at 8 P.M., quite puzzled, says reproachfully: "You used to say one hour after *aksham* was too late. Now you say it is too early!"

How the people exist in summer on the small amount of sleep they take, I cannot imagine; they do not seem to require a siesta.

The sleep I needed was a standing joke—no one really believed it, and they conspired to prevent me at first, without the least idea of the torture they inflicted.

At Bridzha I had a room to myself and could undress. Supper of course was late, but I meant to sleep out my sleep next morning.

It was but 5.30 A.M. when I was waked by a thunderous banging at the door.

"What is the matter?" I asked.

"Are you ill?"

"Ill? No. What do you mean?"

"The sun has been up more than an hour. Why don't you get up?"

"Because I want to sleep. Go away."

"But it is so late. You must be ill. Let me fetch you some *rakia*."

"Go away."

I fell asleep at once only to be roused again at seven, this time by a whole party. "Are you still ill? Here is some *rakia*. The sun has been up," &c. &c.

It was useless to try for further rest. I got up and came out. Great joy from all the worthy people to see I was alive and well. They were sorry if they had disturbed me, but they had got up at 3 A.M.—for no valid reason—and when hour after hour passed, and they found I had locked the door and they could not get in, and did not answer when they first knocked, they thought perhaps I was dead! Thank God, I was safe, but it was very unwholesome to sleep so long.

The old man came to take me to his house to see his great-grandson. And there in the little mud-floored hovel—where nearly all that was left of the four generations dwelt crowded together—he told me the tale of his life. His father had died when he was a child. An uncle took charge of him, and set him to watch goats on the mountain-side. "And always I wanted to learn. I knew I could. I am not stupid. I feel that I have something here." He touched his forehead. "One day in Scutari a gentleman—a foreigner I think—talked with me. He asked me if I would like to learn, and said to my uncle, "The boy is clever. I will put him to school and pay for him." Ah, how I wanted to go! But my uncle said it was nonsense. He wanted me for his goats. I lost my only chance. Then all my young days there was war. Ah, those days when I was young and we thought we were fighting for freedom! But it was all in vain. We are a lost people. The strength is going from my arms. The land is always poorer and more miserable. I am a poor old man that can neither read nor write, and I shall die as I have lived, among the goats on the mountains."

Afterwards and from others—for the old man never boasted of his own exploits—I learned that he it was who had gathered the tribesmen and come to the rescue of the town of Tuzhi, when the Powers ordered it to be ceded to Montenegro. The Turkish troops had already been withdrawn when he started on his forlorn hope—but the resistance he and his offered was such that the town of Tuzhi has not been ceded to this day. Nor did the saviours of Tuzhi meet with any reward from the Turkish Government for which it was saved.

The old man spoke sadly about it, and with much bitterness. I ventured to ask if it would not have been better to have accepted Montenegrin rule for the purpose of having law and order.

"No," said the old man, "Nikita is a brave man. For the Montenegrins he is very good. If we had a Prince like that, we should be much more grateful than they are. But he is our enemy. For thirty years he has had Albanian subjects; their little children are forced to learn Serb. They may have no school in their own tongue. Better to wait and hope for freedom some day than take a rule that tries only to kill our faith and our nationality. In all these thirty years he has built no church for his Albanians in Cetinje."

And this was the universal opinion throughout the Christian tribes. But for the attempt to Slavise them, very many, probably whole tribes, would ere this have thrown in their lot with Montenegro.

It is strange that all the centuries have not taught

even the great Powers, that all attempts to forcibly suppress a language result only in bitterness unspeakable—and race hatred that slumbers never, but lies ever waiting its opportunity.

This land, for which they have so suffered, is no *justissima tellus*. For endless toil it yields back little. Its great stretches of bare rock, its grim valleys, are symbolic of long lives of futile effort and unfulfilled hopes.

At night we sat at supper with the Padre, who had just returned, when suddenly the stillness without was broken by four gunshots.

"Ah!" he cried, "some one is killed." We leaned far out of the open windows. The whole desolate, trackless land lay silent under the cold moonlight—as though all the world were dead.

He hurled a question from out our house in a long howl that tore through the night like a shell; and the answer rang back swiftly. A certain family had just finished making a limekiln, and the shots were to celebrate the event. The Padre drew back into the room, and crossed himself with a sigh of relief.

I remember the episode with curious vividness; for it was the first. Some weeks later, such is the force of habit, I often did not notice gunshots at all.

Two Head-shaves—Scutari.

CHAPTER IV

SELTZE, VUKLI, BOGA, RECHI

WE left early next morning for Seltze-Kilmeni, piloted by the old man, and followed a stony track to Rapsha, whose people derive from Laj Gheg, son of Gheg Laz.

Here we found one of the Albanian virgins who wear male attire. While we halted to water the horses she came up—a lean, wiry, active woman of forty-seven, clad in very ragged garments, breeches and coat. She was highly amused at being photographed, and the men chaffed her about her "beauty." Had dressed as a boy, she said, ever since she was quite a child because she had wanted to, and her father had let her. Of matrimony she was very derisive—all her sisters were married, but she had known better. Her brother, with whom she lived—a delicate-looking fellow, much younger than she —came up to see what was happening. She treated me with the contempt she appeared to think all petticoats deserved—turned her back on me, and exchanged cigarettes with the men, with whom she was hail-fellow-well-met. In a land where each man wears a moustache, her little, hairless, wizened face looked very odd above masculine garb, as did also the fact that she was unarmed.

From Rapsha we made a tremendous descent on foot, zigzagging through fine beechwood down a bad stony track to the river Tsem in the land of the Kilmeni—a descent of not much less than 2000 feet. Beyond the river was Montenegrin territory, the land of the Triepshi tribe. From far above, the old man pointed out the

spot on the right bank of the green torrent, where two
Franciscans were cut to pieces by Moslems two hundred
years ago. A crude chromolithograph of their martyrdom,
widely scattered among the Christian tribes, still cries to
the people for blood-vengeance. In the mountains there
is no *Deus caritas*, but only the God of battles. The
ensanguined figure of Christ on the Cross calls up no
image of redemption by suffering, but only the stern cry :
"We are at blood with the Chifuts (Jews), for they slew
our Christ. We are at blood with the Turks because
they insult Him. We are at blood with the Shkyars
(Orthodox) because they do not pray to Him properly."
And strong in this faith, the mountain man is equally
ready to shoot or be shot for Him.

I thought, then, rather of the martyrdom I should
have to suffer in crawling up this height on the return
journey. The Franciscans were out of their pain, and
had done with Albania, and I was not yet half-way
round.

Han Grabom, at the bottom on the river's edge,
welcomed us heartily. There was a large company of
men and beasts.

Montenegro was but a few yards away across the
Tsem. Hard by were the ruins of a Turkish blockhouse,
attacked and destroyed last summer (1907) by the
Montenegrin troops, who, at the same time, plundered
the *han*. The people complained bitterly of Montenegrin
aggression. Nor could I learn the rights and wrongs of
this frontier fray. Montenegrin officials replied to me
that the *kula* was burnt because it was on Montenegrin
territory, but its ruins are certainly—according even to
their own maps—on the Albanian side of the border.

The *han* was plundered because the Kilmeni helped
the Turkish Nizams in the *kula's* defence. I asked why
—as they so hated the Turks—they had given help. It
was because Montenegro was Kilmeni's worst enemy.

They could not let Montenegrin troops come over their border without fighting them. "It was for our own land that we were fighting." The Kilmeni-Montenegrin frontier, drawn arbitrarily by the Powers after the Berlin Treaty, is one of the many running sores then created; frontiers that seem to have been designed only in order to make lasting peace impossible.

The border, said Kilmeni, was properly marked with stones where it was not river, but the Montenegrins never kept to it.

It is interesting to hear both sides of a case.

I had heard another version of the same tale five years ago on the other side of the line which blamed Kilmeni.

A local hero at the *han* insisted on standing us drinks. He had roused great excitement last year by challenging a man of another tribe to fight a duel, a rare thing now, though it was common thirty years ago, when each man wore a yataghan. People were braver then, he said. "Now it was thought a fine thing to pick off a man from behind a rock; *that has been brought in by civilisation.*"

Four or five hundred armed men, of either tribe, flocked to see the fun. It seemed certain the "duel" would end in a pitched battle between the tribes. The Elders, greatly anxious, made a sitting, and saved the situation by inducing the two foes to swear brotherhood.

Having eaten, I lay down on some planks outside the *han*, meaning to have an hour's sleep while the men fed within.

But the first Englishwoman at Han Grabom was too great a novelty to be wasted. I was just "off" when I was poked up by the *kirijee*. He had told the company that I could "write" (*i.e.* draw) people. They had never seen people written, and I must come and write some to prove the truth of his words.

I went into the stuffy *han*, and drew the *hanjee* making

coffee and another man at the *sofra*, which gave vast satisfaction to every one, except myself, for by then it was time to start.

Following the Tsem's left bank to where Tsem Seltzit and Tsem Vuklit meet, we crossed Tsem Vuklit on a fine stone bridge—Ura Tamara: old Turkish work, which seems to show that the Tsem valley was formerly a much more important thoroughfare than now—and went up the valley of the Seltzit; the track, remarkably good, having been lately put in complete repair by a tribesman at his own

Kavajee.
Han Grabom.

expense. The scattered houses of Seltze lie at the valley's head, where it widens and is fertile. Springs gush freely from the ground. A cataract leaps from the mountain above.

The houses are well built of hewn stone. Seltze has a greater air of well-being than any other district of Maltsia e madhe.

The people are of a fine type and most industrious. The cultivable land is well watered by little canals, but there is not enough to provide corn for all. Seltze lives mainly on its flocks. Each autumn the tribesmen migrate

with great herds of goat, cattle, and sheep to seek winter
pasture on the plains near Alessio, where the tribe owns
land, the women carrying their children and their scant
chattels upon their backs; and toil back again in summer
to the pastures of the high mountains a long four days'
march with the weary beasts.

Blood feuds among the Seltze folk are almost non-
existent. This is due largely to the sweet influence of
the Franciscan, their Padre, a man much beloved, who
has been twenty years among them, and refused lately to
be made bishop for he would not leave his flock.

Upon the Montenegrin frontier he admitted sadly
there was much trouble. Either party appropriates the
beasts that it finds on what it claims as its own side of
that "floating" frontier. And there is naturally a flavour
about mutton so obtained which the home-grown does not
possess.

So was it on the borders of Scotland and England
"in the brave days of old." Seltze rejoiced at having
captured a hundred and fifty sheep; the Vasojevich across
the border retorted by lifting a hundred and ten. The
hundred and ten belonged not to Seltze but to the next
bariak, Vukli. "We scored," said Seltze, greatly contented. Two years ago matters culminated in a fight;
Seltze repulsed two Montenegrin battalions and killed
sixteen of the enemy.

The Padre had very many times kept the peace.

His church was crowded on Sunday, though it was
not a feast day. And the eager attention with which his
flock, asquat on the floor, listened to a very long sermon,
showed he had chosen well when he refused to leave
them.

An Albanian congregation is a quaint one to preach
to. When it is moved, it groans in sympathy and assents
loudly. And when it does not agree—it says so.

After church, to the Padre's great entertainment, the

congregation mobbed me, as pleased as children with a new toy.

Specially introduced to me by the men was one of the "Albanian virgins," a very bright, clean woman of about forty, clad in *enteri* and cotton breeches and a white cotton headwrap like a man's. She was most friendly, said she had no brothers, but stood as brother to her sister who was married. She had never meant to marry, and had always dressed as a man. Had a gun at home, but rarely carried it as she was afraid. She thought for women "this was best." She fumbled in her breast, and pulled out a crucifix and rosary which she held up as a defence. The men indignantly said this was not true—she was as brave as a man really.

The Padre said a herdsman's life was the only way to get a living. A woman who will not marry must adopt it, and is safer in a man's dress from the border Moslems. Formerly a great many women went thus as herds. He had now only a few in his parish.

A girl from the neighbourhood of Djakova is said to have served undetected many years in the Turkish army.

This is the tale of Kilmeni as told by the Padre, some Kilmeni men, and the old man.

It is a large tribe of four bariaks, Seltze, Vukli, Boga, and Nikshi, and is descended from one Kilmeni (Clementi), who had four sons, from whom the four bariaks originated.

Most families, said the Padre, can give complete genealogies.

There is also other blood in the tribe. The bariak of Seltze is divided into two groups, of which the one Djenovich Seltze is brother to Vukli. The other, Rabijeni Seltze, is of another blood, and came, according to the old man, from Montenegro near Rijeka, but this the Padre strenuously denied, saying its origin was not known.

The four bariaks are intermarriageable one with another.

The tribe holds much ground, occupying three valleys that, roughly speaking, lie parallel with one another— Seltze in the valley of Tsem Seltzet, Vukli and Nikshi in the valley of Tsem Vuklit, and Boga at the head of the valley of the Proni Thaat. Seltze (300 houses) is entirely Catholic, as are Vukli (94 families) and Boga (75 families). Nikshi out of 94 families has 10 Moslem.

Kilmeni's adventures have been many. Never content to submit to Turkish rule and fearful of its extension, the tribe, seizing the opportunity when Suliman Pasha, beaten in Montenegro, was in hot retreat (1623), swooped down on him from the mountains and cut the Turkish army to pieces.

The Turks sent a punitive force. The headmen of Kilmeni were executed, and the tribe expelled. But with unbroken courage it bolted back on the first opportunity, and again attacked the Turks in 1683, when they were fighting Austria. Later, in 1737, when Austria was striving to wrest from the Turks that portion of Servian territory which she still desires to possess, she called on Kilmeni to help. But in the fight at Valjevo Austria lost very heavily. The surviving Kilmeni troops dared not return home and face Turkish vengeance, but fled with their allies and settled in Hungary.

Some of their descendants visited Seltze two years ago, and told how they still married according to Kilmeni customs. The bride is led three times round the bridegroom's house, an apple is thrown over the roof, she is given corn, and as she enters the house must step over the threshold with the right foot, and beware of stumbling; and must take a little boy in her arms (this is to ensure bearing a male child, and is common to Montenegro and Albania). Then she is led three times round the hearth.

The corn recalls the *confarreatio* of the Romans.

Seltze was half empty, folk having not yet returned from the plains. Such as were there received me very hospitably. I sat by many an open hearth, and heard of Kilmeni life. Much we talked of that dire being the Shtriga, the vampire woman that sucks the blood of children, and bewitches even grown folk, so that they shrivel and die. All Kilmeni, and indeed all the tribes, believe in her. She may live in a village for years undetected, working her vile will.

Kilmeni had a sure way of catching her. It is to keep the bones of the last pig you ate at carnival, and with these to make a cross on the door of the church upon Easter Sunday, when it is full of people. Then if the Shtriga be within, she cannot come out, save on the shoulders of the man that made the cross. She is seen, terrified, vainly trying to cross the threshold, and can be caught.

She, and she alone, can heal the victim, who withers and pines as she secretly sucks its blood.

A Djakova man told vividly how his father had saved a child.

" It was the child of a neighbour. I saw it. It was dead—white and cold. And my father cried, ' I know who has done this.' He ran out and seized an old woman, and dragged her in.

" ' You have killed this child,' he roared, ' and you must bring it to life again ! ' My God, how she screamed, and cried by all the saints that she was innocent ! ' Spit in its mouth ! ' cried my father, and he held her by the neck—' Spit, spit ! '

" For if she did not spit before the sun went down, it would be too late and the child could not live again. But she still screamed, and would not. And my father drew one of his pistols and clapped it to her head—' Spit, or I shoot ! '

" She spat, and he threw her outside and she ran away. We waited, and after an hour some colour came to the child's face, and slowly it came to life. My father had saved it. And I swear by God this is true, for I saw it with my own eyes."

The Shtriga can torment her victim by aches and pains. The wife of this same Djakova man was horribly overlooked, and had pains in her joints and limbs so that she could scarcely walk. Nor could they find the guilty Shtriga. All remedies failing, in despair, though Christians, they sought help of a Dervish well versed in spells. He cut some hair from the top of her head and some from each armpit, and burnt it, saying some words of power. And as the hair burnt, the pains fled and came back no more.

A grim safeguard there is against Shtrigas, but it is hard to get. You must secretly and at night track a woman you believe is a Shtriga. If she have been sucking blood, she goes out stealthily to vomit it, where no one sees. You must scrape up some of the vomited blood on a silver coin, wrap it up and wear it always, and no Shtriga will have power over you.

A hapless woman in Seltze had lost all her children, and believed that her mother-in-law was the Shtriga that slew them. Infant mortality in North Albania is cruelly high. The wretched mother that sees one little one after another pine and die knows not that they are victims of ignorance—the cruellest of all Shtrigas. The child, tight swaddled, lies always in a wooden cradle, over which is bound, with cords, a thick and heavy woollen cover, the gift of the maternal grandmother when the first child is born. It is as thick as an ordinary hearthrug, and shuts out almost all air. If the child be a healthy one, it is taken out of doors and carried about a good deal, and as soon as it can crawl has plenty of fresh air, but if sickly it is released only from its prison by death.

It is always indoors; the unhappy mother takes the most jealous care that not for a single moment shall it be uncovered. She even gives it suck by taking the whole cradle on her knee, and lifting only the tiniest corner of the fatal cover. To touch it with water she thinks would be fatal. Filthy, blanched by want of light, and poisoned by vitiated air, the child fades and dies in spite of the amulets hung round its head and neck to ward off the Shtriga and the Evil Eye.

One mother had lost all seven of her children, each under two years; and another five, and was in agony over the sixth. She believed her breast had been bewitched and that her milk was poisonous. She turned back the suffocating cover for me to see the child. It had no symptoms, so far as I could learn, of its food not agreeing. But it was white as a plant grown under a pot. I begged her to uncover it, wash it with warm water, and take it out of doors. In vain. Children were never uncovered; it is *adet* (the custom). And what is *adet* is unchangeable. Only the very strong survive, and they become extremely enduring.

No words can tell the misery of the sick in these lands, who, swarming with lice, rot helpless on a heap of ferns or filthy rags in a dark corner till death releases them. No doctor has penetrated these wilds, nor any teacher save the Franciscans, whose medical knowledge is usually of the slightest.

Seltze told me a quaint moon superstition. Hair, if cut at the new moon, soon turns white. It must be cut with the moon on the wane, and then always keeps its colour. A man with a white moustache said it was owing to his having clipped it at the wrong time.

The houses are a far better type than those of Kastrati and Hoti. Solidly built, with two rooms—one often ceiled and with shelves—with high-pitched shingled roofs, some even with a chimney—and seldom with a

stable under. They are some of the cleanest I met
with.

Seltze is the only place in Maltsia e madhe that has
a school—built and taught by the Padre, the Man-who-
would-not-be-bishop.

He stood, a dark figure, against the church as I left.
I turned in the saddle at the top of the slope to shout
"a riverderci" to him, with the hope that it may come
true. For he is one of those who have made a small
corner of the world the sweeter for his presence.

Vukli was my destination. But the snow lay thick
on the pass 'twixt it and Seltze, half-molten, unpassable
for horses. We had to return down the valley to Ura
Tamara, and ascend the valley of Tsem Vuklit—the track
fair and the vale wide and grassy, a great loneliness upon
it, for neither man nor beast had come up from the plains.
Some primitive dwellings, made by walling up the front
of caves in the cliff high above, caught my eye. At
the head the valley is wide and undulating. We rode
straight to the little church and its house, which formed
one building. Out came the most jovial of all Franciscans,
Padre Giovanni, stout and white moustachioed, but bearing his seventy-five years lightly, An Italian by birth,
one of the few foreigners left in the Albanian Church. he
has spent forty years at Vukli—said he was now Albanian,
was priest, doctor, and judge, and that in Vukli he
meant to end his days.

We sat on the doorstep, while he made hospitable
preparations within.

The old man was heartily welcomed as a legal
expert. He was honoured and respected everywhere.
Vukli, as Seltze, was almost free from blood within
the bariak, but one of the few cases of blood was at once
laid before him for his opinion.

We sat round, while the Man-that-claimed-blood told
his tale. His only son had wished to marry a certain

widow, and gave her in token thereof a ring and £T.1. But her parents, whose property she was, would not recognise this betrothal, and sold her to another.

"My son," said the man, "would have paid for her fully, and she wished to marry him. Then was he very angry, and would shoot her husband. But he bethought him, the husband was not guilty, for perhaps he knew not of her betrothal. The guilty ones were the men of her family who sold her. To clear his honour, he shot one of her brothers. Then another brother shot my son, and I have no other. I want blood for my son's blood. They are to blame. They first put shame on him, and then killed him."

The old man thought long over the case, and asked questions. Then he said one was dead on either side, and it were better the blood were laid. He advised a sitting of Elders (a *medjliss*) to compound the feud— which was also the Padre's advice. All who heard agreed with the old man, save him who heard the cry of his son's blood, and he would hearken to nothing else.

What was the woman's point of view? In these tales, she has neither voice nor choice—*adet* (custom) passes over her like a Juggernaut car.

To judge by a twentieth century and West European standard the feelings of a people in such a primitive state of human development would be foolish. It is perhaps equally foolish to attempt to analyse them at all. Here, as in Montenegro, women tell you frankly that, of course, a woman loves her brother better than her husband. She can have another husband and another child, but a brother can never be replaced. Her brother is of her own blood —her own tribe.

On the deck of an Adriatic steamer, at night under the stars, an Albanian once told me the Tale of the Mirdite Woman, with a convincing force which I cannot hope to repeat.

The Mirdite woman was sent down from the mountains and married to a Scutarene. She dwelt with him in Scutari, and bore him two sons. Now the brother of the woman was a sworn foe to the Turks, plundering and slaying them whenever chance allowed. And they outlawed him and put a price upon his head. But he feared no man, and would come at night into the town to sup with his sister and return safely ere dawn. The Turks heard this, and went to the woman's husband with a bag of gold—two hundred Turkish pounds—and tempted him. He had never before seen so much gold. And they said, "It is thine when thou tellest us that thy brother-in-law is here."

On a certain night the outlaw came down from the mountains to the house, and, as is the custom, he disarmed in token of peace. Scarcely had he given up his pistols, gun, and yataghan, when the Turkish soldiers rushed in and slew him, helpless.

His sister, weeping in wild despair, went back with his body to the mountains of Mirdita, singing the deathwail. And they buried him with his people. She came back, still mourning, to her home. And lo! her husband was counting gold upon his knees. She looked at it and asked him, "Whence comes this gold?"

Then he was afraid, for he saw in her eyes that she knew it was the price of her brother's blood. And he spoke her softly, saying: "All knew of thy brother's coming. If he did not wish to lose his life, why came he? Sooner or later the Turks would have slain him. It is better that we have the gold than another."

But she answered not. Then he told her of the much good that the gold would buy, and she answered "Aye" dully—as one that speaks in sleep. But ever she heard the cry of her brother's blood. And when it was midnight and all was still, she arose and took her dead brother's yataghan. She called on God to strengthen her arm—

she swung it over her sleeping husband and she hewed the head from off his body. Then she looked at her two sleeping children. "Seed of a serpent," she cried, "ye shall never live to betray your people!" And them too she slew. And she fled with the bloody yataghan into the night and into the mountains of Mirdita.

It is an old tale. I cannot fix its date. In its raw simplicity it is monumental, and embodies all that there is of tribal instinct and the call of blood.

The Man-that-claimed-blood rose, unconvinced by the old man's judgment, and went away to his lonely hut. The talk, from blood, naturally drifted to wounds. The old man was not only a legal authority but a surgeon of repute. He had recently gained much fame and the large fee of thirty florins—the largest he had ever received—for saving a soldier's leg, and told the tale with modest pride. The soldier was kicked by a horse; the result was a compound comminuted fracture with both bones badly shattered. He demonstrated on his own leg the position of the bones and the point of fracture. The Turkish military doctor wished to amputate—the wound was very foul. The soldier refused to lose his leg, left the hospital, and sent for the old man.

"If the ankle is broken," said the old man judicially, "you can never make it right again. If a man is shot through the knee he generally dies—but three finger-breadths above the ankle and below the knee is safe. You can always save the leg if you are careful."

With his home-made forceps he removed seventeen splinters of bone. When he was sure he had removed all, he washed out the wound thoroughly with *rakia*. (*Rakia* is distilled from grape juice; when double-distilled it contains a considerable amount of alcohol.) Never, said he, should a wound be touched with water— always with strong *rakia*. He then plugged and dressed the wound with a salve of his own making — the ingredients are extract of pine resin, the green bark of elder twigs, white beeswax, and olive oil. The property of the elder bark I do not know. The pine resin would provide a strong antiseptic. He brought the ends of the bones together, bound the leg to a piece of wood, the bones united in three weeks, and in six the man was walking about again with a rather shortened but very serviceable leg.

In gunshot wounds he was expert. For "first aid" his prescription was : Take the white of an egg and a lot of salt, pour on to the wound as soon as possible and bandage. This, only temporary till the patient could be properly treated with *rakia* and pine salve as above. The wound to be plugged with sheep wool, cleaned and soaked in the salve. The dressing to be changed at night and morning, and at midday also if the weather be very hot. Should the wound show signs of becoming foul, wash again with *rakia* as often as necessary.

This treatment he had inherited from his grandfather, who had had it from his. The exact proportions and way of making the salve he begged to be excused from telling, as they were a family secret.

It is an interesting fact that antiseptic surgery should have been practised in the Balkan peninsula a couple of generations, and who knows how much more, ago, while West Europe was still washing out wounds with dirty water.

Of rough rule-of-thumb knowledge he had a good deal—showed where the main arteries ran, where it was dangerous to cut and where safe. I asked how one learned surgery. He said first you must have good hands and good fingers (his own were very fine), and you must think a good deal, and remember what you had seen in one patient and apply the knowledge to the next similar case. Above all, never be in a hurry, and be quite sure before you cut. You must think things out for yourself. Of anæsthetics he naturally knew nothing, and his very deliberate methods would be more than a West European could bear. But the Balkan peasant does not appear to feel pain so acutely, and suffers scarcely at all from "shock."

Apoplexy, he said, was caused by too much blood in the head. He had recently been called to a woman who was struck suddenly speechless and quite paralysed down one side. He bled her from the temple on the afflicted side and seven times from the arm on the other side. Next day she was better. He bled her five times. She made a good recovery and was now walking about, though slightly lame.

One must be guided by circumstances. A man came to him a short while ago with a crushed finger. When he had removed the fragments he found the ends of the bone too pointed and splintered to set well. So he sawed them straight with a little saw of his own making, set them, and made a good finger, but short.

Knowing that the Montenegrin native surgeons of old were well known for trephining, I asked the old man what he could do for a badly broken head. "Ah," said he, "the head is very difficult. It is like an egg. First there is the shell, then the skin, then the brain. If that skin is broken you can do nothing—the man must die. But if the broken bone only presses on it you can save him. You cut like this"—he indicated a triangular flap on the head of the man next him—"and turn it back. Then you pick out the broken pieces very carefully and raise the bone from the brain. But you cannot leave the brain unprotected. You must cut a piece of dried hard bottle-gourd to fit the place—it is round like a man's head. You can find a piece that fits exactly. It must be quite hard. Then you replace the flap over it and sew if necessary and dress with the salve, and his head will be as good as ever."

The *kirijee* at once said, with enthusiasm, that he had been so treated at the age of sixteen; had been knocked on the head in a bazar riot, brought home unconscious, and only recovered when the bashed-in bone was removed. Had had a large piece of gourd in his head ever since. It made no difference, except that he had to scratch his head oftener that side than the other.

The company examined his head with much interest. The old man had never cut out bone himself, only removed broken pieces. But there was a man in Mirdita, he said, very clever at skull-cutting. He had recently removed a very large piece from the skull of a badly injured and unconscious man. (A very large part of the left parietal, according to the description.) Had replaced all with gourd, and made a complete cure.

The company listened with deep interest to the old man's tales. We had another of the successful extraction of a bullet, and heard how he had slung a horse with a broken leg and healed it. He was greatly pleased with my interest, but sighed and said: "I know nothing. You were born in a happy land. I could have learned. I have it here." He touched his head. "I might have been some use. Now I shall die as I have lived—a poor old man among the goats on the mountains."

The old man squatting on a rock became a sublime and tragic figure—the victim of a pitiless Fate—a wasted power, whose skill might have benefited half Europe. My heart bled for him—but at the back of my consciousness I asked myself if he would be any happier hurrying from one fashionable patient to another in a thousand-guinea motor-car through streets that stink of petroleum.

The Padre meanwhile was very busy housekeeping. We should have sent him a wireless telegram, he said. Telegraphing in Albania was far quicker than in any other land. Which is a fact. All news is shouted from hill to hill.

"Shouting" gives no idea of it. The voice, pitched in a peculiar artificial note, is hurled across the valley with extraordinary force. Any one that catches the message acts as receiver and hurls it on to its address. And within an hour an answer may be received from a place twelve hours' tramp distant. The physical effort of the shout is great. The brows are corrugated into an expression of agony, both hands often pressed tight against the ears—perhaps an instinctive counterpressure to the force with which the air is expelled from within—the body is thrust forward and swayed, face and neck turn crimson, the veins of the neck swell up into cords. There are few places where it is harder to keep an event secret than in the mountains of Albania. News spreads like wildfire. The fact that a man has been shot up-country reaches Scutari next day at latest, often with many details.

"Theft is impossible in Kilmeni," said the Padre, laughing; "the whole tribe hears the description of an article as soon as it is missed. Every one knows if some one has a few more sheep than yesterday."

At supper the genial old Padre sat at the head of the table, flanked by the two largest, fattest cats I ever saw. If he did not give them tit-bits fast enough, they slapped him smartly with their paws, which highly delighted him. I think he is the one perfectly contented human being I ever met.

"If I were born a second time into this world, I would again be a Frate," said he; "and if a third time, a third time Frate, in the Albanian mountains, with my people and my little house, and my books and my cats. I hope to die here without ever seeing a town again."

My unmarried condition pleased him much. He enlivened supper with an extremely plain-spoken sermon *de Virginitate*, till Marko protested that he had led a virtuous married life for twenty years, and did not consider himself a sinner. Which called down on us a yet plainer spoken address *de Matrimonio* and *de*—sundry other things expounded in much sonorous Latin, which, fortunately, Marko did not understand, and which "called a spade a spade."

Vukli, all Christian, consists of ninety-four families, all from the same stock. It marries chiefly with Seltze. A wife is cheaper than in Hoti, and costs twelve napoleons. The houses are, as usual, scattered far and wide. An Albanian parish is no easy one to work. A priest has often a four hours', even six hours' tramp to reach a dying man, and no matter what may happen at the other end of the parish, cannot get there in the same day. As at Seltze, the people are very industrious, are pastoral, and have plenty of high pasture. Vukli has a fair share of cultivable land, well cleaned of stones, which are all used for wall-making. Big boulders are laboriously drilled with crowbars and blasted with gunpowder. It often takes a week to destroy one rock—but they do it. And the larger part of the population migrates to the plains in winter with the flocks, wasting weary days on the march over rough tracks and bearing their burdens on their backs.

The houses are, like those of Seltze, clean and well-built. The head of the entrance-door is, as is usual in many parts of North Albania, semicircular, and the arch formed not of voussoirs but hewn from a solid block. This, almost always the case with arched doors' heads throughout the land, shows that arch construction is not at all understood.

It is in the graveyard that Vukli's originality is to be found. This, as is usual where timber is cheap, is full of wooden crosses; but local art has stepped in and transformed the emblem of Christianity into a "portrait" of the deceased. The *chef-d'œuvre* is that of a doughty warrior. His face is carved above, two arms are added, his Martini and revolver are shown on the arms of the cross. It is incomparably grotesque. A serpent wriggles up one side to show, I was told, his fierceness. The serpent not unfrequently appears on graves, and may be connected with now forgotten beliefs. On the other hand, it is customary in the ballads of the Montenegrins to call a great fighting-man *ljuta zmija* (fierce serpent). But in the course of time new meanings may be attached to old symbols.

The Padre laughed when he found me admiring this cross. "Very un-Christian," he said, shaking his head; "but they *do* like it so." Vukli, as Seltze, suffered much from the Shtriga—one wretched woman had lost all her eight children—and also from the Evil Eye (*Syy kec*). So powerful is this, that a man had recently, to prove his power, gazed at a bunch of grapes, which had withered upon its stem and dropped to the ground before the awe-struck spectators.

Syy kec is one of the curses of Albania. Against it, throughout the land, folk wear many charms. Blue glass beads adorn the halters of most of the horses; children have a coin tied on the forehead; the Catholics wear crosses, sacred hearts, medals of the saints (these mostly from Italy), and amulet cases, triangular, holding such Latin texts as they can get the priest to write for them. These, too, are bound to the horns of cattle and the manes of horses, to prevent the latter from being spirit-ridden by night by *oras* or devils.

There is a very good charm (*Djakova*) against all these. You must kill a snake, and cut off its head with silver. The edge of a white medjidieh (large coin) sharpened, will serve—you must dry the head, wrap it up with a silver medal of St. George, have it blessed by a priest, and it will protect you so long as you wear it. A piece of a meteorite is a protection against gunshot. Were it not for these safeguards, it would be hard to live in the land. The devils appear often at night, as fiery sparks dashing about, and then, no matter how well the traveller may know the way, he cannot find it. Nor until the first cock-crow (about two hours after midnight) can he go farther. After that they are powerless, and vanish—as did Hamlet's ghost under similar circumstances. Albania lives in the primitive times when real miracles happen that none doubt—when man has no power over his own fate, but writhes impotent, smitten on the one hand by the wrath of God and tormented on the other by the powers of evil. He faces his doom stoically. *Eghel*—" It is written."

It is good to live in this atmosphere. Many is the tiny, giddy ledge I have crept round without hesitation, driven forward by the cheery shout: "Go on! It is not *eghel* that you will die here." Which I could not have done had an English friend been screaming: "For God's sake, don't try. You will break your neck!" There are countless advantages in travelling with natives only.

Vukli was fascinating, but the time for going came. I was bound for Boga and Shala. Again the heights were not passable for me. I must go back on my trail by Kastrati and Skreli, and ascend the valley of the Proni Thaat. I could do it in two days, but must start early, said the Padre. He advised 3 A.M. He saw to the re-shoeing of the horses the previous afternoon. They need nails or shoes renewing about once a week on these tracks. Three A.M. is a dree hour. I pleaded for five, but was bidden remember the heat. I did. I thought of the way to Gruda as a nightmare of agony. So I agreed, but said I must go to bed early. According, however, to Albanian custom, it was little short of 11 P.M. when I succeeded in lying down on some sheepskins. There was not enough time to waste over dressing and undressing. I seemed to have scarce laid down, when knocks aroused me, and I was told coffee was ready—

and the horses. Giddy with sleep, but terrified of waiting for the sun, I crawled out half conscious. The
Padre, as gay as ever, hoped I had had a good night.
He had—very. The regulation two nips of black coffee
woke me a little, and I said good-bye regretfully to my
jovial old host, went out half dazed into the chill, grey,
sleeping world, and started down the hill over loose
stones, on foot. The effect of the coffee wore off before
I was half-way down. I reeled with sleep, and fell heavily
with a clatter that woke me. Marko and the old man
were distressed, but I had fallen much too limply to be
hurt.

"You woke me too soon," I said. "You know I
don't like it."

"But to get up very early is so healthy!" persisted
Marko.

"I can't help that. Four hours out of the twenty-four
is not enough. I went too late to bed. Supper was late."

"But it was quite early! Only two hours after
sunset!"

I did not enter into the fruitless argument about the
sun setting late in summer, because in Albania it always
sets at the same time—twelve o'clock. "In England
maybe the sun sets later in the summer, but with us
never."

At the foot of the hill I mounted, slung the bridle
on my arm, hung on to the saddle-bow with both hands,
shut my eyes and dozed, waking with a jerk whenever
the horse stumbled or I nodded forward.

Half-way down the valley the old man had friends.
He hailed them loudly, and out they came with a bowl
of fresh milk and some cheese. We breakfasted. It
was the old man's prescription to wake me up properly.

We got to Han Grabom without adventure. Here I
was greeted by another of the "Albanian virgins" in
male garb, who begged me to take her with me to

England. She said she always had to come home along
the Montenegrin frontier, was terrified of being picked
off by Montenegrin sharpshooters, and had no money to
buy a gun. She would like to live in a safe place. She
had no brother, was one of five sisters. Two were
married. The other three all dressed as men, and worked
the family land.

After Han Grabom was the ascent to Rapsha.
Luckily you can ride up places you cannot ride down.
Part walking—in the most risky bits—part riding, we
came to the top in good time. Though it was quite hot
enough, the sun was off.

At nightfall we pulled up at a *han* in Kastrati. It
was one of the occasions when I have really appreciated
a *han*, for I was drenched with sweat and bruised with
tumbling about. The *hanjee* lit a fire, and I dried by it
while Marko chopped the head off a fowl and set it
stewing.

I woke next morning to the sad fact that I must say
good-bye to the dear old man. We were in Kastrati.
Hoti and Kastrati were in blood; he had safe-conduct
back, but must go no farther.

He made a touching farewell speech, begged me to
write to him from London—the Padre would read it to
him. Afterwards he visited me each time he came to
Scutari, haunted by a vague hope that I could do something for his unhappy land.

The *hanjee* piloted us down to Brzheta in Skreli,
where we picked up another man and went on to Boga
by an easy trail up the dry valley of the Proni Thaat on
its right bank, crossing to the left near the village of
Skreli.

Boga—seventy-five families, all Catholic—unlike its
brethren of Vukli and Seltze, was rather badly in blood.
Two brothers had recently been shot by their own
relatives.

For those interested in "dove crosses" I may mention that at Boga and at Snjerch (St. George), near the mouth of the Bojana, now Montenegrin territory, the finest examples are to be found.

The priest and his old mother welcomed me, but, on hearing I was bound for Shala, begged me not to attempt the pass. The snow was very deep, half molten, and sliding, and the descent on the other side extremely precipitous. In no case could the horses cross it. I took their advice. The return journey down the valley was amply worth while for the quite magnificent spectacle of the snowy mountains of Skreli, dazzling against the turquoise sky above a dark pine belt. Just above Brzheta we crossed the stream bed, and struck away from it southwards to Rechi, through Lohja—a small tribe of one bariak, made up of eighty Moslem and forty Christian houses. It has a mosque and a *hodza*, and shares a priest with Rechi, the tribe next door—also mostly Moslem. Rechi-Lohja is of mixed stock, mainly originating from Pulati and Slaku, and was originally all Catholic.

Grizha, another small, one-bariak tribe, hard by, is, I believe, all Moslem, also Kopliku on the plain below.

Rechi we reached through a forest of monumental chestnuts. The church and house, which are new, stand high on a shelf with a great free view over the sweep of plain and the lake of Scutari. The priest of Rechi, a keen student of Albanian custom, was full of information both about Rechi and Pulati, where he had spent several years.

He told us of oaths which, if very solemn ones, are always sworn in Rechi and among all the Pulati tribes on a stone as well as on the cross: "*Per guri e per kruch*" (By the stone and the cross). The stone is the more important and comes first. At a gathering of Elders to try a case, the accused will often throw a stone into the middle of the circle, swearing his innocence upon it.

A man when he has confessed something extra bad, and received absolution, generally says, "I suppose I must bring a stone to church next Sunday?" The stone is carried on the shoulder as a public sign of repentance. And, though told it is not necessary, he usually prefers to bring it. The priest of another district held that the publicity of stone-bringing had such a good moral effect that he never discouraged it. His parishioners sometimes brought very large ones. Whether in proportion to the sin, I know not.

The priests say that, in spite of all their efforts, their parishioners all regard the shooting of a man as nothing compared to the crime of breaking a fast—eating an egg on a Saturday. Fasting in Albania means complete abstinence from any kind of animal food.

In the autumn of 1906 the Albanian clergy went to Ragusa to greet the Archduke Franz Ferdinand, who represented the Emperor Franz Josef, Protector of the Catholic Church in Albania. It was arranged that on Saturday they should dine with the priests of Austria, and upon the same fare. This made something like a scandal among their Albanian parishioners, who thought it a plot to seduce their priests from the right path. "That Pope," said a man to me, "is only an Italian after all!"

We talked of soothsaying—the reading of bones—a custom I first saw in the mountains of Shpata, near Elbasan. The bone must be either the breastbone of a fowl or the scapula of a sheep or goat. No other will serve. It is hard to get people to explain the manner. Putting together facts obtained from the Rechi priest, a man from Djakova, and others, the result is as follows.

To read your own future the bone must be that of an animal you have bred. One bought is useless. A fowl must be decapitated; if its neck be wrung, said the Djakovan, the blood will go the wrong way and spoil the marks.

A good seer can tell at once if the beast be bought or bred.

The bone is held up against the light and the markings of marrow, &c., in it interpreted. The art of how to apply them correctly is jealously concealed.

"I asked a man," said the Rechi priest, "how he read the bones. He said, 'When you see little black marks on paper you know they mean "God," "man," and so forth. I cannot read them, but when I see little marks in the bones I can read them and you cannot.'"

The very best is the breastbone of a black cock with no white feathers on him. The keel is the part used. The fate of the owner of the cock and that of his family is read in the thickness at the end (A)—up it runs a line of marrow; a hole in this in-dicates his death; a break, an illness, or catastrophe. Their situation shows the time at which they will take place. Deaths or accidents to the

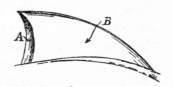

family are shown in branches of this main line. Red spots mean blood. Public events are foretold on the sides of the keel (B). Marvellous tales are told of the truth of these prophecies, and they are widely believed. So absolutely indeed, that there seems little reason to doubt that the terror they inspire has actually caused death.

An only son, well known to the Djakova man, was at a family feast. He held up a fowl's breastbone, and threw it down with a cry. His father asked what was the matter. The son said, "In three days you will bury me." The horrified father picked up the bone, and saw it was only too true. He wailed aloud, "In three days we shall bury you!" All his kin cried over him, the youth blenched and sickened, and could not eat. And in three days he was dead, and they buried him.

"When he read in the bone that he must die, he died," said the Djakova man.

Seeing that I looked sceptical he added, with very much more truth than he was aware of, "It would not kill you because you do not believe it. *We believe it, and so it is true to us.*"

It is conceivable that the panic wrought by a vivid imagination and the pitiless insistence of all his family, would kill a subject with a weak heart—the condemned man dying, so to speak, of "Christian Science."

When Shakir Pasha was made Vali of Scutari, a mountain man, picking up a bone, cried out, "He will only be Vali six months!" This was so unusually short a time that the man was laughed at, but the Vali was transferred in six months' time.

At a wedding feast the bone said that one of those present would be found dead near a rock in a short time. A fortnight later the bridegroom fell over a precipice and was killed. And so forth.

Such is the faith in the bones, that I have more than once been met with a refusal to read them on the grounds that it is better not to know the worst.

As I write the rough draught of this, in Scutari, at the end of November 1908, with war clouds thick on all the frontiers, and discontent already smouldering against the Young Turks, the mountain men are seeing blood in all the bones, "perhaps before Christmas, certainly by Easter."[1] When the elements of war are near, the balance of power may be upset by such a trifle as a fowl's breastbone, and things come "true because we believe them."

The people, said the priest, still hold many pagan beliefs of which they will not talk. They put a coin in

[1] And shortly after Easter the rising in Constantinople took place.

the mouth of a corpse previous to burial, but seem unable to give any explanation beyond that it is *adet* (custom). There is also, he said, a lingering belief in *lares*. He had seen a vacant place for the spirits of the dead left at family feasts. And at Pulati he had found traces of a belief in two powers, one of light and one of darkness, and thought that the sun- and moon-like figures found as a tattoo pattern are concerned with this.

On Sunday the sick and the afflicted flocked from an early hour. The priest had had several years' medical training, and cares for the bodies as well as the souls of his people. His church is always well filled. A crowd of out-patients waited at the door on Sunday. Mass on Sundays is not celebrated in the mountain churches till eleven or later, to give the scattered parishioners time to come. While waiting, we were interviewed by a local celebrity, an old man of Lohja, who boasted that, though a hundred and ten years old, he had sinned but twice in his life. Nor would he admit that in either case he had been guilty. The sin each time was theft, and he had been led astray by bad people. I asked how many men he had killed. He said with a cheerful grin, "Plenty, but not one for money or dishonourably." He was an alert, hooky-nosed old man with humorous grey eyes. When some one doubted his age, he poured out a torrent of historic events which he vowed he recollected. It was suggested then that I should "write" old Lohja. He was immensely flattered, and sat a few moments. When every one recognised the sketch a look of great anxiety came over his face, and most earnestly he prayed me never to destroy what I "had written about him." The same moment the sketch was torn he was certain he should drop down dead—and after living a hundred and ten years that would be a great pity. I duly promised never to part with it and relieved his mind.

The priest chaffed him about his "two sins," saying

he was a very bad old boy and had done all the things he should have left undone, and never came to confession. The latter charge he admitted very cheerily—after a hundred years, confession was not necessary; moreover, he had confessed his only two sins years ago, so had no more to say.

We left that afternoon for Rioli, but a two and a half hours' walk over a ridge and up the valley of a crystal-clear stream that turns many corn-grinding and wool-fulling mills, both of the usual Balkan pattern. In the fulling mill a large wooden axle, bearing two flanges, is turned by a water-wheel. The flanges, as they turn, catch and raise alternately two large and heavy wooden mallets, made preferably of walnut, which falling, pound and hammer the yards of wet hand-woven woollen material (*shiak*) which is heaped in a box beneath them. In forty-eight hours it is beaten into the cloth that is the common wear of Bosnia, Montenegro, and North Albania.

Corn-mills are often very small—a tiny shed on posts over a little cataract that shoots with great force through a pipe, made of a hollowed tree-trunk—the exit hole very small—against a small turbine wheel. The upright axle passes through the two stones, turning the upper one. The corn is fed from a wooden hopper, its flow ingeniously regulated by a twig that plays on the surface of the upper stone. Mills are generally private property of a group of families, each grinding its own corn in turn.

The church of Rioli stands high on the right bank of the valley, that is here richly wooded. In the cliff on the opposite side is the cave in which Bishop Bogdan refuged from the Turks in the seventeenth century.

Rioli is a small tribe of one bariak, I believe of mixed origin. It belongs to the diocese of Scutari.

We now left the Maltsia e madhe group and the diocese of Scutari for Pulati.

CHAPTER V

PULATI—GHOANNI, PLANI, THETHI

PULATI is divided into Upper and Lower Pulati. It is not one tribe, but a large group of tribes under one Bishop. Lower Pulati consists of four tribes, Ghoanni, Plani, Kiri, and Mgula, each of one bariak. Upper Pulati consists of the large tribes, Shala, Shoshi, Merturi, Toplana, and Nikaj. These form also part of the group called Dukaghini, the district that was ruled by Lek, and they cling tenaciously to his law.

Pulati seems to be mainly an ecclesiastical division— the Polat major and minor described by the French priest in the fourteenth century.

The tale that the name derives from a man who possessed nothing but one hen (*pulé*) is scarcely worth repeating.

The Pulati people differ considerably from those of Maltsia e madhe, partly because they are even less in touch with the outer world ; partly, undoubtedly, because of some difference in blood.

As a whole, the physical type is not so fine in Pulati. The big, fair, grey-eyed man is less common—the small, dark, round-headed type very frequent. Costume, especially that of the women, differs much. Custom differs also. But it is always possible that Maltsia e madhe has grown out of customs still existing in Pulati.

The priest of Rioli sent a woman with us as guide, no man being handy. In times of blood between two tribes, a woman guide is far safer. In this case it was peace.

The mountain ridge that here forms the frontier of
Pulati rose like a wall.   Even the pass—Chafa Biskasit—
looked unpassable from below.   The track is very rough,
loose stones and large rocks, nearly all unrideable.   The
heat was intense, the air heavy and thunderous.   But for
the shade of the woods that clothe the heights I could
not have got up.   The two men sweated freely; the young
woman, used to crossing such tracks with 40 or 50 lbs.
of maize on her back, never " turned a hair."

Some people find mountain air exhilarating.   I am
only conscious of the lack of oxygen, and climb with the
sad certainty that the higher I go the less there will be.
What is a pleasant exercise at sea-level is a painful toil
on the heights when gasping like a landed fish.

The way to Paradise is hard, says Marko.

The top of Chafa Biskasit is about 4500 feet.   Then
came the joy of the descent.   Below lay the valley of the
Kiri, in which live the four tribes of Lower Pulati.   The
farther side of the valley, the great range of mountains
that is the watershed of the Kiri and the Lumi Shalit,
forms the frontier of the tribes of Shala-Shoshi.

Tribe frontiers have never yet been mapped.   They
are very well known to the people, who point out some
tree or stone as one crosses the line.   I am not able to do
more than roughly indicate their position.

We came late to Ghoanni, though the distance was
little.   The track was broken away; the horses had to
slide down what looked like an impossible slope, with
a man hanging on to the head and tail of each to break
the speed, and we made a long circuit.   When we came
finally to the Palace of the Bishop of Pulati—a ramshackle
little place in native style, with a crazy wooden balcony—
his Grace was having an afternoon siesta.   To my horror
he was waked up to receive me, but such was his
Christian spirit that he took me in and fed me.

The Palace is snugly stowed among trees, and running

water in plenty flows hard by. It is characteristic of the land that no decent path leads to it. I lay and lounged in the meadow at the side. The air was leaden-heavy, there were lordly chestnut trees near, and a drowsy humming of bees. All the world seemed dozing. The peace was broken suddenly by two gunshots that thudded dully down in the valley—then two more—and silence.

" What is that ?" I asked, mildly interested.

" A wedding, probably," said Marko. " It is Monday—the marrying day with us."

We strolled from the field, and scrambled along the hillside towards a group of cottages. The first woman we met asked us in to hers at once—a most miserable hovel, windowless, pitch-dark in the corners ; a sheep was penned in one and a pig wandered loose. She began to blow up the ashes and make coffee. Life was hard, she said—maize dreadfully dear. You had to drive ten kids all the way to Scutari and sell them to get as much maize as you could carry back. Shouts rang up the valley; a lad dashed in with the news. The shots we heard had carried death. At a spot just over an hour away an unhappy little boy, unarmed and but eight years old, had been shot for blood, while watching his father's sheep on the hillside, by a Shoshi man.

The Shoshi man had quarrelled some time ago with a Ghoanni man, who in the end had snatched a burning brand from the hearth and thrown it at him. A blow is an unpardonable insult. The Shoshi man demanded blood and refused to swear *besa*.

He had now washed his honour in the blood of a helpless victim, whose only crime was that he belonged to the same tribe as the offender.

The child was the elder of two. The father, very poor and a cripple, had gone to Scutari to seek work. Ghoanni was filled with rage. That Shoshi had the right to take blood of any man of the tribe they freely admitted, but to kill a child was dishonourable. They would not do it.

I discussed this case in many places afterwards. Feeling on the whole was against it. Many who thought the law actually justified it considered it a dirty trick. Others held that male blood of the tribe (this is the old usage) is what is required, and in whose veins it runs is a matter of no moment—it is the tribe that must be punished. Even an infant in the cradle has been sacrificed in obedience to the primitive law.

By recent legislation some tribes now restrict blood-guiltiness to the actual offender (as in Mirdita) or his house (as Shala). A Shala man said the Ghoanni case was a bad one. He would not like to have to kill a child, but "if it is the law to kill one of the same house, and the murderer has fled and left no male but a child, then you must. It is a pity, but it is the law."

Could he not wait the return of the offender, or till the child was of age to bear arms? "No; you could not wait because of your honour. Only blood can clean it." I suggested it was the honour of the wolf to the lamb, which surprised him, but he stuck to his point. "Till you had taken blood every one would talk about you. You could not live like that." Mrs. Grundy is all powerful even in Albania!

A man may be shot for blood though ignorant that his tribe owes it. When working elsewhere he will often alter his costume that the district he hails from may not be recognised at sight, lest he have to pay for a crime of which he has not yet heard. Blood seekers, suspecting the origin of such a man, will challenge him, "Whence art thou?" It is not etiquette to lie. Moreover, to proclaim a false origin, if ignorant of the latest blood feuds, might equally make him liable for blood. He may reply:

"From wherever you like."

"What is your name?"

" I was baptized once," and so forth. Answers of this type are given by men on their way home after a long absence, if unaware of the local political situation.

One must not trespass on any one's hospitality, much less on that of a Bishop. At 6 A.M. next day my horses were ready. The Bishop assured me that the track was excellent to Plani, and jocularly promised to call on me " next time he came to London."

As we started, the mountains rang with the shouts that summoned the tribe to the funeral of the slaughtered child. This, our guide remarked, would complete the ruin of the family. Honour compelled it to supply meat and drink to all comers. Some districts, Thethi, for example, have made a law to restrict the number of such guests to near relatives, and so limit expenses.

The Bishop's idea of an excellent track must have been the strait and narrow way. It was execrable. With great difficulty were the horses dragged along. We scrambled and sidled on foot along narrow ledges or crumbly shale that breaks and goes rattling down into the valley below. Shade there was none, nor any breath of air. I have no idea what the scenery was, as I saw nothing but the next possible foothold in a dizzy reel of almost intolerable heat, keeping well ahead of the horses, as they always break off lumps of the track with their last hind-leg.

Not long ago these hills were well wooded, but here, as in many districts, every one cuts and no one plants, and the loose soil is disintegrating with alarming speed. Each rainy season the water tears down the earth in tons, whirling all away to silt up the Bojana and build a bar across its mouth. Blocking its own exit to the sea, the water spreads and festers, fever-stricken, over the plain, leaving desolation behind it in the mountains. The land melts rapidly before the eyes of the poor people, who lament and say that the Government ought to build walls, but cannot understand that they must cut carefully and replant.

In the few foreign schools that exist in Scutari, "book larning" and nothing practical is taught. The pupils are filled with the wish to obtain a clerkship abroad rather than the knowledge of how to develop their own land.

We reached Plani at midday; it lies at the head of the valley of the Kiri. The church stands in a most charming spot. A small cataract leaps down from high above, through a wooded gorge—a bower of coolness and greenery after the roasting track.

Plani, a tribe of one bariak, traces origin from three stocks which are intermarriageable. One hails from Kilmeni. Fifty years ago, people say, they dressed like Mirdites; but I heard no tale of relationship with them.

Plani owed very little blood within the tribe, but was in blood with several neighbour tribes.

When a feud is reconciled in Plani (and in some other districts I believe), a woman brings an infant in a cradle and turns it upside down between the foes, turning the child out on to the ground. As it is always tied down tightly by the cradle cover, it can be gently released —the ceremony is not so violent as it sounds.

There are a good many ceremonies about the laying of blood to be learnt.

The deputy Bariaktar welcomed me to his home—a house of thirty members. He spoke strongly against blood feuds, having lost father, brother, and son, all in the same one. Threatened with ruin if it continued, he had paid blood gelt, 300 guldens in all, and now was doing well.

Plani, like Hoti, has a celebrated surgeon. Unluckily he was absent. Diseases of the eye were his speciality. For inflamed eyes I was told the following is infallible:

the juice of Wall Pellitory mixed with a little salt.
Three drops in the eye twice a day is the dose.

A proverb says : " Each disease has its herb."

A popular dressing for cuts and wounds is the
common St. John's Wort (*Hypericum perforatum*) well
pounded and put into a bottle of olive oil. This must
be placed in the sun for several days, and is then fit for
use. It has such a reputation for healing that I think it
must have some antiseptic property.

A remedy for jaundice, a common complaint in the
mountains, is : catch a little fish, put it in a basin of
water and stare at it steadily as it swims round. After a
few days the yellow goes out of your eyes into the fish,
and you are cured.

A wondrous plant is that which breaks stone and
iron. Should a hobbled horse, out grazing, touch it with
the hobble the iron flies asunder. Valuable horses have
often thus been lost. None knows where the plant grows
but the tortoise.

When you find, as is not infrequent, some tortoise's
eggs, you must build a little wall round them of stones.
Then hide and await the mother tortoise. She will be
very angry and strive to butt down the wall with her
head, lest her children should hatch inside it and be
starved. Failing to butt it down she will go and fetch a
leaf of the plant, touch the wall with it, and at once
down goes the wall !

You can then take the leaf from her, and use it for
burglary and other household purposes. Where she finds
it none knows, and she will not fetch it if followed.

Tortoises swarm in Albania—oddly fascinating beasts
that bask in the sun and peer at you with little beady
eyes, or walk along serenely, craning their wrinkled
necks and browsing with deliberate bites off the leaves
they fancy ; sad things are they in a sprouting maize or
bean field. It is not surprising that their grotesque form

has inspired a folk-tale: How the Tortoise got its Shell.

When Christ was crucified all the beasts hastened to condole with the Virgin Mary. The poor little tortoise was deeply grieved, and did not know how to show his grief; so, on the way, he bit off a large leaf and covered himself up. When the Virgin saw him coming along with only his little head sticking out, he looked so funny that she could not help laughing aloud in spite of the painful circumstances. And the tortoise has been covered up ever since.

Plani knows many strange things. There is a group of houses not far from the church, which has had a curse upon it for many years, so that the families never increase in number. I visited one small house; it contained eighteen people, so perhaps the failure to increase is rather a blessing than a curse.

Talk ran on the *chytet* (fortress), very ancient—who knows, perhaps, a thousand years. Was it far? I asked, for I was tired. "Oh no," said the Franciscan, "we can go and come back easily in an hour."

We started; the track degenerated into a narrow ledge crawling along the side of the mountain, betwixt heaven above and the river below; and at the finish, the spur of the hill, there was a rocky pinnacle to climb.

An extraordinarily wild spot. The sharp peak rose high, with a deep valley on three sides of it. In the gap between it and the range of which it was the final point are traces of the *chytet;* the remains of three wells, now choked with stones. Part of the rock face is roughly hewn, and a few small ledges are cut in it. A rudely-built bastion overhangs the precipice.

"No, we must go to the top," said the wiry little Franciscan, who skipped from rock to rock like a chamois. I was not shod for climbing; having been promised an hour's stroll, and wore a long skirt. "The

way," said the Franciscan, after a vain attempt at the
near side, " is best on the precipice side." Marko did not
like the idea at all ; however, we crawled round and
started. The upright blocks of rock were all too big for
my stride, but there were bushes between, by which to
pull up, and there was something like a thousand feet
below, straight down, to fall. Luckily I am never giddy,
or I should have gone overboard years ago. In the
Balkan peninsula giddiness is unknown, and people
start you along any ledge at any height cheerily and
recklessly.

Half-way up, the heat being appalling, it occurred
to me to ask if there was much of the *chytet* to be seen
when we did get up. Hearing that there was none, and
that we were going up merely for the sake of going up,
I cried off, to the disappointment of the wild-goat
Franciscan. It was a game not worth the candle.
Marko thanked God fervently when I was no longer
overhanging space. He had sworn to bring me home
alive, and had been greatly uneasy.

The fortress was most probably a Venetian outpost
to guard Drishti from the attacks of up-country tribesmen. A bronze cannon was found a good many years
ago buried in the mountain-side below, but was taken
away by an officer and some soldiers.

Plani has little corn land, and has to buy. Some men
and very many women were toiling in long weary strings
over Shala to Gusinje, climbing two high passes—a
frightfully severe two days' march—maize being cheaper
there than at Scutari. The return journey of wretched
beings, staggering under loads of 60 or 70 lbs., is horrible
to see. The cords that bind on the burden often cut right
into the shoulder. The maize lasts little more than a
week, and the weary journey begins again. Small
wonder that the toil-broken people begged that the
Powers would enforce the making of a railway to Scutari.

Time was flying. I wanted to see all High Albania.
It was time to move on. The *kirijee* then said he had
a bad foot and was tired of the journey, so the Padre
kindly lent me his own man to take me to Thethi. We
had a second as escort. The way, said the Padre, was
good, but after sitting my reeling, struggling beast for
some ten minutes over large rocks, to shrieks of " Jesus,
Maria, Joseph ! " which were supposed to encourage it, I
dismounted, and was in for another roasting tramp.

The ever-rising track swung round the head of the
valley, above the source of the Kiri, and over the Chafa
Bashit (some 4000 feet), into Shala.   Once up and over,
all Shala lay before us and below us, a long, lorn wall of
huge, jagged mountains, still snow-capped, with the Lumi
Shalit flowing in the valley at their feet.

I daresay you have never heard of Shala. I have
looked towards Shala and the beyond for years—the wild
heart of a wild land.

Do you know the charm of such a land ? It has the
charm of childhood.   It has infinite possibilities—if it
would but grow up the right way.   It has crimes and
vices ; I know them all (that is to say, I trust there are
not any more).   But it has primitive virtues, without many
of the meannesses of what is called civilisation.   It is
uncorrupted by luxury.   It is cruel—but so is Nature.
It is generous as a child that gives you its sweets.   It can
be trusting and faithful.   And it plays its own mysterious
games, that no grown-ups can hope to understand.

I hurried forward.   There was grass underfoot, and—
always a joy—we were to go down-hill for hours and
hours.   Our two men were not so inspired.   They said
they wished to call on a friend, and left us under a tree
with a Martini, saying that any one who passed would
recognise the weapon (decked with silver filagree), and
consider us properly introduced.

And sure enough the first-comers recognised it at once,

and were most friendly.   The glee with which they learnt how many brothers I possess—married or single, how old—&c., their pressing invitations that we would at least come and have a cup of coffee or *rakia*, or stay the night at any of their respective houses and accept " bread, salt, and my heart," whiled away the time pleasantly till our two men returned.

We descended to the river's bank by Gimaj, a village of Shala, and followed up the valley.   The river became a torrent, leaping from rock to rock—the pine-clad mountains towered on either hand, and the houses were all *kulas*—tall stone towers, loopholed for rifles.

A final ascent brought us to the plain of Thethi, a grandly wild spot where the valley opens out.   The ground is cultivated, and well watered by cunning little canals.   Great isolated boulders are scattered over it, on which stand *kulas*.

The eyes, some one has said, are the windows of the soul.   In extreme wrath, at fighting-point, when a man goes white and strikes, the pupils of his eyes contract to black specks.   So do the blank, windowless walls of the *kulas*, with their tiny loopholes, stand ever threatening.

I think no place where human beings live has given me such an impression of majestic isolation from all the world.   It is a spot where the centuries shrivel ; the river might be the world's well-spring, its banks the fit home of elemental instincts—passions that are red and rapid.

A great square-topped cliff on the left was covered with broken fir trunks, torn down by a heavy snow-slide in the winter.   Bleached and white in the sun, they lay scattered like the bones of the dead.   Others stood erect and gaunt.   "It is the altar of God, with candles upon it!" cried one of the men who was with me.

At the very end of the valley rises the range of mountains called the Prokletija (the Accursed Mountains), so named, I was told in Shala and Lower Pulati, because it was over them that the Turk came into High Albania. Other routes seem more possible; but for my own part I believe in local tradition. And the bitter truth remains that over all the land is still the curse of Turkish influence.

Thethi is a bariak of Shala. The church and churchhouse of Thethi stand in the midst of the plain—a solid, shingle-roofed building, with a bell tower. It is largely due to the personal influence of the young Franciscan in charge that Thethi is almost free from blood. In rather more than four years but two cases have occurred.

We arrived at a moment of wild excitement; crowds of mountain men hurrying up, shouting, yelling, talking at the full pitch of their throats—a regular hurry-scurry, with the little Franciscan buzzing about, commanding, entreating, gesticulating, at once. All the heads of Shala were met *me ban medjliss* (to hold a parliament), nearly a hundred of them. They crowded into a large empty room on the ground floor. The President of Council here is elected by the people (the hereditary Bariaktar in Thethi has no rights as head except in battle; this system is spreading)—a big dark man, not at all prepossessing, who looked an ugly customer to tackle. The window was iron-barred; a woman outside, her face pressed close to the grating, listened eagerly. It was a most important meeting on home and foreign affairs. The noise was terrific, and deafened us even in the room above. The Padre came panting upstairs with his arms full of pistols, flintlocks heavily mounted in silver. "Thank God, I got these from them!" he said, as he stowed them in the cupboard with the cups and plates; "they are dreadfully excited to-day!" The room was already stacked with Martinis, deposited in sign of good faith. The question under debate was peace or war.

Shala and the other Christian tribes that border on Moslem ones are always making and repelling raids.

Recently the position had become acute.   In the previous autumn the Moslems near Djakova captured and imprisoned a Franciscan for many weeks.   At the same time the whole of the Moslem tribes were mysteriously supplied with Mausers and quantities of ammunition, it was said by the Turkish Government.   Exultant and boasting, the Moslems had just sent in an ultimatum to the Christians that all who had not turned Moslem by Ramazan would be massacred.   Krasnich, the next-door Moslem tribe, boasted 350 Mausers, Gasi 300, and Vuthaj 80 ; Christian Shala but some six or eight, and these only smuggled in with difficulty.

Nevertheless, filled with rage, Shala swore *besa* of peace with its Christian neighbours, Shoshi and Merturi, and passed a resolution to warn the Vuthaj and Gusinje Moslems that in seven days from receiving notice, Shala-Shoshi and Merturi would be on a war footing with them.   The decision was arrived at in a wild clamour, and the Franciscan fetched to record it; which he did, when he had vainly talked himself tired in favour of peace.   The local priest, being the only man who can write, always has to act as Chief Secretary for State at a *medjliss*, and must write its decision whether he approve or not, and preserve the document for future reference.

The exhausted and excited *medjliss* then started again on local grazing rights, and finally broke up shouting, having decided nothing further.   The wary Franciscan retained the pistols of the five most influential men till the morrow, when all was to be concluded.

The *medjliss* met early next morning, and this time in a great circle out of doors.   I meant to photograph it, but was dragged away by Marko and the Franciscan and sent indoors, as they feared firing at any minute.   Four of the five chief "heads" had agreed the day before to

the decision of the majority. The fifth stood out furious
and vowed neither he nor his *mehala* would accept it.
As he was head of fourteen houses and ruled sixty-four
individuals, his agreement was necessary to any grazing
right changes. After a most stormy hour or two on the
perilous brink of blood, he was talked round. The
motion was carried, and the heads came upstairs for
their pistols, but the affair had been touch-and-go.

"I am afraid they find it dreadfully boring," said the
Franciscan. "They say no one has been shot for two
whole years! We nearly had a row at a *medjliss* a little
while ago—(that was why I got the five chief pistols this
time)—I heard a fearful noise, and as I ran out a lot of
them all got up into a bunch like bees, and raised their
rifles. They were just going to fire. They would not
listen to me. I rushed into the church and rang the
bell as hard as I could. It had a splendid effect. As
soon as they heard the bell, from habit they all shoved
their pistols in their belts and took their guns in their
left hands, and began to cross themselves. No one knew
what had happened. They poured into the church to
see. By the time we came out again and had had a talk
they were quieted."

Such was my coming to Thethi. I stayed some
time, and came back to it, and hope to go again.

Shala, Shoshi, and Mirdita, says tradition, descend
from three brothers, who came from Rashia to escape
Turkish oppression, shortly after that district was occupied
by the Turks.

One of the brethren possessed a saddle (*shala*); the
second a winnowing sieve (*shosh*); the third had nothing,
so he said "good-day" (*mir dit*) and withdrew. The tale
as it stands is doubtless fabulous, but the fact that to this
day Mirdita does not intermarry with either Shala or
Shoshi is, to my mind, conclusive proof of original close
consanguinity.

When Shala and Shoshi settled, they found inhabitants already in the land, who, they tell, were small and dark. In Shala, eight families are still recognised as of this other blood. The rest, a very large number, migrated "a long time ago" (probably when the Serbs evacuated the district), to Dechani and its neighbourhood, and are now all Moslem.

I remember in 1903, when at Dechani, being much struck with the small, dark-eyed Albanians there, for then I was familiar only with the fair, grey-eyed type.

As the Turks overcame Rashia earlier than they did Bosnia, it is likely that the emigration of Shala-Shoshi's forefathers from Rashia was earlier than the Bosnian migrations into Maltsia e madhe, already noted.

It may even have been at the end of the fourteenth or beginning of the fifteenth century. Local tradition in Shala tells that three hundred and seventy-six years ago (*i.e.* in 1532) the bariak of Shala had sufficiently increased in numbers to be divided into three main "houses" —Petsaj, Lothaj, and Lekaj—which, as separate bariaks, still exist. This is evidence that at that date they must have been settled for some time. Lothaj and Lekaj have recently decided that they are sufficiently far removed to be intermarriageable. But Petsaj still refuses on the ground of consanguinity.

The bariak of Thethi consists of 180 houses, of which 80 form the village of Okolo at the extreme end of the valley.

Thethi can, and does, grow enough corn for its own support, and has passed a law strictly forbidding the export of any, as has all Shala. The only near corn-supply is the Moslem Gusinje, and in case of that being cut off by "blood" or war, there is no nearer supply than Scutari, a dear and distant market.

Life at Thethi was of absorbing interest. I forgot all about the rest of the world, and having paid off and dismissed the *kirijee* and horses, there seemed no reason why I should ever return.

It was the time of ploughing and harrowing. The harrow is a large bundle of brushwood, on which some one squats to weight it down.

All day long folk came and holloaed under the window, "Oy Padre," and received spiritual consolation, or doses of Epsom salts. Often they came merely to see me, in which case their curiosity was satisfied.

The relations of a parish to its priest are amusing. They refuse to call him by his name, if they do not like it; hold a *medjliss*, and solemnly decide on a better one, by which he is henceforth known. I came across no less than four of the mountain priests thus renamed.

Numbers of sick came for help. In spite of the magnificent air, the death-rate is appallingly high. Thethi had been devastated four years ago by smallpox, which rages every few years through the unvaccinated Turkish Empire, while vaccinated Montenegro next door goes scot-free. No medical assistance came to the wretched people, who died in great numbers. Only the plucky Franciscan trudged from one deathbed to another, and kept up the courage of the survivors. And this they have never forgotten.

Under the awful conditions of life all epidemics— cholera, typhus, smallpox, even influenza—assume terrible proportions whenever they occur in the mountains. Neither isolation (in a house with one dwelling-room, where perhaps thirty people sleep together), diet, or nursing are possible. The children die off like flies in autumn. Helpless and powerless, the people wait for the storm to pass over. *Eghel*—"It is written."

But apart from epidemics the death-rate in the mountains is high. The blood-feud system accounts for the death of many men, some in feud within the tribe, more in feuds with neighbour tribes.

Baron Nopcsa, a most careful observer, after collecting the list of killed in a large number of tribes, estimates the average in the Christian tribes as 19 per cent. of the total male deaths. This list includes the wildest of the Christian tribes, and does not include some of the quieter ones, so that the average for the whole is probably rather lower. Shala-Shoshi and Mirdita stand high on the list—Toplana, highest of all. Of the Moslem tribes no statistics have been taken. Matija has the worst reputation. The Moslem average probably does not differ from the Christian one; religion does not affect national custom.

As for the statement recently published by a self-styled "Observer," that many people are daily shot in Scutari, I can only say that some one had been "pulling the poor gentleman's leg" very badly, and not on that subject only.

In spite of the shooting, there are more men than women. People say it is because God in His infinite wisdom sends an extra supply to Albania, where He knows they are needed.

It is more probably because there is a very high death-rate of women. The very young age at which girls are married—often at thirteen—and ignorant treatment causes great mortality at childbirth; also much evil arises from working too soon afterwards.

Shala is one of the tribes that suffers much from a form of syphilis said to have been recently introduced, as do all the tribes with which it intermarries. In some places I was told that there are scarcely any healthy married women. Mirdita, on the other hand, which is consanguineous, is said to be quite free.

When a blood feud is compounded in Thethi with a family not consanguineous, it is usual to cement the friendship by a marriage—not always successfully. A man some years ago, when laying a feud, sold his daughter to a Gusinje Moslem in spite of her protests. She managed, when fetching water, to induce her companions to go into a house. She then fled and hid, and by night got over into a Christian tribe, where the Padre helped her to get to Scutari. A blood feud was the result.

The border Moslems will pay high prices for Christian girls, ten napoleons even above the Christian rate. Moslems rarely sell girls to Christians, but both Moslems and Christians abduct one another's girls freely. Hence much blood.

The lot of a woman who wishes to escape from a Christian husband is even harder. Recently a Christian woman—married into a Christian tribe—who lived most unhappily with her husband, ran away from him, meaning to go to a Moslem at Ipek and turn Turk.

Passing through Thethi, she was recognised and stopped. The tribe she had fled from was informed. Six men of her own tribe and five from her husband's came and took her back to her husband. It was far better for her, said Thethi, to be unhappy with a Christian than happy with a Moslem.

Should a woman be very badly used by her husband and fly for protection to her family, they may, if they think her flight justified, refuse to give her up. In this case they may summon a *medjliss* which, in extreme cases, permits her to remain at home. Should the family keep her without permission from the *medjliss*, a blood feud with her husband arises.

This custom prevailed also in Montenegro till fairly recent times. I was told of a case in which thirty men were shot in a fight that ensued when a family refused to give up a refugee daughter to the husband who had ill-treated her.

Trouble, as the Franciscans were never tired of impressing on me, was brought into the world by woman.

Thethi had lately been much upset by a fair widow.
Married very young in Thethi, her husband was killed
within the year. As she was childless, she was the property of her own family. The *xoti i shpis* (lord of the
house), her nephew, sold her again at once at an enhanced
price. The second husband also came to an untimely
end almost at once. She had now a great reputation for
beauty, and was in much demand. Her nephew had an
immediate bid of five purses (22 napoleons) for her and
accepted it. Followed a second bid of rather more. He
threw over the first and accepted this; but there came a
third, of no less than eight purses. His aunt was indeed
a gold mine. He jumped at the eight-purse man. A
terrible quarrel ensued. The five-purse man took his
money back and was appeased, and the second also
was talked round. Then a fourth man appeared and
said the widow had promised herself to him, and she
confirmed his statement.

Eight-purses insisted she was his. The nephew, too,
was highly in his favour. The matter was laid before
the priest. He, finding the woman was quite decided
for number four, supported her choice, for, as he philosophically remarked, " It is really no use marrying them
to the ones they don't want ; they only run away." The
nephew said he would be satisfied with a fair price, so
the couple hooked their little fingers together, exchanged
rings before the priest, and were pronounced properly
betrothed.

Eight-purses arrived in a fury, and forbade the banns
on the grounds of consanguinity. A relative of the
bridegroom had been *kumar i floksh* (head-shaving godfather) to a relative of the bride. They were head-
shaving second cousins, and not intermarriageable. The
Padre briefly said "Rubbish," and married them. Eight-
purses and all his house flew in wrath to the Bishop and
accused the Padre of celebrating an incestuous wedding,

demanding his immediate expulsion. His Grace told them to "be off!" Vowing vengeance, they went to Scutari for Government help against both Bishop and priest, but, obtaining none, they finally dropped the matter.

The Upper Pulati tribes are greatly given to the custom of taking a deceased relative's widow as concubine. Against this the Padre was waging active war. One man gave as his reason for taking his sister-in-law that he was a poor man and could thus get a wife for nothing. Nine weeks, Sunday after Sunday, was the pair excommunicated. Then the man said he would leave her if the Padre would find him a cheap wife. An Albanian Franciscan will undertake any job to assist his flock. In a neighbour tribe he saw a likely-looking widow, found she was going cheap, and sent for his strayed sheep to have a look at her. The man was delighted. Her owner "swopped" her for an old Martini, the triumphant Padre married them and received him back to the bosom of Mother Church.

In the wilderness I never want books. They are all dull compared to the life stories that are daily enacted among the bare grey rocks.

A father and mother came sorely anxious to the Padre. Some time ago they had sold their daughter and received the purchase-money. Now, when it was time to send her, they found he had taken his uncle's widow and also his cousin's as "wives," and wished to add their daughter as a legal one to the family circle.

They did not wish her to be one of three, and said he must first dismiss the other two. He refused, said he had bought the girl, and she was his and must live as he chose. They said the deal was "off," and offered to return the purchase-money. He swore vengeance. They were terrified lest the girl should be forcibly abducted, and begged help. The Padre put the girl in charge of his mother, and hurried off to find a respectable man who would marry her and take her to a distance. This he quickly succeeded in doing, and she was safely smuggled away.

Very slowly does tribe usage yield to Church law. Some customs one cannot wish to preserve. Others, that are denounced as Pagan, one regrets. Some years ago it was the common custom to burn a Yule log at Christmas, and with it corn, maize, beans—samples of all the land yields—and to pour wine and *rakia* on the flames as offerings, doubtless to a half-forgotten God. The ashes were scattered on the fields to make them fertile. But an energetic Franciscan argued, " Why waste good food and imperil your souls by Pagan rites, when you might save both by behaving as Christians?" And the picturesque and harmless custom is fast dying out. (It is still practised in Montenegro.)

The belief in what is *eghel* wars with Christianity and sometimes conquers. An old, old man lay mortally ill. The Padre hastened to him, but he refused to confess and did not want absolution. "I cannot die," he said, "it is not *eghel*. Never before have I had such a flock of goats, nor such store of corn and dried meat. I cannot die with all that food to eat." But he had mis-read the Book of Fate, and died *sine sacramento*.

Thethi is one of the few places in North Albania that has not lost the old art of chip-carving. The graveyard is stately with big wooden crosses, well carved, the arms ending in circles adorned with a rayed sun. A little child died in the night, and hither next morning came the funeral party, bearing the little corpse in its wooden cradle.

It was beautifully dressed, and had been washed quite clean, probably for the first time, poor little thing. On its breast lay three green apples. The women sat round and sang death-wails while two men dug the very shallow grave. This was because the child's head had not yet been shaved. After that ceremony it would rank as an adult, and the grave must be dug breast-deep. No coffin was used, but the grave roughly lined with planks.

The wild wailing of the women and long-drawn sobs of the father, while one woman sang a death-chant, were painful in the extreme. But just as I was feeling broken-hearted the song ended, and the party began to chatter and laugh as though nothing were the matter. Some people, on the way to Gusinje to buy maize, stopped to look at the corpse, and all were talking cheerfully when, suddenly, a woman began another death-chant, and at once the sobbing began again.

They then cut a lock of the child's hair, and laid the body in the grave with the three apples on its breast. The Padre arrived, and they asked him if the apples were necessary. He said not, and they were removed and tied in a handkerchief with the hair.

The funeral service was quite drowned by an old man who stood at the head of the grave with his rosary in his hand and shouted a hotchpotch of every scrap of Latin he could remember from any service, at the top of his voice. A plank was laid on as lid, the earth hoed over. No one displayed the least emotion, and the party trailed away carrying the empty cradle. Both in Montenegro and Albania the cradle is often broken and left on the grave, a most pathetic monument. Of the apples I could only learn it was an old custom to put them in the grave. It prevailed till lately in Montenegro also.

The days passed. I visited dark *kulas* perched on rocks, and met everywhere the same frank hospitality and courtesy, though it weighed on my soul that I was receiving it under false pretences; for, in spite of my frequent and emphatic denials, all Thethi persisted in believing me to be the sister of the King of England come to free them, and addressing me always as Kralitse (Queen).

But though happy at Thethi my soul hankered ever after Gusinje. Gusinje, said every one, was impossible. I had tried for it in 1903 from Andrijevica, in Montenegro, but no one would take the risk of piloting me. The Turkish Government gave no permission—the natives would admit no stranger. In former days a consul or two had visited it with an escort. Lately it had become the Lhassa of Europe, closed to all; though several had tried.

The longer I stayed at Thethi, the more I thought of Gusinje. Marko would not hear of it. I gave it up at last, and ordered mules to take us to Lower Shala, and went for a walk with the Padre up the valley to Okolo. It is a wonderful valley—wide grass meadows with a crystal-clear river through them, fed by countless bubbling springs.

Okolo is well-to-do. Many of its eighty *kulas* are large and fine, and some quite new. Were it not for the curse of blood, Okolo should flourish. In land, wood, and water it has all that a village needs. But though it has been at peace within, for four years, a field full of graves, but a few years older, shows that it is not for nothing that Shala is reputed a fighting tribe.

On a summer evening a party of men strolled down the valley, sat upon the ground lazily, and watched the stars come out.

Then, pointing to a certain star, one said : " That is the biggest," and another said : " No, that one there is bigger." A fierce dispute took place; some took one side, some the other; rifles cracked, bullets sang. When the smoke cleared and the first excitement was over, there lay seventeen dead men—slain for a star—and eleven wounded. Their comrades buried the dead where they fell—for they died in sin—*sine sacramento.*

At the very end of the valley towered Mal Radoina, said to be the highest of the Prokletija range, and Mal Harapit thrust up a sharp pinnacle to the sky with a deep square-cut pass on its shoulder—Chafa Pes—the pass that leads to Gusinje. Beyond that mountain wall lay the Promised Land, and I had ordered the mules for Lower Shala to-morrow.

A headman of Okolo invited us to his *kula*. We followed him, and then wonders began to happen. At his door was tethered a beautiful little grey saddle-horse. It was the horse of one of the headmen of Vuthaj, a large Moslem village but an hour from Gusinje, and he was guest at the house. My spirits rose; there by the hearth sat a long, lean Moslem, smartly dressed, armed with a new Mauser—a man of means evidently. He greeted the Padre heartily—for the Padre had once visited Vuthaj, and prescribed successfully for some sick —was much interested in my travels, and told of the beauties of Vuthaj. Vuthaj, if not the rose, was next it. Anxiously I asked if it could be visited; the Moslem promptly invited us. He belonged to one of the two chief houses, and said he could guarantee our safety.

But as he was bound for Scutari he could not escort us. I was ready "to see Gusinje and die"—the Padre had friends and would be safe—but Marko said it was impossible, and he had a wife and children to consider. I was torn betwixt a desire to go and a fear of getting any of my men into trouble. But a few days before, Thethi had sworn to declare war against this very district —the land of Mausers. After much talk, sheep-cheese and *rakia*, we said adieu with the matter undecided.

As we turned the bend of the valley, and the square-cut pass was lost to sight, I felt I had lost all I cared about. So near, and yet so far. The sporting Padre returned to the charge: "What about to-morrow?" He enlarged upon the ease and safety of the expedition;

he suggested that he and I should go and Marko wait for us. Marko refused this absolutely; he had sworn to bring me back safely, his honour was concerned in it; if I died, he meant to die too. God would protect his wife and orphans.

"Nothing will happen," said the Padre firmly. "I will go," said I. No sooner said than arranged. Our host at Okolo volunteered to be escort and provide two mules. He had to go, or send some one, at any rate, as he had promised to send the Moslem's grey horse back. The Padre's servant was to come with a rifle; we were to take no luggage of any sort, and only food enough for the outward track. It took six hours, if you went fast, said the Padre. We were off before six next morning, I fondly believing we should arrive by one o'clock, and return next morning—which, after nine years' experience of the Near East, was extremely foolish of me.

CHAPTER VI

THE PROKLETIJA, SHALA, AND SUMA

"Ah, 'tis an excellent race, and even under old degradation,
Even under hodja and Turk, a nice and natural people."

As far as Okolo it was easy going; there we lost over an hour waiting for our escort, who was waiting for a mule, which was waiting for a man, who was unavoidably delayed because, &c. &c. By the time we got to the mountain-foot it was hot. It had not occurred to me before that it was possible to find a way over what looked like a wall at the end of all the world, but I followed the Padre, who rode the Moslem's horse, and we started up a steep, very steep trail that zigzagged over masses of loose rock and boulder that had crashed down from the mountain above. The higher we got, the steeper was the track that crawled on a narrow edge. I wondered each time we turned a corner where my beast would find footing for his four hoofs, and the loose stones bounded into space.

About half-way up is a great cavern formed by a mass of overhanging strata, and blackened by the fires of the wayfarers who rest here. We dismounted. Above us rose a cliff with sprawling pine trees here and there. Nevertheless, except that the trail crawled along edges with a sheer drop, and was very narrow, it was not bad, for pine logs laid across it in all the steepest parts made a rude staircase. We climbed it on foot, and the mules followed; the Franciscan was by this time enjoying himself extremely. He flew ahead, reached the top of the pass, and roused the echoes by yelling a demoniac laugh of his own invention till the mountains rang with gigantic mirth.   I struggled up the rocky steep, happily believing that we were at the top and only had to trot down into Vuthaj, and turned the corner to find the Franciscan, his brown habit girded to his knees, rejoicing in front of a wall of snow, some twelve or fifteen feet high, that blocked the pass.   I was astonished—Marko aghast.   " Oh, it's nothing ; you wait and see ! " cried the Padre.   He proposed the local drink—snow beaten up in milk—which, by the way, is very good—and mixed some.   We started again, and scrambled up on the top of the snow.   It was thawing in the sun, soft and very heavy.   I was wearing native raw-hide *opanke*, and was soon wet half-way up to the knee. The dazzling snow-slope cut sharp against the sky.   A few yards more ploughing upwards and we should be really over the pass ; but we got to the top, and, behold, a white desert of snow—a deep, snow-clad hollow, a sharp rise, snow-peak over snow-peak—snow as far as could be seen.   The Franciscan gathered his skirts around him, squatted, gave a yell, and shot down the slope, and ran round and round at the bottom in wild circles like a playful dog, shouting German and Albanian equivalents for " Oh, let us be joyful ! "   The mules tried zigzagging, gathered speed rapidly, and landed in a heap.   So did I.   Marko was indignant.   " Why didn't you tell us there was snow ? " he asked.

" Because I knew you would not let her come, and now she is going to Vuthaj !   Going to Vuthaj," he sang. " Oh, there's lots more of it !   I don't suppose we shall arrive till late in the evening.   We aren't half-way yet."

" But you said six hours ! " said Marko.

" I said six hours *if you went very fast !* and in this snow, of course, you can't."

We ploughed on up the next slope.   The hollow was a sun-trap.   I clawed and slithered on the molten surface, sometimes going in knee-deep. My feet were dead with cold, and the sun was scorching my back.

We came out on a hard snow level, mounted, and rode over a considerable piece—much to my relief, though a bit risky. The snow, where it had in places melted away from the side-walls of rock, showed twenty and more feet deep. Then came another long slither through wet snow, ankle-deep. Getting off the snow on to *terra-firma* took time, as in places it was thin, and it was possible to fall through into deep holes between the rocks.

We got down into a valley where grass sprouted through puddles of snow-water among great boulders, and halted to feed man and beast.

There came a long descent on foot, zigzag through magnificent beechwood, and out into the valley below. Along this we rode cheerfully, passing a small lake, very blue and deep, but made, I was assured, entirely of snow-water, and dried up in the summer. We were now in the Forbidden Land, the Prokletija. Marko was anxious; the Padre carolled gaily—sang " The English are going to Vuthaj," and became more and more festive.

In all that happens in the Balkan Peninsula there is more than meets the eye. I now learned the wheels-within-wheels that worked this expedition. A certain Austrian some time previously had given dire offence to a native of Thethi, and blackened his honour. The said Austrian had tried to get to Gusinje, and failed. It was believed that if an Englishwoman got farther than he had, he would be most intensely annoyed. I was a pawn in the game of annoying Austria. Nor was the game to be so easy as had been said.

A halt was called. I was told that I figured as the sister-in-law of one of the party, and that I must take off my kodak and fountain pen, as they were not in keeping with the part. Also, though the people of Vuthaj mostly spoke some Serb, I had better remember that I was in a Moslem land, and hold my tongue.

I was not at all pleased at this, as I had meant the expedition to be all above board. But it was far too late to go back—nor did I want to. Bound not to risk a blood feud by indiscreet conduct, I acquiesced unwillingly, and on we went, still descending the stream.

The valley opened and widened, and there lay the scattered houses of Vuthaj, spreading up the mountainside, over whose flank ran the track to the other forbidden city, Plava.

Vuthaj valley is rich with green pasture, large, well-watered fields, and large, well-built *kulas*, with high, shingled roofs. In the midst stood a small mosque, with wooden minaret. There it all lay in the afternoon sun. My kodak was thrust into my hand. "Quick, before any one comes. You are the first foreigner as near as this!" Click!—and the camera disappeared again. My escort now all became silent and anxious. Folk came out, and stared at us doubtfully. The Padre hailed an acquaintance, and was well received. We dismounted, and were led to the *kula* of the owner of the horse—the man we had met at Okolo.

It was a fine house, the best in Vuthaj—gaily painted with horses, a large crescent and sun, and many other objects and twiddles, in a wide frieze below the roof. And it was two storeys high, above the ground floor. As had been agreed upon, I followed my three men humbly and at a slight distance, my eyes discreetly downcast, only taking mental notes asquint as I passed.

We went through a high gateway into a walled yard—which stank, and enclosed a smaller house and a stable—and were led upstairs into a fine room on the upper floor of the big house.

A goat-hair matting covered the floor with gay red rugs upon it. A fretwork and carved screen on one side

formed the front of sundry cupboards and niches. The
walls were clean white-wash, and the hearth open. A
showy European chiming clock stood on a carved bracket,
and a smart paraffin-lamp hung from the ceiling. All
glass either comes from Scutari by the same route as I
had, or comes up from Cattaro *viâ* Montenegro and
Gusinje, as does everything else imported. How it arrives
intact is a marvel—but Wedgwood used after all to
send his china on mule-packs not so very long ago in
England.

The head of the house received us most courteously.
Of course it was not etiquette for him to take notice of
me. I sat on the floor in a corner as bidden, held my
tongue, and looked on.

The room was light, for the windows on the yard side
were large. Some millstones lay handy, to fortify them
at a moment's notice. The shutters were well chip-
carved.

We were in a fine Moslem stronghold in the Prokletija,
the Forbidden Land.

The sick swarmed in to consult the Padre, who was
kept busy writing prescriptions and brevets, marked
with a cross and beginning " Excellentium crucis," for
which there was great demand. And quite a crowd
came merely to look at us, for I was said to be the first
foreign female and the first female dressed *alla franga*,
in Vuthaj; and the first foreigner of any sort that had
come right into Vuthaj.

The housemaster made and handed round coffee and
tobacco incessantly. The room was crowded with tall,
lean men, few, if any, under six feet—many over—all
belted with Mauser cartridges; the Mauser tale was
true. The men are of a marked type—very long-necked,
often very weak-chinned, with a beaky nose that gives
an odd, goose-like effect. I saw this type later among
the Hashi and Djakova Moslems. Many were weedy

and weakly in appearance, but swagger in bearing. I wondered if this marked type were produced by constant in-and-in marrying on the female side. The costume increases the long, lean appearance. The tight trousers are worn very low—only just to the top of the pelvis—and the waistcoat exceedingly short, so that there is an interval of twelve or eighteen inches between the two which is tightly swathed in sashes and belts, sometimes three broad ones, one above the other, with spaces of shirt between. This gives an extraordinarily long-waisted look, as of having double the proper number of lumbar vertebræ.

The Franciscan suggested that we should go for a stroll, but it was negatived firmly. We were to stay on show, and write prescriptions. The air was stifling ; often as many as thirty visitors crowded the room, and stared.

The Franciscan had boasted, just previous to reaching Vuthaj, that he would walk me down to Gusinje, and that we should start back to Thethi about noon next day. But he had reckoned without his Moslems. In a lull in the prescriptions he whispered to me that we must stay all next day at Vuthaj. If we persisted in leaving perhaps we should be fetched back. What did I think? The headman next in importance to our host wanted us to pass the next night at his house. I agreed to stay.

Much talk of *ghak* followed. Our house was in blood with that just over the way, within easy gunshot, and they had been peppering one another from the windows; whence the millstones. The centre hole in a millstone serves admirably to fire through. Their new Mausers had been " blooded."

They fell into blood thus. The other man's haystacks had been burnt; he accused our house. A council of twenty-four Elders had tried the case, and acquitted our housemaster. Over-the-way persisted in the charge, and, on various pretexts, had the case twice re-tried, always with the same result. Our house was exasperated with the constant re-trying. A free fight took place, and one of Over-the-way was killed. They fired at each other's houses many days. Our house had spent over 600 piastres in cartridges. Now a fortnight's *besa* had been given, and the case was to be shortly re-tried. Our housemaster lamented bitterly the conditions that made such things possible—the absence of a decent Government and the amount of money that had to be wasted in weapons for self-defence. " Where there is no proper Government, the bad rule," he said.

He was in sad earnest in his desire for better things. Nor need one go as far as the Prokletija to find folk with unrealisable ideals. As he had received us and had spoken so freely, I whispered to Marko to ask him presently whether the district would permit a railway to cross it. He said his house would welcome one, but admitted that some would oppose. The district is one of the most fertile in Albania, specially noted for cattle and horse breeding. With a good road or a railway, he said, they would soon be rich. Now they could only sell their corn to their next neighbours, and send their horses down in droves through Montenegro to Cattaro (whence they are mainly shipped to Italy)—a long and weary tramp.

I looked at the room full of long, lean cat-o'-mountains, and wondered whether it would benefit anybody— let alone themselves—to turn them all into fat corn and horse dealers.

> " Civilisation is vexation,
> And progress is as bad.
> The things that be, they puzzle me,
> And Cultchaw drives me mad."

More visitors streamed in. They sent for *rakia*, and, in consideration of our feelings, drank the first glass ceremonially—" *Kiofte levduar Christi* " (May Christ have praise). I know no Christian village anywhere that would be similarly considerate of Moslems.

A theological discussion began. One of the guests had a friend who had been to Jerusalem and heard on good authority that Christ had not been crucified, but had gone straight to Heaven, and that another had been crucified in His place. The Franciscan, in a whisper, asked me if he should argue the point and improve the occasion. I said, "Don't. They have received us as their guests, and we must not make trouble." And the subject dropped.

It was now 10 P.M., and we had eaten nothing since noon. But still we continued to attract spectators who came, gazed, and commented and threw cigarettes at me, all of which were duly collected and smoked by Marko and the Franciscan. A man—a most weird creature, with dark eyes, a great pallid face and clean-shaven skull—came in with a tamboora and played and sang interminable ballads, his lean fingers plucking strange trills and wonderful shakes from the slim, tinkling instrument. The room was foggy with tobacco smoke and reeked of humanity. I rocked and dozed in my corner. The Franciscan whimpered pitifully, "Oh, I am so hungry." Marko looked careworn. At last the women —who had long been peering at us through the doorway—came in, unveiled as are all the mountain Moslems —and laid the *sofra*. They fingered me curiously, and spoke freely to many of the men, brought the *ibrik* and soap; we washed, and I was invited to eat with the men of the house, and Marko and the Franciscan. The head dealt round wooden spoons, and gave us each a huge chunk of hot maize bread. The women set a large bowl of boiled lamb and *pillaf* (rice) on the table. Some one recounted that the former Padishah, Abdul Aziz, used to have twenty-four fowls stewed down daily to make the juice for his *pillaf* to be cooked in.

The company fell on the soup, and the meat—in an incredibly short time—was left high and dry. Our host then tore it up with his fingers, and flung a lump at each of us. The Franciscan, as honoured guest, was given the head, and politely threw it back. It passed backwards and forwards, and they finally tore it in half—" honours were divided." I was helped last with what was over. They ate like wolves, tearing off the meat, bolting great lumps —apparently whole—and flinging the bones behind them. Eating boiling-hot, greasy mutton that slips and scalds, and will not be torn to convenient mouthfuls by one's unaccustomed fingers, requires much practice. In a few minutes all was cleared. The shoulder-blade was held up to the light, and gave good omen. The empty bowl was whisked away, and one of *kos* (sour milk) followed —a dish which is poison to me, though I am assured that it is not only wholesome but is used as a " cure." I made up by chewing maize bread laboriously. The *kos* was finished before you could say " Jack Robinson." I doubt if the whole meal took more than fifteen minutes.

Meanwhile the visitors sprawled on the floor in heaps, drinking black coffee, and the harsh voice of the singer and the thin, acid notes of the tamboora rose and fell amidst the buzz of talk. The women came and removed the *sofra*, and we washed. There seemed no signs of bedtime. The Franciscan and I were both dropping with sleep, and woke one another up at intervals. It was past eleven when the last of the visitors uncoiled his length from the floor and strolled off.

Then the women came and spread the mattresses. I had expected to be sent to sleep in the women's quarters, but after a long debate it was considered proper to put me in one corner and place the Franciscan across it, and to arrange the six men of the house and the men who had come with me, in a row on the other side of the room. The Franciscan — believing, as most Christians do, that the Moslem faith can be distinguished by its peculiarly unpleasant smell — was pleased with this arrangement and remarked cheerfully, "How lucky for me! You do not stink."

It was nearly midnight when we were all arranged. I dropped asleep as soon as my head touched the mattress. And at 4 A.M. in came the housemaster with a clatter, made a terrible noise lighting the fire and making the morning coffee. Every one began to arise and shake themselves. I was sick with unsatisfied sleep, and knew not what to do. Squinting from under my cover, I perceived the Franciscan still slumbering sweetly and decided to sleep again. But the populace, though having nothing particular to do, was bent on Daylight Saving. Soon the room was crowded, as it was the night before, all coffee-drinking, in the cold grey dawn.

Sleep was banished. At seven o'clock, somewhat rested, I arose dishevelled, and asked Marko for the little packet of soap, comb, toothbrush, and towel, that had been rolled in my coat and strapped behind my saddle— all I possessed in the way of toilet apparatus. Alas! at the top of the pass some one had rearranged the saddles, and the bag was lost. I was depressed at the idea that for the next ten days I was doomed to go uncombed and untoothbrushed, but Marko was truly delighted. He thanked God and rejoiced whole-heartedly. "Now we shall get away alive. We have had our misfortune! We've lost something. And," he added cheerfully, "you don't *want* the things. A toothbrush!" In England a toothbrush is no great rarity, but the gods of Albania had possibly never before received such a rare and precious gift, and may wait long before acquiring another. At any rate, propitiated they were.

The Franciscan, who had also arisen and shaken himself, now told me he had been definitely forbidden to take me to Gusinje or go himself. I wanted to go quite alone and chance it, and believe it would have been possible, but as my men insisted they would follow, and it would certainly have got them into trouble, I dropped the cherished scheme.

The Franciscan then asked leave to go for a stroll. A great debate ensued. Then a large company came out with us, and walked some hundred yards to a plum tree. Here we were told to sit down, and sit we did, encircled by our escort. And after half-an-hour we were taken back again.

Incarcerated once more in the room upstairs and left with instructions to stay there, Marko became very anxious. "You would come," he said; "now we are prisoners, and God knows what will happen."

I was obsessed with the idea of seeing Gusinje—harped only on that, and thought of nothing else.

The Franciscan looked odd and anxious, but industriously kept up rather forced merriment.

Dinner was the same as supper. We were again left alone, and told to wait till the other house was ready for us. So I went to sleep, and Marko whiled away the time by blaming the Franciscan for getting us into this mess. When I was waked at three o'clock, and told the horses were ready, they were both cross and depressed.

We were escorted downstairs. Our host, courteous and dignified to the last, said good-bye at the gateway, and pointed out how the angle of the wall had been whipped and chipped by Mauser balls in the recent fight. Some men of the house walked with us, and handed us over to men sent to meet us.

Our new host was in his "country house," for the purpose of pasturing his flocks. It was in the valley along which we had come.

When we had gone a short way, the Franciscan told the men to go on with the horses, and said we would follow. No objection was made. We climbed a rocky hillock in the middle of the valley, and followed its ridge till we could see round the corner.

"Is there light enough to photo?" he asked.

"Photo what?" said I.

"Gusinje!"

And there across the fertile plains, half-buried in trees, lay the little town about two miles away.

I had by now given up all hope of seeing it and stared amazed.

"Childe Roland to the Dark Tower came," flashed most inappropriately into my mind, for the spot was sunny, cheerful, and verdant. The river serpentined towards it. The plain was scattered with little white houses.

It was five years since I had first tried to see this Promised Land, and now I had to be satisfied with seeing it from the heights. But I had seen it at last.

One of our escort came to find us. He explained now why we had been kept shut up. News had reached Gusinje that a foreign Giaour was in the neighbourhood, and a *suvarri* had been sent to reconnoitre and arrest. But our gallant host had been loyal—had kept us concealed, and only sent us out when the coast was quite clear.

The sun was setting as we turned from the hill. It was almost dark when we reached our new quarters.

The scene within the house was magnificent. It was nothing more than a huge, rudely-built stone cattle-shed —vast, cavernous—lighted only by a pile of blazing logs. Great curtains of cobweb hung from the smoke-blacked rafters above. The walls and the posts that bore the roof glittered with cartridge-belts and brand-new Mausers, the weapons of the four-and-twenty tribesmen gathered to meet us. The ground was thickly strewn with heaps of newly-cut bracken. An Homeric meal was served on many *sofras*. The twenty-four men-at-arms, brave, with heavy silver chains and silver-mounted revolvers, couched like panthers in the ruddy glare, was a sight to remember. Two serving-men held flaming torches aloft, by the light of which we tore and worried the seethed lamb. The roof rang with laughter, song, and the tamboora. The door was shut and barred, the fire was roasting hot, and the smoke almost blinding. The warriors, replete with fat lamb, sprawled on the ferny beds. The women squatted in a far corner and devoured the remains of the feast, then performed their prayers, rising and falling, genuflecting and prostrating, dim figures through a curtain of coiling smoke. The men prayed not, nor genuflected, but lay down to sleep in a long row, packed close under sheets of felt or their own hooded cloaks.

The house-master came and put me and my two companions in a row, spreading a large *yorgan* over me.

"With respect," said the Franciscan, gazing wildly round—"here one gets lice!" It was a point I could not be bothered to argue. I shoved my coat under my head and slept at once, waked frequently by the poor Franciscan whining miserably: "Ah, I sleep so badly! I think always of these lice. I think I feel them now."

Before four the women were already making the daily bread, wrestling with the dough in a big dug-out trough as the grey dawn struggled through the chinks in the roof. The atmosphere of the yet unopened house was asphyxiating. I strode over the bodies of the sleeping men and hurried to the door. Marko followed, rousing up our guide and sending him to catch and saddle the mules. We had meant to start at five. We did not. The Franciscan had gone to sleep, at last, in spite of his fears, and now nothing would make him arise. When we brutally woke him, he said he was going to sleep again, and did so. By the time he emerged and was ready, a large party of excited men had arrived from Gusinje. A noisy parley ensued. No stranger, they said, ought to have been admitted into the district. Marko became very anxious, and was sure we should be detained. The leader of the party had me asked if I had "anything written that showed where treasure was hidden." Countless treasure was buried somewhere near. I was not to take it. After a long hour's pow-wow they trooped off back to Gusinje, and as soon as they had turned the corner we mounted and rode quickly away. Nor was it too soon, for men were sent out from Gusinje two hours later to capture us.

At the top of the pass, flocks of sheep and goats trailed single file over the snow in long dark line, the first up from the plains. The drovers shouted that if we wanted mutton we could look for a sheep that had fallen over the precipice—they had no time to lose—must be over the mountains before sundown.

This inspired my party. We hurried on, and at the top of the zigzag, where the edge dropped sheer away, the faint cry of the wretched beast rose from the depths. Our guide lay flat, craning over and clinging to the pine roots, and saw the sheep on an inaccessible ledge below. A rifle-bullet killed it, and a shower of rock dislodged it. At the bottom Marko, the Padre, and I waited while the other two mutton-hunted and returned triumphant with the bleeding carcase. A great disembowelling took place at the river's source, and there wandered up a ragged old man, who collected the coil of slippery guts in his arms and begged—if we did not want them—that he might have them to make soup. We left him asquat on the stream bank, washing his treasure-trove. That night we supped off shot sheep. And this is the story of how I did not get to Gusinje.

Of the origin of the Gusinje people I learnt only that they derive from many stocks; that before turning Moslem they were Orthodox, and had never been

Catholic. Also that they can almost all speak Serb as
well as Albanian. Which all points to a possible Serb
origin, though much intertribal "sniping" now takes
place between them and the Montenegrin border tribe,
Vasojevich.

Of the even more remote and reserved folk of Plava,
on the mountains above Gusinje—who have driven away
more than one Turkish Governor and troops—it is said
that part derive from the Catholic tribe of Hoti (I had
this from a Hoti man), but that others, who are "very
impudent and defiant," are "very, very old," and a long
time ago were called Pagani. I asked what was the
religion of these Pagani, but my informant knew only
that now they are Moslem. The word had no meaning
to him. It would be interesting to find if they passed
straight from Paganism to Islam. It is not impossible.

I left Thethi early next morning from Lower Shala
with two fine white mules, and their owners, who lived
in a *kula*, high on a crag. The trail along the left bank
of the Shala River is good, rising higher and higher on
the mountain-side. About half-way our two men suggested
a halt at a big *kula*—for water and a rest—a great rude
four-square tower, with a stone staircase outside to the
first floor.

The *xoti i shpis* (lord of the house), a tall, lean, eagle-
eyed old man, welcomed us to his eyrie.

A wooden ladder led up inside to the top floor—the
family dwelling-room, where thirty-one human beings
lived together under the autocratic rule of the old
man. The sickening stench of crowded humanity was
heightened by the presence of two large sheep, penned
fetlock-deep in manure, on one side, and two small
loopholes were the sole means of light and ventilation.
Fresh brushwood was cast on the half-dead embers of
the hearth in the centre, and the dense resultant smoke

temporarily overcame the other odours. The heat under
the stone sunbaked roof was suffocating.

The house-lord, as is etiquette, himself made coffee.

There was a confused din of squalling children.
Three, all under two years old, alternately made staggering rushes to the edge of the unguarded trap-door
—and were rescued just in time to prevent their com-
mitting suicide in the depths—and rushes to obtain
refreshment from the breasts of their mothers, which
were conveniently exposed.

The men listened eagerly to the questions which the
house-lord showered upon us—on the injustice of the
Government, the miserable state of the Christians—the
hopelessness of any improvement so long as the Turks
governed—what did I think and advise? I said the
first thing to do was to check the blood feuds.

The old man looked up keenly. "Have you a King
in your country?" he asked.—"Yes." "Can he read
and write?"—"Yes."

"And he makes war on his enemies?"—"Yes."

"Well," said the old man firmly—"we are all poor
men. We have no school, we know nothing. If your
King, who can read and write, kills his enemies, why
should not we poor men kill ours?" This sentiment was
greatly applauded. "If one man shoots another man in
your country, what does your King do?"

"He sends the *suvarris* to catch the murderer, a
medjliss is made to judge, and he is hanged."

This the old man considered a dirty trick. Shooting
is far better. As for trusting the arrest to gendarmes—
every one knows what gendarmes are! They would
catch any one, and swear he was the man. Nor had
he any opinion of a *medjliss* made by the Government.
He knew what governments were. I assured him our
medjliss was conducted justly. He replied, "Why spend
all this time when it is far more convenient and satis-

factory to shoot your enemy yourself?" I told him that in our land people do not carry guns always. He could not understand how in that case a man could protect himself from horse-stealers from over the border. Nor could he realise a state of society where such things do not happen. It filled him with respect for my King, who, he opined, must have killed vast quantities of thieves to have produced such a result. And he begged me to tell my King of the sad state of Albania, and ask him what could be done. If he were really very rich, and would do a lot for the country, perhaps he could be King of Albania too. The great thing was to get rid of the Turks. Any of the Seven Kings would be better than that.

So deeply interested was the old man that he begged us to stay till to-morrow to discourse on these subjects. The extreme filth made this unthinkable, but I left regretfully, for the shrewd old man, with the extraordinary dignity and state with which he offered hospitality and the unhesitating obedience that his subjects all gave to his stern commands, was a human document worth studying. In flocks he was wealthy, his *kula* fit to stand a long siege, and he had goodly store of wine and *rakia*. The family lived in one room simply because it was comfortable and convenient, and not from necessity, and, lastly, the sheep lived with them because they bring fertility.

We drank many noble sentiments in strong *rakia*, among them the health of my King, and I rode away.

The Padre of Abate, the church of Lower Shala, was away, but his servant put us up. In the evening we sat out under the trees, and discussed Shala affairs with them that came to see us. They seemed much pleased with their reputation for a high death-rate. Four men had been killed a few days before in a quarrel, but that, said some one, was nothing. "Sometimes we shoot a lot all in one day. Once," and he roared with laughter at the

mere recollection, " twelve were killed for one of these "—
he dropped a cartridge from his belt to illustrate his tale.
A man missed a cartridge from his belt, or said he did—
at any rate it was not there—and accused the man next
him of having picked it up. He denied it. The first
man shouted "Thief!" the second, "Liar!" The whole
company present took sides and a battle ensued.
"Every one was shooting and shouting, and when we
left off there were twelve dead and a whole lot wounded.
Oh no! we never found the cartridge. Very likely he
had left it at home."

As an instance of the detailed way in which local
history is handed down, I noticed with interest that all
the names of the killed were given, though the affair
took place a dozen years ago. Peace be to their ashes!
The manner of their death still is a joy to their tribe.

We left for Shoshi early next morning, walked down
a steep descent to the river, which we crossed on a high
wooden bridge protected by a shrine to St. Antony.
Following the right bank of the Shala River a little way,
we struck up the hill through most magnificent chestnut
forests. Shala, under better law, might be a happy
valley. It has a superlative water-supply, springs that
bubble crystal-clear from out the rock; it is well tim-
bered, and such cultivable land as it has is very fertile.
Nor is there any lack of pasture for flocks. We passed
many big *kulas*, and the fields of sprouting maize were
all guarded by wooden crosses painted white.

Descending, we crossed a small stream, a tributary of
the Shala River, ascended, and arrived at Kisha Shoshit,
the church of Shoshi.

The Franciscan (a Tyrolese from the Italian-speaking
district), who has spent a large part of his life with Shala-
Shoshi, has been collecting and transcribing manuscripts
from the churches, and painfully putting together details
that throw light on the history of the country. But so

many churches have been burned, with all that they contained, that records are few. The earliest he showed me was of 1648, and recorded the assassination that year of five Franciscans; one at Podgoritza.

The Podgoritza Moslems—renegade Serbs and Albanians—were famed for ferocity. Under Montenegrin rule a curious thing has happened. When the town first became Montenegrin a very large part of the Albanian inhabitants retired to Turkish territory. Since then Albanians have been slowly and peacefully reconquering their lost town. The Moslem left, but the Catholic tradesman has taken his place. Almost all the trade of Montenegro is in his hands, and he it is, chiefly, that is employed by the Italian tobacco company there. For the Montenegrin has no genius for trade. Podgoritza is the richest town in Montenegro, but the money is mostly in Albanian hands. The conquered is eating up the conqueror.

According to local tradition, it was to Shoshi that the hero, Lek Dukaghin, came on fleeing from Rashia. A rock—Guri Lek Dukaghinit—that stands high on the hillside across the valley, marks the spot where he first stayed.

Next Sunday was Whit Sunday. The little church was crowded. Many had come a four-hours' tramp.

And always when I went to mass I asked myself fruitlessly, "What does their religion mean to these people?"

That they place great importance on its symbols there is no doubt. The cross is a sort of a charm, marked on bread, planted on every hill, scratched or painted on every door, set on the gable of roofs, worn round every neck, and tattooed on the hand, arm, or breast of the greater part of the Catholic population as a protective charm. But of the real teaching of Christianity they seem to have no idea. The Jesuits have, unfortunately,

made an appalling and revolting series of pictures, showing the tortures to which the sinful mountaineer will be
subjected, and with these strive to terrify him into obedience.   Of *Deus caritas* I fear he has heard little.

And the pictures defeat their object.   When I once
heard a man threatened with hell-fire for taking his
sister-in-law as concubine, he replied, "We should not
be so cruel, and God is not crueller than we are."

The Padre of Shoshi has great understanding of and
sympathy with his people.   I heard more than one tale
of how in mid-winter he had risked his life, fighting his
way through snow and swollen torrents, to reach a dying
man.

The congregation filed out into the sunshine before I
had come to a conclusion about them.

On the space in front of the church a great *medjliss*
took place.   The Elders sat in a circle on the ground or
on stones.   The subject of debate was the case of the
child who had been shot at Ghoanni by the Shoshi man.
Shoshi, to its credit be it said, was violently indignant
over the affair, and public opinion ran so high that the
ghaksur had not dared to remain in the tribe, but had
fled.   The *medjliss* now was held to decide whether his
house should be burnt as punishment.

Many were in favour of this.   The difficulty was that
there was no law under which this could be done.   The
blood had been taken *outside* the tribe, therefore was not
a crime against the tribe, and not punishable by it.   The
duty of vengeance lay with the dead boy's family.   All
agreed that if they liked to come and fire the house,
Shoshi would not oppose them.   But, as the near
relatives were a crippled father and a child, they were
incapable of executing justice.

The question caused great excitement.   The burning
of the house would entail passing a new law to punish a
man for a crime against another tribe.   This would mean

an entire reconstruction of the code, and nothing less than considering themselves as a nation, and not as detached tribes.

I asked whether it were not possible at least to pass a law to punish any man killing a child not of age to bear arms.

It was pointed out that if Shoshi did so, and neighbour tribes did not, Shoshi would be at a disadvantage.

The old man of Shoshi.

I asked whether the punishing in this particular case could be trusted to the Turkish Government, but was told that the man had fled none knew where, so that he could not be given up, and that to invite Turkish soldiers in to burn a Shoshi house would be a bad precedent.

The question was discussed for two days, and was undecided when I left.

The proceedings of the *medjliss* were very orderly, save for the great noise; usually a man was heard out with few interruptions; only now and then several shouted at once. Most of the time the case was argued by two men—one on each side—the others assenting or dissenting, but not breaking into the debate. A fine old man, one Nik Lutzi, said to be an hundred years old, the headman of all Shoshi, was one of the chief speakers. Lean, shrunken, but full of life and energy, with a heavy grey moustache and a flintlock pistol, he sat alert and emphatic, thundering his views with a great voice.

I looked on all the afternoon till the meeting broke up. There was an odd fascination about watching the

expounding of Lek Dukaghin's law, close to the spot
where he is said to have first settled.

According to custom, male blood of the tribe can be
taken so soon as the child's head has been shaved. For
this reason, I was told, mothers with one little boy sometimes delay the shaving a little. But it is not thought
correct.

Popular feeling now seems to be in advance of tribe
usage, and it is to be hoped child-blood will cease soon
to be liable for vengeance. Till free from the risk of
blood, children can never be sent long distances to
school.

From Shoshi a fairly good route took us by Chafa
Kirit, over the mountains that form the watershed
between Shoshi and Lower Pulati, to the church of Kiri,
and thence down to and across the river Kiri, tame and
shrunken by summer drought. A short ascent on the
other side, a descent to cross a tributary stream took us
to the church of Suma by about seven.

The priest was away, the house locked up, but we
had not long to wait for quarters. A fine young man
came down, and asked us to be his guests. The house
was a stone one of the shed pattern, one long, windowless room ; three men and two women were its inmates,
and all at once set to work to make ready for us. One
man hurried off, cut great bundles of walnut branches,
and made me a springy and deliciously scented couch
on the ground just outside the door, where I rested
luxuriously. Another rushed to the rising ground above
the house, and yelled aloud to the four quarters of the compass : "We have guests ; a man from Scutari, two from
Shala, one from Shoshi, and a strange woman." The cry
echoed around. The house was in blood, and this was
to warn all whom it might concern that to-night was
" close time for shooting." A house with guests in it is
exempt ; and again, as the light faded from the sky, rang

the warning yell, "We have guests." For it is in the gloaming that the blood-hunter seeks his prey.

Thus had they fallen in blood : The young fellow who had invited us had been engaged from infancy to a girl. When she was ripe for marriage, her father sold her to another; the youth had never even seen the girl, but this was of no moment, his honour was blackened. He went forth and shot a man of the girl's family, and cleansed it; now the family of the slain man hungered for the blood of him or his. He looked on the situation with grim satisfaction, for he knew he had acted righteously.

I lay and listened to the tale while the three men, intent on feeding us sumptuously, slaughtered a kid on a hurdle by the doorstep, and were busy cleaning and quartering it.

Just as they were bloody to the elbows—dan! rang a rifle and phew-ew sang a bullet close over our heads from behind the corner of the wall. Down fell the flaying-knives; the three snatched the Martinis that hung handy from the stone brackets by the door, and dashed off in hot pursuit. A yell of laughter followed at once. A neighbour with a strong sense of humour had fired, just for a joke, to make them jump! I lay on my walnut leaves, for I was tired and had not bothered to get up, and enjoyed the joke hugely.

With Marko's help I explained that girls in England were very apt to break off engagements in a light and casual manner, even when the gentleman was their own choice, and to take another, and that no shooting took place. The man had to put up with it, and find another if he could.

They were horrified. The jilted one cried loudly that such creatures could not be called men ; such cowardice was incredible. The girl's father ought to be shot for letting her behave so. He could make her obey if he chose. They agreed that this was what one must expect if women were allowed opinions.

It was dark by now. We went into the house and lay round the central fire on couches of fern while the kid was transformed into four courses—soup, chunks of liver and kidney roasted on a spit, boiled kid, and kid baked with herbs. By this time it was past ten, and I was asleep, and had to be waked to eat. And I was asleep long before the lively party had picked all the bones. We all slept on the floor except the head of the house, who slept in a little room, or rather box, of hurdle, hung like a swallow's nest upon the wall and supported below by a post. The house was remarkably clean, and the two women very neat and gay. Hearing from Marko that I liked milk, they had a large bowlful ready for me when I woke in the morning. And it will be long before I shall forget my hospitable and gallant hosts who took me in and gave me of their best, and who lived up to their code, counting their lives as nothing when it was a case of keeping honour spotless. It is by no means every one in a "civilised" land who is prepared to do this.

From Suma we rode up to the top of the mountain ridge that ends in Maranaj, the square-headed mountain conspicuous from Scutari, and saw a wondrous panorama of all Scutari Lake, the parched and yellow plain, and the mountains, peak beyond peak, fading into infinite space in a dazzle of sunlight.

Down we went to the Kiri again, where it pours from out the valley, and the ruins of Drishti stood sharp against the sky on the summit of the hill beyond.

The spell of the wilderness was upon me, and even Scutari seemed too civilised, but we did not enter it in a wholly commonplace manner, for our two men, who had come all the way from Thethi and served us excellently, suddenly announced that for private reasons they dared

not enter the town.   I fancy Shala owed the Government
money, and they feared lest their beautiful white mules
should be seized.   We had to unsaddle at a *kavana* outside, and find a man to carry harness and saddles into the
town.   We had sneaked out in the grey of the morning;
we trailed in at even by the back way.

The first news was that the opinion of the Vali need
no more be considered.   Nor that of Ezzad Bey, the
commander of the gendarmerie.   The soldiery, sick of
waiting for pay long deferred, had peacefully revolted,
stacked their arms, and refused to do more drill till
things were righted.   It was rumoured that the pay had
stuck in the Vali's pocket, and that his position was
most precarious, and Ezzad Bey, the tyrant of Tirana,
had "left for his health," and was travelling abroad—
political fever, it was said.

He had, it would appear, had rumours of the
approaching events, and withdrawn to a safe place till
he knew "which way the cat hopped."

And all this was the cloud no bigger than a man's
hand that heralded a mighty storm—but as yet we knew
it not.

CHAPTER VII

DUKAGHINI—DUSHMANI, BERISHA, NIKAJ, SHALA

"The thing that hath been is that which shall be ; and that which is done is that which shall be done."

A FEW days in Scutari sufficed to reply to a very belated correspondence and gather an idea of what had been happening in Europe, also to have the girths, crupper, and breast-strap of my saddle looked to—for one's life may depend on the strength of a couple of buckles—and I was ready to start again for the wilderness.

The Vali's opinion, after his recent humiliation, was considered of no importance, so leaving the town righteously and as bold as lions—with two very good horses and an excellent *kirijee*—before 6 A.M. we were well on our way to Shlaku.

Following up and then fording the Kiri, we struck up country by a narrow shady lane, near Muselimi, rich with great clusters of wild purple clematis. Green and steel-blue dragon-flies flashed in the sun, and countless big scarlet-winged grasshoppers danced in dizzy round, whirring harshly. All nature seemed full of the joy of life. The maize grew fat and luxuriant in the well-tilled fields. There were great fig and olive gardens, and the few vineyards looked flourishing. This, some years ago, the best wine-growing land of the district, was devastated by Phylloxera, and replanting has but just begun. It belongs partly to Moslems and partly to Christians. The desolate stony wastes that now border the Kiri were similarly rich, but floods have torn down all the soil and left ruin behind.

We ascended the valley of a small tributary, and cultivation ceased. The low hills of crumbly red soil are fairly clothed with vegetation and the track good; but neither a house, nor a beast, nor a soul was to be seen, nor any sign of man. Higher up was some culti-vated ground, and some men hard at work making an aqueduct, leading water from the stream through a channel they had banked along the hillside and bridging a gap with dug-out wooden troughs on trestles.

To the right of the track, on a wooded hill, stand the ruins of an old church, Kisha Shatit. Deserted churches throughout Albania often stand in thick woods, as some superstition prevents even the Moslems from cutting wood near them.

The ruins are large. The remains of a tower still stand, and walls of large buildings, said to have been a bishop's palace and a monastery, cover all the hilltop. Within the church lay heaps of human bones, for the natives have grubbed up all the floor in vain search of hidden treasure.

A rude altar, built with sticks and boards against a tree, showed where mass is still served once a year. It is not known when the church fell into ruin, but it must have been long ago. The present church of the district is at Mazreku, hard by, and is included in the diocese (but not the district) of Pulati.

At the top of the hill we were hospitably entertained by the owner of a small house. Marko had expected to find an acquaintance here, but he had gone the way of many a *maltsor* (mountain man), and been shot a year or two ago. Half the house—it had been two cottages in one block—was a heap of ruins: burned for "blood." Its owner, our host's cousin, had fled.

We rested under a large mulberry tree. A most primitive ladder, like the bears' pole at the Zoo, served

as a way up it, and the *kirijee* feasted largely on the
sickly-sweet white mulberries.

From here onward the country was barer and barer,
rocky and waterless; the houses were few and wretched.
And we came to Kisha Shlakut (Church of Shlaku) about
five in the evening. The village—some dozen scattered
houses—is called Lot Gegaj.

The priest was absent—had been sent for up country.

I have been in many melancholy spots, but Lot Gegaj
is one of the worst. All around the parsonage was a
desolation of huge slabs of rock. It splits in narrow
strata, and the cleavage is so sharp that it appears
machine-cut—the remnants of a giant factory of roofing
slabs. Only the scantiest vegetation manages to cling
in the crevices. Deep down below flowed the Drin,
turbid and yellow, half empty, with bare tracts of shingle
on either side, but still flowing rapidly between the
forbidding flanks of the grim valley. I thought of the
Lake of Ochrida, whence Drin springs, of the squalid
dens of misery on its shores, of fever-stricken refugees
and putrid gunshot wounds in the spring of 1904, after
the Bulgarian revolution, till Drin seemed one of the
rivers of Hades, and its waters flowed only to mock the
parched and starving heights.

Three months' unbroken drought, destined to last three
more, had already brought the people to dire straits. It
took two hours to fetch a small barrel of water to the
church, and other houses were much farther away. The
wretched, half-starved goats and sheep were driven to
water once in twenty-four hours. Shlaku tribe consists
of about three hundred houses, all Christian. It is an
offshoot of the tribe of Toplana. A third of it lives by
charcoal-burning, the others by keeping goats. There is
very little cultivable land.

One sample of the life of grinding misery will suffice.
A man—most honest and hard-working—supported him-

self, his widowed sister-in-law, and her child, by charcoal-burning. Weekly, he took as much as he could carry, and drove a loaded donkey down to Scutari, exchanging the charcoal for the maize on which they lived. But he fell ill, and entrusted his donkey to a neighbour, who ill-treated it, and the wretched beast died. Ill, he crawled to Scutari with all the charcoal he could carry, but it was no longer enough to buy the week's food. Only by spending a whole day in the town and begging scraps of food, which he carried home, could they manage to live. A Scutarene took pity on him, and gave him enough maize to sow his little field. He sowed it, but the cruel drought killed almost the whole of it. The sickly, under-fed child and its mother—who was crippled with acute rheumatism—could do nothing to help in the charcoal-burning. And thus do folk in Shlaku drag out a miserable existence.

If this luckless family would turn Moslem they would almost certainly have their wants relieved. But this they will never do. Some poor wretches came and prayed me to tell them where they could find water. They did not mind how deeply they must dig, if I could only tell them where. And they were woefully disappointed.

I left Shlaku, glad to escape the sight of misery which I could not relieve.

A Shlaku man came with us as escort, and put on a clean shirt and gold-embroidered waistcoat, to accompany us worthily. We started by a sharp ascent, up the shoulder of the big mountain, Tsukali, bare at first, then covered with the low scrub beech which is cut for charcoal, and came into the most magnificent virgin forest of monumental beeches—miles and miles of it—great straight silver trunks some hundred feet high, giants centuries old.

Our luckless horses had had no drink since noon the day before, and we made for the nearest spring. It was a mere trickle, and the dug-out trough was empty. But

by clearing the channel of beech leaves, and letting out
some water that had collected above, enough was obtained
in twenty minutes to give them each a drink.

We tramped on through beech leaves, sometimes
knee-deep. Only the swishing of our feet in the dead
leaves broke the heavy silence of the forest. In one
place some one had thrown down a light, and long arms
of black ash sprawled up the slopes, the fire crawling
smouldering, without bursting into flame. A thin
column of blue smoke showed a live spot. My men
would not trouble to try and stamp it out, saying that
if no wind blew it would be all right. And thus are
acres of forest burnt every year, when the dry season has
set in.

High on the mountain we suddenly came out on to a
fine grassy plain, where two men were busy haymaking.
On all sides it was walled in by beech forest, and up
above towered the bare peak of Tsukali.

The men came up most kindly with a large jar of cold
water, and spread hay for us. We lay in the shade and
ate and drank, and they told of the dangers of the forest
in winter—endless, trackless, shrouded in snow,—how
a woman and child who tried to cross it last December
never came out again. Vainly were they searched for
many days, and their remains were only accidentally
found in May, in the depths of the forest, when the snow-
drifts melted.

Marko, talking to the two men, referred to them as
" brothers." The elder burst out laughing. " Brother !
That's my son ! "

Even Marko was surprised. " How old are you ? "—
" Thirty-one." " And your son ? "—" Fifteen. I married
young, I did. They wanted another woman to do the
work of the house, so they bought me one. They said I
was quite old enough, and you see I was." He roared
with laughter.

I asked how old his wife was when they married.
"Twenty-five," said he, and added it was a great bother,
"for now she is very old, and no good at all.   I must get
another somehow."

The boy was a fine-grown specimen. They were
both of the small, dark type prevalent in all this part of
the country so far as I saw.   Grey and blue eyes are
very scarce here.

The characteristics of the small, dark type are: round
head, face short and rather wide across the cheekbones,
brown hair and eyes, varying in darkness to almost black ;
eyebrows level, often nearly or quite meeting over the
nose, which is usually short and straight, maybe slightly
aquiline, but never has the long, drooping point characteristic of the fair type of Maltsia e madhe, and the fair
people of Montenegro, Bosnia, and Central and South
Albania.   The hair on the face is sparse and straggly ;
that on the head grows very low on the forehead, and
there is often a distinct trace of hair along the temporal
bone to the outer end of the eyebrow.   This small, dark
Albanian type differs markedly from the large, dark type
of Montenegro, in which the skull is extremely wide at
the temples and cut straight off at the back, and the
individual is tall, broad, and heavily built.

I fancy there is no Slavonic admixture at all in
the small, dark Albanian type.   There are certainly no
Slavonic place-names in the parts where it predomi-
nates.

We descended on foot through forest—cool, green,
and silent—and came out suddenly on to scorching rock,
under a blazing sun.   The descent was steep and bad at
first, and then came a   saddle " even worse, where the
horses were dragged along with difficulty.   The heat was
intense, and the men, parched with thirst, called a halt
in a patch of shade.   To make sure of obtaining water,
they yelled to all points of the compass that a priest was

dying of thirst on the mountain-side. A most charitable youth climbed up from his house—half-an-hour distant—carrying the largest bottle-gourd I ever saw, wrapped in a wet cloth and full of cold spring water (far too cold, I thought, to drink in such heat), and a tin pot. My men drank till I thought they would burst. One drained the tin pot seven times (considerably over three pints), and said he felt much better. Half a potful was enough for me, which surprised them. The men of the Balkan peninsula all have an incredible capacity for water-drinking. Thus revived, we started again, Marko and I by a "short cut" impossible for the horses, which were sent around by the water-bringing youth.

The "short cut" was a path some twelve inches wide along the face of a cliff. Barring the fact that there were some hundred feet to fall, there was no difficulty about it, but the reverberation of heat off the wall of rock was awful, and to avoid being sunstruck I hurried along as fast as I could in spite of Marko's imploring shouts behind me, "*Kadal, kadal*" (Slowly).

Then came a very deep descent, and we saw the church of Dushmani far below on a little green oasis, and lower still the river Drin, all walled in by grim, iron-grey ramparts of rock.

Dushmani—consisting of two bariaks, Dushmani and Temali—is one of the wilder tribes.

It is part of the district of Postripa. Postripa consists of Mazreku, Drishti, Shlaku, and Dushmani. Ecclesiastically all are included in the diocese of Pulati, but are not properly part of the Pulati group. Dushmani takes its name from Paul Dushman, a chieftain of the fifteenth century. Dushman is a Turkish word, meaning enemy—possibly a nickname given him by the Turks. The tribe is wholly Christian.

The bariak of Dushmani consists of a hundred and sixty houses. Of these no fewer than forty were, at the time of my visit, in blood within the tribe. As for external bloods, they were countless.

Dushmani believes in Lek Dukaghin as the One-that-must-be-obeyed, and that he ordered blood-vengeance. The teaching of Christ, the laws of the Church, fall on deaf ears when the law of Lek runs counter to them. But they believed vaguely in the symbol of Christianity, for I found, on asking, that most men had a tiny cross tattooed upon the breast or upper arm. Then, in case of being found dead in a strange place, they would be certain of Christian burial.

Yet many of the grave-slabs in Dushmani churchyard are rudely scored with mysterious patterns in which the sun and crescent moon almost invariably occur, and the cross seldom—the symbols of the pre-Christian beliefs that still influence the people. I vainly and repeatedly asked for their meaning, but only met the old answer, " *Per bukur* " (For ornament). No other graveyard yielded me so many of these, but I could not hear that the sun and moon were ever a tattoo pattern here as in other parts.

Bones, and fragments of them, were strewn all over the place. The explanation was that a huge feast has to be held before each funeral. Any one in the tribe can come to it, and, owing to the long distances that folk have to journey, it is very late before the interment takes place. It is, therefore, often half dark before—when the feast is over—the relatives of the deceased dig the grave, and they dig heedlessly anywhere, digging up the former remains. There appears to be a great prejudice against digging the grave some time before, as various unlucky things may happen to it. No one may step across it, nor may it be left empty—something made of iron must be placed in it—was all that I could learn.

One of the tribe bloods has lasted for five generations. The chief man in this feud—grey-eyed and fair-haired, but with the other physical characteristics of the local dark type—lamented his position bitterly. Five generations were too much. The quarrel had had nothing whatever to do with him, but he was liable to be shot for it after all these years. I asked why he did not pay blood-gelt and compound the feud. He replied indignantly that his side was the innocent one, so why should it pay?

The Franciscan — priest of Dushmani — laughed heartily. "They are all innocent!" he said, "every one of them, according to their own account, and all at blood with some one or other." He added that because of "blood" they would very rarely come to confession. His own servant, for example, had killed three.

This youth was entirely delightful. Bubbling over with animal spirits, full of jokes, and most good-natured, he was wildly jealous of his honour, and had an almost tigerish thirst for blood. His instincts were primæval, and he rejoiced in his exploits so whole-heartedly that I could not but sympathise with even the bloodiest.

Aged two-and-twenty, dark, slight, active as a cat, with wide cheekbones and a sallow skin, he was no beauty, but his cheerful smile and his naughty, sparkling eyes, as he told his tales, made up for all deficiencies. He was one of the happiest creatures I ever met. He had drawn his first blood at the age of twelve, which is certainly something to be proud of. A Moslem derided Christianity in his presence, whereat he had at once whipped out his revolver and fired. The Moslem, slightly wounded, returned the fire at once, but missed clean. The little wild-cat then rushed in, fired four shots into the Moslem, dropped him severely wounded, and got away unhurt. As he sat asquat, with his rifle across his knees, he rolled with mirth at the mere recollection. After this exploit, it was thought as well that he should leave the scene of action for a while, so he went to Scutari, where—of all things in the world—he took service with a Moslem family that was unaware of his past history. Here he was so well fed and had such a fine time, that some of the priests in Scutari were afraid he would be persuaded to turn Turk. This struck him as peculiarly humorous. The idea of his being anything but a most exemplary Christian was too ridiculous. A fellow who has shot a Moslem at twelve turn Turk!! One of the Jesuits, intent on rescuing him, talked to him in the street and got him to walk to the Jesuits' school. Several came and spoke to him. They said he should live there; they would feed him just as well as the Moslems, and teach him to read and write. He saw the other little boys. The door was shut. He felt like a fox in a trap. Never, never, could he bear such a life. But he was afraid to say so, lest they should refuse to let him out. He said instead that his Moslem master owed him a napoleon: might he go and fetch it first? He would come back at once.

"And as soon as I was safe outside the door, I ran for my life and got away to the mountains. Oh, I kept out of the way of Jesuits, I can tell you! If I had stayed there, I daresay I should have been a priest by now—perhaps in this very parish! I am a good Christian—always have been and always shall be. No schools for me; I don't want to read or write—it is no use whatever."

I asked what would be of use.

"What we want," said the Primæval youth, "is a new Government—a good Government that would do something for us, a good King; any one, so long as he is rich and not a Turk; your King, now—why can't he come?"

"You would not like it if he did," said I. "He would not allow you to take blood any more."

"What would he do?"

"He would send his *suvarris* to catch you, and you would be hanged."

This took every one aback.

"But if a man owed me blood?"

"Then you must tell the Governor, and the *suvarris* would catch the man and he would be hanged. You must not take the blood yourself."

"That would not clean my honour," said the Primæval one; he pondered. This idea of a Government was quite new to him.

"The King of England is very good," he suggested; "if he knew about the man that killed my cousin he would pardon me."

"No," said I.

"Well," said he resolutely; "after all"—he grasped his throat and squeezed it experimentally—"hanging is not much—one would die quickly. I would shoot my man first, and then your King could send his *suvarris* and hang me if he liked. I should know my enemy was dead, and one must die some day."

"Your body must," said the Franciscan, "but your soul will not—what of your soul?"

"My soul? When I am dead, what does it matter to me?—my soul can fly where it likes!" He flapped his hands airily to illustrate his soul's departure, then he roared with laughter. "Do you know," he asked, "about the *maltsori* (mountain man) who was dying? He said to the Blessed Virgin: 'I know that I am much too bad to go to Paradise, but I pray you to put me there just to spite the devil; it will annoy him extremely.'" He was wholly content with himself, and quite irrepressible. "I often think," he added cheerfully, "we *maltsori* will really find it very hard to get to heaven. *When the Last Day comes, we shall have to have the most awful fight with Christ!*"

And this was the man who had shot a Moslem for speaking ill of Christianity. Later in church I watched him, quite fascinated, as he robed the priest, lit the candles and censer, and assisted at the altar with incomparable precision and decorum. What ideas had he inside that shaven skull, on top of which a great shag of dark hair stood upright grotesquely ?

Said the Franciscan, half apologetically, as we came out, " I must have a servant of some sort, and they all owe blood; what *is* one to do ? What indeed! And the Primæval one, his church duties over, squatted on the balcony and washed cartridge-cases, setting them to dry in the sun previous to refilling.

He had sworn a few weeks' *besa*, with a man to whom he owed blood. Yesterday he had visited his foe and been handsomely treated in the way of victuals and drink. To-morrow the *besa* expired; he would be liable to be shot, and was looking forward joyfully to the renewal of hostilities. He gave no quarter and expected none ; avenging a blood gave him the same sort of satisfaction as winning a race at Henley, or scoring heavily at a cricket match, does to his contemporaries in England.

Nor, looked at from an unprejudiced point of view, is there much difference between them, for man-hunting is undoubtedly the finest form of sport, and he played the game quite honourably and according to rule—generously even, for he had once plunged into the Drin, saved an enemy from drowning, and afterwards sworn peace with him for evermore.

Talk ran all on *ghak*. A neighbour house had been in blood for fifteen years. The man had abducted his wife from another tribe, she coming willingly to escape marrying the man to whom she had been sold as a child. Her father's family and that of her betrothed had been at blood with her husband's ever since, and he never went out without three or four comrades.

In a like case, the man and his wife had fled from the wrath to come, and are living safely abroad, but the three families wage continuous war at home, and twenty-five men have already been shot : " Not a woman but a devil for the mischief she has caused," said the narrator. My suggestion that the blame attached to those that had bought and sold her was incomprehensible and quite new.

A remarkable characteristic of all the mountain tribes is that they have almost no amusements ; games I asked for vainly, and I never saw a dance but once. The singing of national ballads is the only pastime. Even children seem to have few games, and almost never to play them. The traditional wrong and its avenging is the chief object on which the mind is fixed ; the Bari-aktar of Dushmani had not yet taken a blood, as was his duty, and had fallen into dire contempt. At a recent *medjliss* he had tried to speak, and was told that'until he had cleaned his honour his opinion could not be heard.

The *besa*, once given, is inviolable ; its power is terrible. It compels a man not only to avenge a wrong done to a friend with whom he has sworn *besa*, but also to any stranger whom he has sheltered for the night, and this law has to be obeyed to the uttermost.

A certain family was at blood with a man, but one member of the family made it up with the enemy—temporarily, at any rate—and swore *besa* with him. This included a vow to protect each other. His own brother then shot the family foe dead ; by the terms of his *besa*, he who had sworn it was bound to avenge the slain, or be for ever dishonoured. He shot his own brother and cleaned his honour, and came to confess, wild with grief, weeping bitterly and lamenting the deed which a cruel fate had forced upon him. He believed it was the only way.

Nor is this an isolated case. It is related that not long ago a Montenegrin — a criminal wanted by the Government—fled over the border and refuged in the mountains of Shala, where he was given shelter and hospitality in a certain house.

The Montenegrin Government offered a sum of money,
a revolver, and a rifle, as reward for either handing him
over alive or producing evidence of his death. During
the absence of the head of the house, his younger brother,
tempted by the reward, shot the guest and claimed and
obtained the reward. The house-lord returned, and the
murder was discovered. "What did the Prince of
Montenegro pay you?" asked the elder brother sternly.
And, when he was told, replied, "He has not paid you
enough! Take that." And, drawing his revolver, shot
him dead on the spot. He too lamented the deed,
but said that the honour of his house must be maintained. It had never before betrayed a guest, and
should never again. And in such a case the house-
lord is rightly held to have administered justice
only.

The days slipped by pleasantly at Dushmani, livened
by song and hospitality and tales. Shlaku, the neighbouring tribe, was very angry with the men of Temali.
Dushmani and Temali had a huge contempt for the
brains of Shlaku. Shlaku men were all fools, they said,
and boasted they would prove it.

The priest of Shlaku went to a meeting at Scutari, and
was to be away a week or so. A Temali man thereupon
stole or borrowed a complete priest's dress, tonsured his
head, and went to Shlaku. Telling the servants at the
priest's house that their master had been taken ill at
Scutari, and that he had been sent to replace him for
a time, he took up his quarters there,—said he was
a foreigner,—spoke but little and badly, and sat pre-
tending to read a foreign paper. Soon—he said—he
would know the language better, and then would be able
to hear confessions. The simple people were completely
taken in, and received the new priest very well. The
impostor took care to clear out in good time, and Temali
sent derisive messages to Shlaku asking, "What about

fools now ? " Shlaku, furious, vowed to shoot the sham priest if only they could catch him.

The Primæval youth laughed inordinately, and regretted only that the sham priest, who was his cousin, had been afraid to confess Shlaku, as then Temali might have learned all Shlaku's secrets, which would have been highly delightful. That the sham priest was now liable to be shot was only part of the joke.

Infant betrothals, as usual, cause many grim doings. Two bright, neatly-dressed women came and talked to Marko and me. They were sisters from the neighbour tribe of Merturi. One was married in Dushmani. The other was an Albanian virgin. Having been sold by her father to a man to whom she absolutely refused to go, she ran away at night, but did not get beyond the tribe land. The men of her family all turned out and hunted for her as for a wild beast, captured her in a wood, bound her hand and foot, and took her home. Here she was tied to a log, but at night she gnawed the bonds at her wrists, freed herself, and again escaped, this time reaching the house of her brother-in-law in Dushmani. He sheltered her, and has kindly given her a home with him; and as she has sworn virginity before witnesses she is now free.

In Pulati and the whole of the group of tribes that call themselves Dukaghini, an Albanian virgin cannot inherit land, as is the case in the Maltsia e madhe, where, if a man leave no sons, the land goes to his daughter should she have sworn virginity, and only after her death to the nearest heir male.

In Dukaghini, the land passes to the next heir male, but should a daughter of the late owner be an Albanian virgin, the heir must pay her yearly out of the estate 300 okas of maize, 18 okas of rakia, and 30 of wine; and she can enforce payment by appeal to the council of Elders.

The council consists of the Bariaktar and a number of heads of houses, except in tribes which have formed at

Dielmia and have an elective head. For small affairs twelve to twenty-four are enough, according to the importance of the case. For matters affecting the whole tribe, a full council of all the chief heads must sit. These fix the price of articles to be sold within the tribe, and in case of necessity forbid the export of foodstuffs. The neighbour tribe of Toplana had just forbidden the export of maize owing to the prolonged drought, and had fixed its price and that of cheese. It had also decided that the Toplana folk should not come to the feast of St. John the Baptist, the patron saint of Dushmani, which was to be held shortly, because of the large amount of " bloods " between the two tribes. In the wilder tribes of Dukaghini no general *besa* is given for Church festivals, and those who come—unless protected by a private *besa* and in company with one or more of the tribe visited—do so at their own peril.

The evening of the twenty-third of June was quite exciting. The Primæval had spent most of the previous evening filling blank cartridges to greet guests. The Franciscans of Berisha, Shoshi, and Toplana arrived in turn. Each hailed him of Dushmani from a distance, and greeted him with revolver shots. Out we rushed, the Primæval dancing and shrieking like a demon, with a revolver in each hand, both of which he fired at once. We had the liveliest supper—four Franciscans, Marko, and myself. The Padre of Toplana had brought a wonderful attendant with him—an elderly, most wiry creature, brave in a red *djemadan*, gayer and even more voluble than the Primæval. The two, who were supposed to wait at table, were inimitable—entered into the conversation, corrected their " masters," smoked, joked, laughed, and had drinks. Old Red Coat talked every one down, and boasted incessantly of his own merits, the chief being his stainless honour. He had shot four men in its defence, had his house burnt down four times, and

HOUSE-LORD OUTSIDE HIS KULA.

BOY OF KASTRATI.

CROSS AT VULKI, WITH PORTRAIT OF DECEASED.

GRAVE, BETWEEN SKRELI AND BAITZA, SHOWING PORTRAIT
OF DECEASED'S FAVOURITE HORSE.

BOY OF BOGA IN FULL DRESS.

ALBANIAN VIRGIN, RAPSHA.

WOMEN OF SHALA (COSTUME COMMON TO PULATI).

VALLEY OF GUSINJE.

SHALA MEN.

ORDINARY PATTERN MILL, SHALA.

PRENK PASHA AND A "YOUNG TURK" AT SHPAL, MIRDITA, ON PRENK'S
RETURN FROM EXHILE.

flourished greatly, and was ready any day to shoot four more. He had rewarded his Martini for its part of the work, with four silver coins driven in between the stock and the barrel. He got on very well with his Padre— was not his servant, but his comrade. Outside, crowds of guests were arriving at various houses near, from Shlaku and Berisha and distant parts of Dushmani, all greeted by volleys of rifle and revolver shots, to which the Primæval replied with a revolverful of blank, and Old Red Coat with ball cartridge out of window, and both with piercing yells. And the little brothers of St. Francis sang songs at the top of their powerful voices. I thought how dull London dinner-parties are, and wondered why people ever think they would like to be civilised. This was as good as being Alice at the Mad Hatter's Tea-party. And so passed the Eve of St. John. No bonfire-burning took place, and I was assured that the custom is unknown in the mountains, though practised by some of the Scutarenes, which seems to show that it is not an Albanian custom, but brought in from abroad.

A great crowd came to church next day. There were stacks of rifles outside, and within their owners sang "*Et in terra pax hominibus.*" The Padre of Berisha preached. I could not understand him, but reflected he could have no better subject than "The Voice of One crying in the Wilderness."

After mass there was a rush for the shooting-ground—the mark was a white stone, and the range short. The Primæval hit often, and a man with a Mauser every time he tried. Those that missed were very close. But it was not difficult, for I hit it myself, with the Primæval's beloved Martini, which he pressed upon me, adorned as it was with silver coins, to reward it for the lives it had taken.

Drunk with noise, excitement, and the smell of burnt powder, he drew out the hot empty cartridge-cases and breathed in their odour with ecstasy, gasping, "By God, it is good!" It was like blood to a tiger, and made him wild to kill his cousin's murderer, who had got safe away a year ago, was now in prison in Scutari on another charge, and to be released soon. I asked why he did not tell the Scutari authorities of the murder and let them punish him, but was told he would only get ten years, "and he deserves shooting, as the poor deserve bread." At this tense moment a rumour spread suddenly that the enemy had been released, and had been seen coming to the feast.

The Primæval dashed off with Martini and revolver, in spite of the shouts of the Franciscans, but it was a false alarm, and he returned unappeased and disappointed—his enemy was still in prison. "Never mind," said he, "he must come out some day." And he sat and nursed his Martini, crooning a song, in which he addressed it as his wife and his child, for he wanted no other—his life and his soul——"Not your soul," said the Padre sharply. "All the soul I want," said he, incorrigible. His "well-beloved" had cost twelve napoleons, the price of an ordinary wife, and he spent eighty guldens a year—exactly half his income—"feeding" it.

The company discussed weapons. The accuracy and repeating power of the Mauser were admitted, but its bullets were too small to be of any use. "They just go through you and don't hurt. You can go on fighting all the same."

A Mirdite had recently taken part in a general squabble, and walked home a long distance. He drank the usual cup of black coffee, and was about to drink a second, when he uttered a cry, collapsed, and died shortly. It was found that he had been shot clean through the body (through the stomach, I believe, from the account); the wound had closed, and there was scarcely any external bleeding. Presumably he was unaware that he had been hit.

To prove the harmlessness of small bullets, a man clapped his right hand against a tree and begged me to fire through the palm with a Mauser pistol; it would make no sort of difference to him. He was quite disappointed at my refusal.

The afternoon passed in paying visits—sitting on heaps of fern in dark dwellings, drinking healths in *rakia*, chewing sheep-cheese, and firing rifles and revolvers indoors; a noisy joy that peppers oneself and the refreshments with burnt powder and wads. In one yard two girls were slowly turning a whole sheep that, spitted lengthwise, was roasting over a large wood fire. It was stuffed with herbs and sewn up the belly, and of all ways of cooking mutton, this is the most excellent.

By night-time we were all too sleepy to do much sing-song. The Primæval had emptied all his cartridges, and was again busy refilling them.

We had passed a true Albanian day, said the Padre of Toplana:

" Duhan, rakia,
Pushke, dashtnia "

(Tobacco, brandy, guns, and love). I suggested that *dashtnia* should come first, because *maxima est caritas*. But they said, not in Albania.

And so ended St. John's Day.

I had meant to go to Toplana, but was told it would be impossible for horses; the tracks were too bad. The heat was intense, so I gave up Toplana for the time being, to the grief of Old Red Coat, who, having taken a vast fancy to me, pressed me to stay as long as I liked at his house, and go out shooting every day. When he left he actually kissed my hand, and announced loudly that I ought to be extremely proud. For a man to show such a mark of respect to a woman was, he believed, rare in the annals of the human race.

I planned a route by Berisha, meaning to take Toplana on the return, and was advised not to start till the Padre of Berisha had returned home.

The feast did not go off entirely without blood. A man was shot dead on the way home in a quarrel, and a Dushmani man wounded accidentally. Some one fired off a blank cartridge close to him, and blew the wad into his fore-arm. It was a nasty ragged hole, full of burnt paper and rag, and his shirt-sleeve was bloody; but he paid not the smallest attention to it. As for cleaning it, he and his friends jeered at the notion. They all had bullets in them, they said, and a wad was nothing. He shoved the thumb of his wounded arm into his cartridge belt to steady it, and rushed off down the mountain with his friends, singing loudly.

We started to Berisha a large party, as the Padre and the Primæval came with us to see us safely over the Drin—the frontier of their territory.

The way down was very bad—all loose, flat stones that slipped and slid. I was well ahead with the Primæval when I heard a terrible cry behind me. Poor Marko had fallen, and was lying with his leg twisted under him. "Compound fracture," thought I, and hurried back in about the worst fright I ever experienced. Luckily it was only a sprained ankle, but that was enough. My pocket-knife was sharp as a razor; we soon had the boot off. I took the puggree off my hat, tore it in strips and bound him up tightly. Then we were in a great dilemma. To climb back was impossible; so was carrying him; so was riding. If we could only get down to the river, we could ride the rest of the way. Supported by the sturdy young Franciscan, he slowly hobbled down in great pain.

Drin ran swift and yellow, and on the farther bank

were the Padre of Berisha and a number of his men, who
had long awaited us. For the accident had lost us an
hour and a half.

On our side the river were many Dushmani men,
ready to ferry us over, stark nude, and bizarre in the
extreme, for each had an inflated sheep-skin fastened on
in front by loops round his arms and legs.

A Berisha man, similarly adorned, crossed the river to
us swiftly, lifted high out of the water by his float, and
using his arms as oars. A great noise began, but as I
was busy bathing Marko's foot in the cold river, I paid
no heed. Our men, meanwhile, were inflating six sheepskins, and lashing them to a hurdle with green withies.
They inflate the skins by simply taking a long breath, and
blowing hard into one corner. The big skin is taut in a
few moments. I believe they could blow out a motor tyre.

The horses were stripped and driven in by a Dushmani
man, who plunged in with them. The current whirled
them away down stream, to the terror of the *kirijee*, who
cried that if a drop of water got into their ears they
would at once sink and drown. They landed a long way
down the other side. A terrible shouting was going on.
The *kirijee* crossed first. He laid flat on his belly on the
hurdle, with his legs tucked up, as it was short. The
saddles were piled on his back to keep them dry. The
Berisha man plunged in with him, grasping the hurdle
and propelling it with powerful leg-strokes. It was the
kirijee's first trip of the sort, and he screamed aloud with
fright, but was landed cleverly not much lower down.
The Berisha man came back for me. I said farewell to
the Franciscan, who laid me on the hurdle and shoved
me off. I had strapped my camera on my back to keep
it out of the water. Away we went—it was better than
any watershoot—and landed just at the foot of the rock
on which the Padre of Berisha stood. He hauled me up.
The sweat stood on his brow; he was girded with a

cartridge belt, had a large revolver in it, and his Martini in his hand. "Has the Padre his revolver?" he asked, as he pulled me up, "and cartridges—plenty of cartridges? They are going to shoot. Oh, my God, what a mess we're in! I ought to be reading mass in the village, but I didn't dare leave them. God knows how many would have been shot." He slipped a Browning pistol from the pocket in his sleeve (Franciscan habits are delightful garments, all made up of secret pockets) into my hand. "They don't know it's mine. Shove it in your belt." I took it, but was mainly occupied balancing on a high rock, and trying to kodak the next hurdle trip. He dashed down among his men, some dozen of whom, sullen and fierce, were dodging from cover to cover, rifle in hand. The Primæval was rushing and dancing wildly about on the other side. The two parties howled at one another. "It is all his fault," cried Padre Berisha, shouting to the Primæval to shut up. "They all want to shoot him. He'll be shot in a minute, my God! My people think it their privilege to bring visitors over. When the first one went over, that mad fellow called him bad names, and told him to go back, and leave the job to Dushmani. The men here are furious. They want to shoot the Dushmani who brought the horses over. Good God! they are sending Marko over with him now! And he swims so badly—ah!" Poor Marko was whirled far down stream, quite out of range of my camera. Padre Berisha howled over the water to Padre Dushmani to get off with his men— another minute or two and shooting would begin. We hurried down to meet Marko, who, poor fellow, was landed among an awful pile of rocks, which he had to climb over.

The Dushmani men plunged back at once, and soon they were all lost to sight among the bushes.

The Berisha men, balked of their prey for the time,

and sulky as bears, turned their attention to us. " In
the first place," said the Padre, " this woman is my friend,
and in the second, she can shoot very well." He then
ordered them to come to mass. We turned to scramble
up the steep bank; they followed growling. It was
short, luckily, and Marko got up with help. We came to
a small house and entered the yard. The people brought
us out seats, but were in a state of excitement. A
number gathered, and the Padre and Marko argued with
them long and loud. One tall, long-faced man was
stubborn as a rock. The honour of Berisha had been
wounded, and nothing but blood would heal it—that of
the Primæval in particular.

We were still on the bloody edge of things. Only
the moral influence of the Padre had swayed them to
come to mass instead of staying to massacre, and it was
obvious that they were sorry they had come.

I said I had come a very long way to see them as a
friend; had visited a great many tribes that had been
pleased to see me. If Berisha did not want me, I would
go back again. I did not wish to make any unpleasant-
ness. "They will be quieter after mass," whispered the
Padre; " wait here, and I will go and make ready."

The noise reduced itself to growling undertones, and
we were served with coffee, which I thought a good sign.
The Padre summoned us shortly to the upper room of the
next house. It was a pitch-dark den, lighted only by
one brilliant ray of sunlight through the roof that fell on
the flour-bin—which the Padre had dressed as an altar—
and some tiny flickering tapers stuck on the stone wall
behind it by melting their ends. Dinner was cooking in a
hooded fireplace. Two goats were tethered in the corner.

The congregation, some twenty men, squat cross-
legged in the darkness—their minds filled with vengeance—sang loudly. The sunlight haloed the yellow
hair of the bullet-headed, bull-necked Padre—a man

more stubborn even than his wild flock. A very ragged
man assisted at the altar, and mingled the wine with
water from a coffee-pot. The goats bleated loudly, two
children toddled about squalling, and over all the great
voice of the Padre thundered sonorous. He raised the
chalice, glorified in the one bar of golden sunlight. It
was incomparably magnificent. I was upon a quest, and
saw the Holy Graal. He aspersed us with a bunch of
basil dipped in a bowl that was a dug-out lump of wood.

We arose, and an old woman hurried up to get flour
from the bin that had just served as an altar. While
dinner was cooking we sat outside, and the whole argument began again. There was the payment for the ferry.
If the ferry were the privilege of Berisha I would gladly
pay, just as if Dushmani had not assisted. This they
flatly refused. They did not want money, but their
honour, and would take payment only for the two transits
they had made. Dushmani had taken part of their job ;
and for this insult no money could pay. The offer,
however, pleased them. They absolved me of blame.
But the next question was whether, as I had come in
such a manner, I ought to be well received, or even
received at all. Perhaps I was a friend of the Turks.
They wanted no friends of the Turks in their land. The
Padre said I came from a Christian country, and was a
friend of the Catholics. They decided that my having
come to mass was a point in my favour.

He then said that at the feast he had seen me shoot
with a Martini and a Mauser. Which was another.
They wanted to see the Browning—which was still in
my belt—and be shown how it worked. This was highly
embarrassing, as I had never had one in my hands before.
"Show them," said the Padre in German, and hastily
explained what to do. I drew out the magazine successfully, to their extreme interest. This won their hearts.
Once on this congenial topic, all went well. Child-like,

they forgot their injuries over this new toy—a strange woman, with a new kind of weapon—and invited me very heartily to stay for a whole year.

The Padre then begged that my coming should not be made a cause of bloodshed with Dushmani, that they should not talk about the episode in the tribe, but that it should be considered closed. They all shook hands on it with us and agreed; but added cheerily that it really did not matter, as they had already so much about which to fight Dushmani.

We parted the best of friends. Marko and I rode up the bed of the Lumi Berishet, as it was a better route for riding than the mountain path taken by the Franciscan. Then a very steep pull up the hillside took us to his house and the tiny church of Alshiché.

The fame of my arrival, of course, spread. No foreign woman had ever been seen before in the land; and next day a number of Heads came to visit me. They questioned me closely about my land and its Government, and, as soon as they were assured I was neither Moslem nor Orthodox, were most friendly, and highly flattered at my having come so far to see them. They were sorry only that I had not brought a lot of soldiers to make a new Government.

"These are our worst enemies," said one, tapping his rifle. "Bring soldiers, take away our guns, make a good Government, and we will obey."

Nor, if they believed in the Government and were fairly treated, would the mountain tribes be very difficult to govern. They have the most wonderful power of obedience where they believe obedience due, and usually obey their house-lord absolutely. There is, for example, a very large group of four houses here which is governed by four brothers, who are now but very distantly related to most of those under them; but they expect and receive entire obedience for no other reason, that I could ascertain, than that the ruling power belongs to that branch of the family.

We had a long sitting to debate both the question of " blood " and of " sisters-in-law," and told them that the King of England disapproved most strongly of both practices, whereon they again requested that he would send soldiers. Blood feuds, they said, were almost all the fault of women. Women were very wicked (here the Padre agreed).

Sometimes they were very disobedient, and you had to beat them a great deal. A man must order his wife three times before he may beat her, and then if, for example, she still refuses to go and fetch water, what can he do but beat her? I suggested that, perhaps, she was tired and the water-barrel was heavy. " Oh no," was the reply, " they are quite used to it." Also, if a man tells his wife not to answer him, and she does, he must beat her, or she would go on talking. Of course, only a woman's father or husband may beat her.

Wife-beating, said I, is punished in England by imprisonment—the King disapproved of it also. This staggered every one—even the Padre. That a wife could be so wicked as to tell the Vali, and let him send *suvarris* to catch her husband, was beyond belief. Said one, " Near Ipek there has been a feud for thirty years about a woman who refused to marry the man to whom her parents had betrothed her. Peace was only made two years ago, and blood-gelt paid after twenty-two men had been shot. All because she was disobedient. That is why women should be beaten."

Said another: " A Berisha girl was betrothed to a man, and refused to go to him. She ran away with a Temali man, and the priest there married them. Now all three families are in blood, and the first betrothed, who had paid for her, wants his money back. Her father will not give it, and says it must be got out of

her husband.   The husband says, why should he pay for
his wife when, most likely, he will be shot before he has
had her any time?   It has only just happened, and a lot
will be killed before it is finished.   She ought to be well
beaten."

Then, to convince me of the innate wickedness of
woman, and the harm of letting her have her own way,
I was told—

The Story of the Woman who was Thrice Married.

This woman was a Devil.   God! what trouble she
has made!   She is of Ipek, and the daughter of a rich
house.

The house-lord is a rich man.   He has shot eight
Turks, two Catholics, and six Orthodox—and has paid
for the lot.   He is so important that he counts as twelve
witnesses in a trial.   But he has been married for years
and has no child.   Now his wife is forty, and will never
bear one.   He wanted to marry again, and found a girl
and had paid twenty-five napoleons for her.   But the
Bishop of Prizren heard of it, and sent three priests to
forbid the marriage.   He was surprised, and said he only
wanted a son.   The priests threatened him with excommunication, so he obeyed.

Well, this girl who made such trouble was the
daughter of his brother, who, thank God, has sons
enough—so the family will not die out.   She was very
beautiful—a great big woman.   When she was quite a
girl you would have thought she was twenty-five.

Her father sold her as a child to a man in Ipek.
But when she was only fourteen she said — the young
Devil—"He is not brave.   He has never shot a man.
I won't have him, and you shan't take me to him alive."

She was to go to him at sixteen, and refused.   She

said she would not have him, but would marry one of her cousins. The cousin was not a very near one—so not forbidden by the Church ; but forbidden by our custom. My cousins to any generation are my brothers and sisters.

Her father was furious, said it was a deadly sin, and drove the cousin from the house. But he came at midnight with his brother and fetched the girl, and they got away to Hoti. There, as they had been living together some weeks, the Padre married them. Her parents and her betrothed were furious, for they held the marriage as incestuous. They could not come to Hoti themselves, but offered to pay twenty-five napoleons to any one who would go and shoot her husband, and within a year of marriage shot he was, and his brother too. She had borne her husband a son, and went with the babe to Scutari. She was very beautiful, and a Moslem wanted to marry her. The priests heard of it, and feared she would turn Moslem. They persuaded her to go back to her own people.

She returned with her child to Ipek, but dared not go to her father, and took refuge with the Franciscans. Her father came and demanded her. He said she had dishonoured the family, and he must shoot her. The Franciscans refused to give her up till he had sworn to spare her life.

She went home. But she was a Devil. She would not live without a man, and wanted to be married again. Her father wanted to give her to the man to whom she was first betrothed. And there was no reason why she should not have him. Really he is very brave, and has now shot four men—(Here I could not help laughing. The narrator was surprised, and asked why?)—He said she belonged to him, and he would marry none other. She said he never should have her—she would run away with another cousin. Her father, in haste to prevent another scandal, found a man for her—a nice man, aged forty. She said he would do, and they were married. And that very day she said he was too old, and for three whole weeks she refused to have anything to do with him. She was a very wicked woman.

Two years she lived with him, and bore him a daughter. Then he died, and she was again a widow.

Her first betrothed was now in blood with her family for marrying her to the man of forty. There had been a good deal of fighting. But he wanted to stop the feud and marry her. He said he knew she was a beast and a Devil, but she belonged to him, and have her he would. But she wouldn't. She ran off with a man of twenty-five —very beautiful—and they were married. She is only twenty-five herself. God knows how many more she will marry!

Her first betrothed is still in blood with her family, and both are in blood with her husband's family. Ever so many have been shot, and plenty more will be. Now you see that I spoke truly when I said all evil comes from women. They are Devils.

Nor will I mar such a fine tale with superfluous comment.

We debated the ethics of wife-beating almost daily during my stay, and neither side was converted. It led to—

THE TALE OF THE MAN WHO COULD UNDERSTAND BEASTS AND BIRDS.

A certain man was gifted with the power to understand the talk of beasts and birds. But on condition only that, should he ever tell that which he heard, he would drop down dead.

One day he overheard the donkey talking to the

horse. The donkey's remarks were very funny, and, as he came from the stable, he laughed.

"Why are you laughing?" asked his wife.

"At something the donkey said."

"What did the donkey say?"

"You know I cannot tell you. I should drop down dead."

But she was wicked, as all women are, and she only answered : "What did the donkey say?"

And all day and all night she gave him no peace, and he had neither sleep nor rest, for still she asked : "What did the donkey say?"

Worn out at last, he could bear no more : "To-morrow I will tell you," he said. He called his little children and said good-bye to them, and told them he must die to-morrow. They cried bitterly and begged, "Oh, mother, do not kill our dear father!" But she answered only, "I want to know what the donkey said."

So the poor man went out to take a last look at his yard, and there he saw the cock standing on tiptoe, flapping his wings and crowing as loud as he could.

"Oh, you wicked bird!" cried the dog, "How can you laugh and sing when our dear master, who is so kind to us, must die to-morrow?"

But the cock only crowed the more : "Laugh!" said he, "I shall die of laughing! Look at him—the silly fool! He has only one wife, and cannot manage her; while I have fifty, and keep them all in order!"

The man heard this. He picked up a large stick, and went back into the house. "Do you want to know what the donkey said?" he asked. "Yes," said his wife. Then he gave her a good beating. "Do you want to know what the donkey said?" he asked. "Yes," said she. So he beat her again. "Do you want to know what the donkey said?" "Yes," said she. So a third time he beat her till he was quite tired. "Do you still

want to know what the donkey said ? " " No," said she.
And they lived very happily ever afterwards.

Poor Marko meanwhile was dead lame, his ankle
badly swollen. Native treatment consisted of frequent
and hot fomentations with a thick decoction of ferns,
Ceterach, and *Trichomanes nigra* boiled with wild pepper-
mint. I prescribed rest, though he pluckily declared he
was ready to push on at any cost rather than delay my
journey.

A friend in need is a friend indeed, and I cannot
sufficiently thank the young Franciscan who made us welcome to stay in his house till Marko was on a fair way to
recovery. His parish is widespread, and, together with
Merturi Gurit, included three hundred houses. Berisha
and Merturi Gurit are a bariak of Puka. The people of
Berisha and Merturi (the tribe on the other side of the
Drin) claim to be the oldest tribes of the mountains ;
and, in spite of the frequency in these parts of the small,
dark type, persist that the fair type is the true Albanian.
One thing seems certain, for most tribes tell a similar tale,
and that is, that for the most part the men, who fled before
the inroads of the Turks, took shelter in the mountains
and are the founders of the present tribes, found on arrival
a dark population, which they conquered. In some cases
they intermarried with them, and in other cases evicted
them. The fact that the older inhabitant is always stated
to have been dark is a proof that the new-comer must
have been fair. As a whole, all the tribes that trace
origin from Rashia are darker and smaller in type than
those of Maltsia e madhe, who say they come from Bosnia.

Berisha holds strictly by the laws of the mountain.
It is not represented in the Djibal at Scutari, but is under
the Turkish Kaimmakam of Puka.

Blood-gelt in Berisha must be paid within two years.
The sum varies from six to seven *chesé* (purses)—that is,

from about £21 to £25,—may be paid in instalments, and need not be in coin. Martinis are often taken in part payment. One purse must be also paid to the Elders who judge, and one to the Kaimmakam of Puka. But the representative of the Turkish Government seldom gets a fee.

Berisha is all Christian, but in the neighbourhood of Ibalje are many Moslems. The Christians there built a small schoolhouse, started by the energy of some of the priests. This vexed the Moslems much, and little more than a year afterwards it was burnt one night by the border Moslem tribe of Krasnich. The Christians believed that the Krasnichi had been summoned to do this by the wife of a certain Moslem who angered them greatly by always making game of the Christian faith. Had she been a man, they would have shot her; but women are not shootable, so they burned her husband's house. He, being a Moslem, appealed to the Turkish Government, which had taken no notice of the burning of the Christian school. The Government then sent 300 Nizams to investigate the affair. The Christians were condemned to pay 150 napoleons, but had not yet paid it, and did not mean to. Further trouble was expected, and feeling ran high.

Berisha was in blood with Krasnichi, in blood with Dushmani, and greatly in blood also within the tribe; And, as befits a primitive land, is full of things magical. I was asked to give my opinion on the magic imprint of a man's hand. We scrambled down one blazing afternoon to some houses, near which the underlying rock thrust its bare bones through the thin soil.

The house-lord and many men came out, and showed me upon the top of a rock the so-called hand, and lower down a rounded pit, said to be the print of a mule's hoof. Only the very wildest imagination could see any resemblance in either case. A man watching goats had accidentally laid his hand in the upper mark, and found it fitted. Search had then revealed the "mule's hoof." Then, in this desolate, bookless land, where nought but bloodshed breaks the monotony of the slowly dragging hours, these people gave their minds to interpreting this "writing on the stones," and decided that long years ago, when the rocks were soft, a certain man had hidden a vast treasure beneath them. To mark the spot he made the hand-print, and as he leaned to do so, the mule on which he was mounted trod into the soft lump below. The question I was to unravel was how to get at the gold. They waited anxiously. After some consideration, I said I did not think the marks indicated gold at all; but this did not satisfy them, and at their earnest request I " wrote " the marks in my sketch-book, and promised that if any priest or *hodza* in England succeeded in explaining the mystery, I would let them know.

They then led me eagerly to a greater marvel, in a hollow not far off. It was carefully covered with planks, and was merely an ordinary trough, roughly hewn from a block of stone. Beyond all doubt the work of human hands, it might have been made at any time, in any land that had stone. But it was believed to be supernatural, very precious, and also fraught with meaning. No man had made it. It had stood there for a thousand years— so their grandfathers and great-grandfathers had reported. It belonged to the days when the Jews ruled the land. I said decidedly that the Jews had never ruled the land, which gave very great satisfaction.

The tale that the Jews once ruled Albania is fairly widely spread. It refers, most probably, to the tradition that there was another religion in the land before Christianity; and as it was neither Christian nor Moslem, the people have decided it was Jewish, as they know of no other. It is highly probable that in the remote mountains Paganism flourished to a fairly late date.

There was no reason why the trough should not have been there when the ancestors of Berisha arrived. But why it was thought to conceal treasure I know not.

As we returned to the humble huts and partook of sheep-cheese and *rakia*, I remembered that many of the tribes of my own land believe in planchette and table-turning—consult palmists and globe-gazers, are "Christian Scientists" and "Higher Thoughters"—and reflected that all the training of all the schools had but little removed a large mass of the British public from the intellectual standpoint of High Albania, whereas for open-handed generosity and hospitality the Albanian ranks incomparably higher.

Marko's ankle was much better, and he vowed he was fit to travel; but it was not well. A rideable track was absolutely necessary. Toplana and Merturi were both out of the question; so was return to Dushmani. The Padre recommended Nikaj, and generously insisted on coming to see us safely over the Drin—the frontier of his territory, lest at this ferry, too, there might be trouble. This meant a six hours' tramp for him, and as many more back—twelve hours' toil to help a stranger guest. The only available mule belonged to a family excommunicated for a sister-in-law affair. They were extremely anxious to lend it, but the stern Franciscan preferred to suffer rather than have any truck with sinners.

We started at 4 A.M. The first ascent was very steep, and I felt very sad for the trouble I was giving. But the Padre tramped well. Once up on the top, the way was excellent—by Merturi-Guchesit, and through a great beech forest along the mountain-side. Far below on the left flowed the Drin, with the rugged, arid mountains of Toplana beyond.

Toplana holds a sinister record; its annual death-rate from gunshot wounds is double that of most other Christian tribes. It is a very old tribe. Shlaku and

Gashi are both offshoots of it. Shlaku and Toplana are both small and Christian ; Gashi, all Moslem, is reported to be rich, and consists of 800 houses. Its territory is as yet almost entirely unexplored.

We rode through the forest—by the way lay a great rock. A maiden, who was so holy that she was almost a saint, had vowed that she would carry it to the church of Berisha. Miraculously aided, she bore it a long way; but here in the forest she heard a shepherd fluting, and she looked upon him, and he was fair and comely. Then she forgot the heavenly things upon which her mind had been fixed, and earthly thoughts seized upon her ; the rock fell from her shoulders, and when she strove to pick it up she found her strength had gone, and there lies the rock to this day.

Between Merturi-Guchesit, and Apripa Gurit, we passed a splendid *kula*, *Kukdoda*, with a great stone watch-tower, all loopholed, and with many of its stones signed with a cross. A second smaller house and a hurdle maize-shed stood in its yard.

At Apripa Gurit, near the Drin, we halted for lunch by a spring. An excommunicated family lavished attentions on us, cut fern for us to sit on, brought *rakia*, and did its best to soften the heart of the Padre. The house-lord, a very old man, begged the Padre earnestly to confess him. " Only when you put a stop to your son's living with his sister-in-law," said the Padre. The son (whose sins were being visited on the father), a remarkably fine young man, wearing a handsome silver chain, was quite impenitent. He had found a girl, and had arranged to marry her in a year ; till then he was going to live with his sister-in-law, and would make it up with the Church afterwards. All the family supported him in this arrangement ; they were so decided about it that I wondered whether the real object of it were to beget a child that should rank as that of the deceased brother, but that I could not ascertain. They were uneasy about the excommunication, and offered the Padre first thirty, then fifty guldens, or beautiful candles or pictures for his church, but he was as stubborn as they. The confessional, he said sternly, could not be bought; when his terms were complied with, he would gladly receive them all back—there were eighteen of them, I think—and not till then.

Meanwhile the ferrymen had been summoned. So far, our way had been easy, but the descent to the river was very bad indeed—a crumbly cliff. Marko managed it by sitting and slithering. The horses came down all of a heap, sending such a shower of stones flying that we had to take cover behind the rocks.

The *trapa*, two very rough dug-outs lashed together with withies, and propelled with the rudest wooden ladles, was under the lee of a rocky promontory; the stream was swift and strong. Stark naked men with inflated sheepskins bound before them, pranced about the shore, and played like kittens. One started with our two horses, creeping out to the tip of the promontory, and then whirling away down stream, striking out violently, yelling to the horses, steering and guiding them. They got over safely a long way down, and it was our turn next. I said good-bye to the Padre, nor could I thank him enough, for, as Marko truly said: "If we were the King of England he could not have done more for us."

The crazy contraption was half full of water. We piled ourselves and the saddles on the centre plank. Three men—one stark naked—guided the affair to the end of the promontory; there the current caught us, whirled us round like a straw, and spun us along, the water slopping over the gunwales. The men paddled madly; we sloped across the stream, and cannoned against a lot of boulders—two of the crew leapt out, hung on to a rope that was a long, dried trail of vine, swam in with it, hauled—the *trapa* swung round, grounded in a shallow, and we scrambled ashore.

The naked man then went back to fetch his best clothes and put them on, as he was to guide us to Nikaj. The rest of the journey was most painful. There was no track. The guide had never taken horses that way before. There was nothing for it but walking, and instead of getting better it got worse. Poor Marko suffered so horribly that I regretted having come a hundred times, but it was too late to go back. A thunderstorm fell, too short to do good to the parched land, but enough to make the surface greasy for climbing, and Marko twisted his foot again.

We arrived at Gianpepaj a melancholy party, to be received by a dismayed Franciscan, whose house was half ruined.

Out of sight is out of mind. In the heart of the wilderness, where more than elsewhere it is urgently necessary to teach the people and save them from Moslem influence, the condition of the churches and the priest's houses is often a disgrace. "Nikaj," said a priest bitterly, "is a land abandoned by God and man."

The tribe is of mixed origin, and consists of some three hundred houses, so widely scattered over a wild country that the one Franciscan in charge struggles vainly with a hopeless task.

Twenty of these houses trace origin from Kilmeni, and are intermarriageable with the others, which are an offshoot of Krasnich. Krasnich, according to tradition, stems from Bosnia. (See under Hoti.) In olden days, when Krasnich was still Christian, shepherds—led by one Nikol—drifted here from Krasnich, and settled. This Nikol had a daughter who was very ugly, and had but one ear; he failed to find a husband for her, and she bore a son by a gypsy. This son was accepted by Nikol, and from him are descended a hundred of the Nikaj houses. They are called Tsuraj, and are not intermarriageable with

the other houses of Krasnich origin because they descend
from Nikol's *daughter*.   This is the only case of descent
traced through a daughter that I have found among the
North Albanian tribes.   The very small, dark type
common in Nikaj and Nikaj's notoriously thievish nature
are popularly ascribed to this union.   The fair, aquiline-
nosed type is scarce.   Nikaj is under no Turkish official,

A Kula
Nikaj.

and (as does also Merturi) owes nominal alliance to the
famous chieftain of Krasnich, Shaban Benaku.

Practically it is without any form of government.
The wild population does not even obey its own council
of Elders.   Wretched, abjectly poor, clad often in rags
that are barely enough for decency, lean, dark men prowl
the wild valleys, knowing no rule but that of their own
most primitive instincts.   And in that forlorn land it was
fated that I should stay.

Further travelling was made impossible by poor

Marko's foot. I paid off the *kirijee* and horses, and dismissed them.

"God cast you into Hell," said a priest to me afterwards, "that you might tell of it in England—that you might cry to every Catholic in England : 'Save these people!'"

The tribesmen received me extremely well. Few things please them more than almost endless pow-wows and arguments. The only thing that they objected to about me was my straw hat. They had never seen one before, and frankly said it was foolish, useless, and ugly. When I discarded it, and tied my head up in a towel and a pocket-handkerchief, in imitation of a tribesman, and then squatted cross-legged on the ground among them, they were quite childishly delighted, and ready to pour out the tales of blood and horror that are part of the dull routine of their lives. Here is the story of how Nikaj fell into blood with Shala. Krasnich is Moslem, and always at blood with one or other, or all, of the Christian tribes. Some six years ago the Krasnichi wished to kill a certain Shala man, but could not come at him. So they bribed a Nikaj man—a known bad character—to do the deed, promising him sixty napoleons. He waited till the Shala man came to Nikaj on business, and then traitorously offered to be his escort back—an escort being necessary. When they were actually within the Shala frontiers, the Nikaj man let his victim get a few paces ahead, and shot him in the back. He then rushed in to cut off the head to take as evidence. The poor wretch was not dead, but too severely wounded to defend himself. Desperately he seized the knife blade with his fingers, which were cut to pieces. Finally, the Nikaj hewed his head off, put it in a bag, took the dead man's Martini also as proof, and started for Krasnich to receive the blood money. But the head seemed to grow heavier and heavier till, as he afterwards told, he thought

it weighed a hundred okas. and he hid it in a hole in the
rocks, and went on with the Martini. This, in turn,
grew too heavy for him, and he arrived in Krasnich quite
exhausted.

Meanwhile the headless body was found at Shala,
and the hacked fingers told of the horrible struggle. All
Shala was furious. Nor was the body identified till it
became known that a certain man had gone to Nikaj and
never come back. The body was buried hurriedly, with no
funeral ceremonies, for the loss of the head is accounted
the most terrible disgrace. Nikaj, when charged with
the crime, was as furious as Shala, for even among the
very wildest tribes the *besa* is held inviolable, and the
Nikaj man, by breaking his, had put himself beyond the
pale. Nor has he ever dared return, but is said to be
living with a Moslem tribe. The Nikaj men begged
Shala not to hold them responsible for the crime, but
Shala thirsted for vengeance, and the two tribes have
been in blood ever since. The head was found a year
afterwards by some shepherds, and buried with the body.
The Martini was not found till nearly two years had
passed.

In cases of blood vengeance it is not correct to take
the weapons or any other property from the body of the
slain. The slayer kills to clean his honour, not in order
to steal.

In the Maltsia e madhe weapons are never taken.
But they are by some of the wilder Dukaghini tribes—
Berisha and Nikaj among them.

Nikaj is now in blood with Krasnich too, and is also
greatly in blood within the tribe. And for tribe bloods,
as usual, all the blame was thrown on the women. They
run away from their husbands and live with other men
—they are devils, in fact, for, of course, the husband and
the other man must shoot each other. A large proportion of the children were, they said, illegitimate, because

their proper wives bolted. But they admitted frankly
that they beat and generally maltreated their wives, and
that the women had no choice whatever as to whom they
married. I maintained that under these circumstances
they naturally bolted. Any one would—I would myself.
This shocked the Franciscan, who protested, "But they
are *in matrimonio.*" Once *in matrimonio*, the worthy
man seemed to think it should be impossible for the poor
woman, even when married to a stranger, for whom she
had no affection, to fall in love with anybody else.

Experience in the tribes had proved to him that
matrimony was the root of nearly all evil. The thing of
which he was quite certain was that both he and I had
acted very wisely in abstaining from it. He quoted St.
Paul, in Latin, in support of this view. And the fact
that I had sworn no vow, and had yet managed to escape,
interested him much.

Even the Laws of Lek are not always obeyed in
Nikaj. The paying of blood-gelt does not always stop a
feud. In a recent case the feud had ceased for years.
But when the son of the man who had ended it grew to
be fifteen years old, and was now head of the family, he
declared that as the family honour had been sold when
he was an infant, he was not bound by the oath, so went
forth with his gun and shot a man of the other house
And the feud began again.

Nor is the law of Albanian virgins always respected.
A hideous example was told me.

An old couple had no sons, but had two daughters ;
both, with their father's consent, wished to remain
unmarried. The other men of the family were very
angry at this, as they wished to make money out of the
girls. They sold both for good prices, and carried them
off by force. One was handed over to an old man, helpless, and forced to cohabit with him. She consented to
being legally married—probably not daring to refuse—

but she hated him.   Seeking means of escape, she made
the acquaintance of a youth in the neighbourhood, and
promised to marry him if he would free her.   When it
was time to go to the forest to fetch firewood the youth
offered to go too and help.   On the way the couple let
the old man walk ahead, and when they came to a precipice shoved him over, and returned saying they had
missed him in the wood, and could not find him.   They
fled together into another tribe, and the body was not
found for some days.   They are now married, and as it is
believed that the woman threw the old man over, no
blood-vengeance has been taken.

Nikaj, of course, swarms with devils ; a very large proportion of the women have dealings with them, and work
much ill.

A Moslem magician—a most wicked man, who is in
league with all the powers of evil—arrived at Nikaj while
I was there, and had the impudence to come and ask for
hospitality and quarters at the church-house—to the not
unnatural wrath of the Franciscan.   Both he and Marko
believed him to be so desperately wicked that they would
not allow him to come anywhere near me, though I
declared I was sure he was only an impostor, and that I
should like to see his tricks.   They were not tricks—
he was known to have sold his soul to the Devil, and
summons his aid by standing on one leg and kicking the
other violently behind him till he streams with sweat and
is exhausted.   He then reads the future and folks' fortunes, and thus does much harm, for all that he says is
diabolically inspired, and people believe in him, and act
accordingly.

I remembered that the tribes near Bond Street are
credulous enough to support many magicians, and that
there is no fiery and earnest-minded Franciscan to chivy
them away.   Perhaps when the Albanian Mountains are
completely and successfully civilised, the women of Nikaj

that now "deal with the Devil," will edit the Fortune-telling columns of the *Albanian Gentlewoman*. Great, indeed, would be the blessings of Progress if any one knew whither they were "progressing."

Then Marko told a perfectly authentic tale of—

A DEAL WITH THE DEVIL.

A certain man had dealings with the Devil, and did so much evil that at last the Pasha threw him into prison. One day the Pasha had many guests, and bethought him that he would summon the magician from prison to do some tricks. Duly brought before the company, he asked for a large bowl of water. This being given him he performed sundry charms over it, and asked the guests what port they would like to see : " Malta," said they. They looked, and there they saw Malta quite clearly—land, houses, sea, and a steamer in the harbour just about to start. " Have I your permission," said the magician to the Pasha, " to depart in that steamer? " " Certainly," said the Pasha. The magician put his foot into the bowl of water, and at once disappeared and *went to America on the steamer*. In America he had more than ever to do with the Devil, and had a wicked servant who aided him.

One day when he had prepared a quantity of magic liquid in large bottles he ordered his servant to kill him, cut him up, and bottle him. The servant refused. He then wrote many letters to all parts of the world, and bade the servant post them : " I shall kill myself," he said ; " you must cut me up and bottle me. Put the bottles in the cellar, leave them for nine months, and tell no one ; I shall answer the letters myself. After nine months you must open the cellar, and I shall come to life again." He killed himself, the servant bottled him ; some time elapsed, and then answers to the letters began to

come, written by the magician himself. The terrified
servant gave information to the authorities. The cellar
was opened, and it was found that the pieces had
actually begun to come to life. Had the nine months
been completed there is no doubt that the scheme would
have succeeded, and this wicked man would have lived
again; but the authorities ordered the pieces to be
destroyed, and that was the end of him.

Except myself, none of the horror-frozen audience
doubted this marvellous tale. " With the Devil," I was
told, "nothing is impossible." Magic is used by wicked
Moslems to pervert Christians. I was told the following,
which took place at Scutari, while I was up in the mountains on my first tour :—

A Turkish officer lodged in the house of a Christian
who had a daughter, a young woman twenty-five years
old; they went out walking together. One day, when
thus out, he put her into a carriage and drove her to a
Moslem house, and told her parents that he was going to
marry her. The parents declared that she had been
forcibly abducted, and appealed to the Archbishop and
clergy. They all demanded her restoration of the Government. The girl, it seems, had already declared her
willingness to turn Moslem and marry the officer; the
Church protested, and she was given back to her family,
which, to make sure of her, sent her straight off to
relatives in Podgoritza (Montenegro). There the whole
mystery was explained; the charm by which she had
been bewitched was found hanging round her neck and
removed. She at once ceased to wish to be a Moslem,
and was perfectly cured—it had all been done by magic.

My kind host feared always that I must be bored.
Life to him was a dull monotony of feuds and raids, to
check which he daily wore out his soul in vain, but to me
time in no way dragged.

Relations between Krasnich and Nikaj were very strained. At night, watch-fires twinkled on the Krasnich mountains, and talk ran on horse-raiding and cattle-lifting. Krasnich had shut its territory to Christians, and barred the route to Djakova, where Nikaj buys such extra things as it needs. Nikaj is three days from Scutari, an almost impossible journey to make with flocks and return with maize. Save stinking and savage Djakova, most Nikaj folk have never seen a town, and that but seldom. One man told me that he went to Scutari and Djakova each once a year. When fighting had seemed imminent in the spring, over the captured Franciscan, Djakova cut off Nikaj's gunpowder supply.

Thus things simmered and sizzled. Shala had a *besa* with Krasnich; but Krasnich harried some Christian villages near Djakova that are descended from Shala. Shala recognises them as blood relations, and does not intermarry with them, and therefore claimed the pro-tection of the *besa* for them. Krasnich refused to recog-nise them as Shala. Shala thereon said the *besa* was " off," and raided Krasnich at night, stealing three mules. Krasnich does not border with Shala, so sent three Krasnich men to accuse Nikaj of having fed and sheltered the mule-stealers on the way. Ten Nikaj and the three Krasnich made a sitting in a circle at the foot of the big wooden cross, and argued the affair for hours. Nikaj loudly protested entire ignorance of the affair, and told them to go to Shala.

A day or two after, Nikaj went a-raiding to Shala, and lifted two fine horses. Shala then sent over delegates, and complained that it was not fair. The horses were not Shala horses, but belonged to some Kilmeni men who were guests, and had come under *besa* to pasture beasts. The horses were under *besa* therefore, and must be restored. To this Nikaj merely replied airily, " Another time don't leave horses belonging to guests straying about." The two horse-stealers, however, offered to sell Shala the horses for five hundred piastres apiece. Shala was enraged. They wrangled long, and put off further debate till to-morrow.

Next day the two horse-thieves—one a fairish man, with a hooked nose, small head, and very weak jaw, and the other a forbidding, dark youth, with a handkerchief bound over one eye, low types both—came in hot indignation to the church-house to complain to the Franciscan and ask his advice. In the night, Shala had stolen the two horses back again, and got safely over the border with them. The Franciscan, Marko, and I, all three shouted with laughter, " Bravo, Shala! " The two thieves were hurt. They told, in all innocence, of the pains they had been at to get the horses in the first place, and now they had been robbed. It was most unfair; the horses were theirs. Nor could the Padre make them see it in any other light; for, by the law of the mountains, robbery from another tribe with which no *besa* exists is rather a virtue than a crime. If Shala had the right, Nikaj argued, to take the horses back, then Shala must restore the mules just stolen from Krasnich. A delegate came over from Shala to debate this nice point, and asked pertinently, " Are you in *besa* with Krasnich? If so, we return the mules."

As Nikaj was badly in blood with Krasnich—had barely a week ago refused to have anything to do with the mule affair—the proposition was unanswerable.

Shala withdrew, leaving the poor horse-thieves very crestfallen, and all Nikaj so angry that possibly by now the comedy has ended in tragedy.

People came to see me almost daily, bringing gifts of honeycomb or *rakia*, all praying me to get them a new form of government. It was in their power, I said, to start a better government at once. They had but to consult the Franciscan before deciding to shoot, and to

follow his advice.   They replied : " How can we obey a
man with a cord?   He has no soldiers to force us.   We
must have soldiers to make us obey ! "

They were at liberty, too, in their *medjliss*, I urged, to
make new rules.   "What is the use?" they said ;   "you
can spend weeks making a new law ; but the first time it
is broken, some one says of the guilty party, ' Oh, but he
is my cousin.'   Then you would have to fight all his
family.   By your plan we should kill each other more
than we do now."

I strove to explain that in England we governed ourselves with a *medjliss*.   But this was beyond even Marko
and the Franciscan.   " You have a King," they said ;
" when he says some one must be shot, he is shot.
Without the King, no one could obey the *medjliss*."   The
King, they maintained, was very rich, and had soldiers
and suvarris, who forced the people to obey him.

I said that we paid for the police and soldiers ourselves ; but that any nation could be so foolish as to do
that they refused to believe.

There they sat—dark, ragged, voluble, conscious of
their own misery, vaguely desirous of something better—
and clamoured to me for a King.

I looked at them with awe ; for I saw them through
a vista of thousands of years.   The river of evolution
had left them stranded—waifs of a day when men had
not yet learnt to form a nation, and had whirled me and
mine through all the ages—through tribes, principalities,
kingdoms—washing, as it went, the Divine right off
kings, and hurrying us none knows whither.   We have
even got back to a *medjliss* to the ruling of which we
object—as does Nikaj.

They waited further advice.   I tried again.

" You say you all want a good government."   " Yes,
they all did."   "Then why do you not try to keep the
laws that you already have ? "   They all assured me that

they wished to, but that they could not because of the bad people. I asked if there were more good or bad in the tribe. The great majority, they protested, were all good. All those present certainly were. Then, said I, they could force the bad ones to obey. For example, they could punish all the thieves — thieving is said to be a weakness of Nikaj. This was impossible, said a " good " man. He himself, of course, would not think of stealing, but suppose his cousin stole a horse, he could not possibly allow his own cousin to be punished.

The old Bariaktar of Nikaj.

They could not unite for the benefit of the tribe except when attacked from without, nor could they see that it was desirable. One's own blood came first. It was a case of "house" against "house," and in all the tribe there was no one with sufficiently marked individuality to sway the rest for good. The old Bariaktar, a man of much force of character, celebrated for his eloquence, had done much good, but was now past work. This fine old man paid me a special visit. He bore his eighty years well, and his grey eyes were still keen. He had an aquiline nose and strong jaw, and his thoughts were all for the saving of Nikaj. He had done all he could for it. Now he was old, and could do no more. If he were but younger he would come with me, no matter what it cost, and go straight to the house of the King of England, and tell him all the misery of the land and beg him to save it. Or he would have exchanged blood with me, and then as his sworn *probo* I should be bound to help him. He was sure I was of sufficiently noble family for him to exchange blood with me.

He did not speak for himself or his family. It was for

the country he wanted help. Thank God, he had no
crimes on his soul and was in blood with no one. And
all his five sons were alive. Four were married, but the
fifth, though twenty-five, was not. "And it is my own
fault. The first four brides were all bespoken unborn.
But for my youngest son I thought there was no hurry.
Now all the maidens of good family are born betrothed.
And I must have one of a good family. Good blood is
what I want for him. A woman of bad stock causes
endless trouble. It is not a question of price. I would
willingly pay a few napoleons more for good blood." He
was looking, he said, for a suitable widow, and he repeated
that the price did not matter.

The old man was celebrated for having fifteen years
ago settled a most difficult quarrel between Shala and
Nikaj which had cost much blood. Twenty-four sat to
debate the case, squabbled endlessly and came to no
decision. Only the old Bariaktar spoke never a word.
Asked why, he said he would not waste his words, as
he knew they would neither listen to him nor take his
advice. Pressed to give an opinion he rose to his knees,
as the custom is, and spoke for twenty-five minutes so
clearly, so forcibly, and so eloquently on the subject that
his advice was unanimously taken and peace made.

The Franciscan asked him to stay for dinner. But it
was a Saturday, and though I had said repeatedly that
fast food was quite enough for me, a little piece of meat
had been prepared for my dinner. The mere sight of
cooked meat on a Saturday would have shocked the old
man severely and made a scandal throughout the tribe.
It was arranged, therefore, that I should eat apart. This
pleased the old man greatly, for it is in accordance with
mountain custom that men and women should not eat
together, and he expressed a high idea of my modesty.

Nikaj believes itself to be pre-eminently Christian.
But nearly every member of the tribe drops his baptismal

name and calls himself by a Turkish one—Said, Suliman, Hussein, &c.—though they hate the Turks.

A youth who had drifted in to see me remarked, quite casually, in general conversation, "My brother shot a Gashi man yesterday," much as an English lad might say "I met old Smith the other day." I asked "Why?" "Because he spoke against the Christian faith," said he solemnly. And all thought the Gashi had been rightly shot.

It is said, I know not with what foundation, that at one time Nikaj was Orthodox. If so, this would indicate that its parent stem Krasnich was Orthodox, which is of much interest, since the two kindred tribes of Vasojevich and Piperi in Montenegro are Orthodox, and the name Krasnich has a very Slavonic ring about it (*Krasan*, beautiful). But Nikaj must have early become Catholic if the tradition be true that there was formerly a Benedictine monastery not far from where the present church stands, and that it was burnt by the Moslems.

Nikaj believes itself to be Christian, and shoots Moslems freely, but, in spite of the penalty of excommunication, sells daughters to the Moslems of Gashi. Moslems will pay thirty napoleons for a Christian girl, and will take even blind and ugly ones. The girls are often bound and handed over by force. Sometimes they run away, and a blood feud is started.

The old Bariaktar talked the tribe into passing a law to burn down the house of any man selling his daughter to a Moslem. But it was never enforced.

Of the three hundred houses of Nikaj, at least fifty have widows of brothers or cousins as concubines.

Nikaj, obeying not the laws of the Church to which it boasts that it belongs, and incapable of sufficient internal organisation to enforce even its own tribe laws, struck me as the most degraded native type that I met. Degraded, I say, because it seems very possible that the refugees in these isolated spots have not stood still, but have relapsed. For in Nature nothing stands still; it either develops or atrophies.

And as they very rarely come to church, it is hard ever to gather them together for any instruction or information. Part of the Tsuraj stock live at the top of an almost perpendicular cliff that rises up from the river.

To ascend it by the short way on foot is three or four hours' hard climb; by the mule track it is a good six hours'. To work such a parish is entirely beyond the strength of one priest.

On Sunday more than twenty men flocked to the church-house before mass. With Marko's help we discussed the usual subjects, while the Padre made ready the little chapel below. But at the sound of the first notes of the church bell, the company arose and all filed off. They had come to see me and not to attend mass. The congregation in the wretched, poverty-stricken little chapel consisted only of the Padre's servant, one or two women and children, Marko and myself.

When we came out of the dark, chilly, little place into the sun, back came all the crowd as eager as ever for an argument with me.

I started, with a view to stirring them up, by saying that when I told people in England that they sold their daughters to Moslems, had several wives (sisters-in-law, &c.), dropped their baptismal names and took Turkish ones, shot one another, stole within the tribe (which they admitted with grins), never came to church, and broke the rules of the Church, no one would believe they were Christians. They persisted that they were, and chorussed that they shot Moslems whenever a decent chance occurred. As for the wives, one of the company, who was excommunicate for having two, protested with great earnestness that the second was his cousin's widow. She had three children to bring up, so must stay in the house;

his honour therefore compelled him to cohabit with her.
She, of course, could not be allowed to marry outside the
house; but she was only twenty-four, and to force her to
live single would be so wrong that, in spite of the commands of the Padre, he could not do it—it would not be
honourable. He deplored the ban of the Church, but
family honour came first.

Of the Turkish names I could get no explanation,
except that they liked them, and, as they could not be
baptized by them, took them afterwards. To the question
why they should shoot Moslems, but like to imitate them,
they could give no answer; but it amused them. As to
selling daughters to them, they frankly admitted it was
a question merely of price. They would always sell to
Christians if they paid as well. Marko begged them to
consider their souls' future. One man argued ingeniously.
He denied all responsibility about his soul. The Padre
said God had given him his soul. "Very well, then, it is
God's business to look after it. I never asked Him to
give me a soul." To Marko's suggestion of eternal
torture, he replied that the torture of his soul would not
affect him after he himself was dead, and that it would
be extremely unjust of God to torture his soul for sins
that his body had committed. His poor soul had done
nothing at all. They all seemed to regard the soul as
something quite apart from their own identity—possibly
as the sort of bird that flies from the mouth of the dying
in cheap religious prints. "When *I* am dead, it does not
matter to me what becomes of my soul," was the general
idea. Two things only did they consider important—to
keep the fasts and to be buried in consecrated ground.
The only reason I could get for the desire to be thus
buried was that the churchyard was theirs, and they had
the right to be buried where they pleased. But the
churchyard was the most neglected and desolate that I
saw in any Christian tribe. Rough stones only marked

the graves; none marked with a cross or any other symbol. Nor did they seem to attach value to a funeral service. The rule of the Church is that no man who has gone out with the known intention of taking blood, but is killed himself, may be buried in consecrated ground, for he has died with the sin of intended murder on his soul. Recently a man had gone to kill an enemy, but was himself mortally wounded. The Padre hurried to confess him. He persisted only in regretting that he had failed to clean his honour, and died impenitent. The Padre therefore refused burial in the churchyard, but the tribe came and buried him there. Orders were then sent peremptorily by the Bishop that the body was at once to be exhumed, and exhumed it was, and buried elsewhere. This made a considerable sensation and much displeasure, and it is possible that it will not have the intended effect.

Church services have no meaning for many of them, and therefore no influence. One woman actually came into the church when the Franciscan was serving mass, walked straight up to the altar, and said : " Padre, I want you to write a letter for me." He took no notice of her, so, as he was raising the chalice, she caught hold of his arm and repeated her request much louder. His servant then, to her surprise, led her out. I could not find that they believed in anything really but " the Canon," and " there are no soldiers to force us, so we can do as we like," summed up their code.

But they can be faithful to their sworn word, and at times scrupulously honest. The odd, old man, the priest's servant, had once gone almost without food for four days, to his master's horror. Left in charge of the the house with plenty of food in it, he had eaten only some broken scraps. The rest, he said, did not belong to him, and he did not know if he might touch it.

He had a peculiar sense of humour. Roaring with

laughter, he told that he had had a very funny thought. "Suppose a cow fell from the cliff opposite. It would be broken all to pieces. Every man would run to pick up a bit for supper. Then suppose, just as they got there, the bits all joined into a cow again and ran away!" The thought of their disappointment tickled him so hugely, he could scarcely tell it for laughing.

The tribesmen love a joke. It is usually a tale of a successful swindle. Thus: A man bought a donkey at the bazar and led it away. Two thieves followed him. One slipped the halter from the donkey, and went off with it. The other put the halter on his own head, and followed the man. When the first thief had had time to escape with the donkey, the second began to pull and groan. The astonished man looked back, and found the donkey gone and a man in its place. "Where is my donkey?" he asked. "Alas!" cried the thief, "I am that luckless being. A wicked magician turned me into a donkey for fifteen years. The time has just come to an end. I have nothing, and know not where to go." The kind man then released him, and gave him some money.

Half-way up the cliff whence the cow was supposed to fall, a treasure of gold is fabled to be hidden. But it cannot be found, for it is *amanet*—trusted to the Earth, who will not yield it till certain unknown conditions be fulfilled.

A good plan, in such cases, is to sprinkle the earth overnight with flour or wood-ash. If, early in the morning, any footsteps be found on it—those, for instance, of a goat, a dog, a bird, even a man—such a creature must be sacrificed on the spot, and the Earth will yield the treasure. It is useless to dig unless you know the requisite spell.

A man once went to bury gold in a forest. But a woodcutter hid and watched him. He of the gold laid it in a hole at the foot of a tree, saying, " O Earth, do not yield this till two mice drag a cart round the tree." He went away believing his gold safe; but the wood-cutter caught two mice, tamed them, taught them to draw a little cart, and drove them round the tree. Then he dug and found the gold. Without the mouse trick, he might have dug vainly for weeks.

The heat wave that had hung over the thirsty land for months, broke in a deluge. Thunder crashed continuously, hurled back and forth from one mountain to the other. "Drangoni is fighting the dragon!" These frightful fights take place in mid-air. Kulshedra (the dragon) strives to overwhelm mankind with floods and torrents, Drangoni beats it back with thunder. When a child is born with a feather under its arm, it is a sign that he will be a Drangoni. His mother must not tell of the feather, or he will die at once. Most likely St. George was a Drangoni. The Drangoni is always male and Kulshedra female. A male animal can be a Drangoni.

Poor Marko's ankle had been on our arrival very bad—enormously swollen, and with signs of inflammation up to the knee.

Local opinion was that three strong men ought to pull it out till it went "pop" and was cured. I knew it was not dislocated, and feared lest they should persist and set up such acute mischief that Marko himself might go "pop." Finally, we set a crowd of leeches to pasture off him. Disgorging leeches is certainly a messy job, but I was surprised to find the disgust it caused to various men who dropped in, blood being the fluid in which they are accustomed to cleanse their honour.

When not a leech was left to cry " More," Marko, limp and depressed, took the blackest view of life, but the inflammation was checked and the swelling reduced.

More rough climbing was out of the question. As

soon as he was fit to travel, we started for Shala (so as to return to Scutari slowly by the easiest route), with two good mules and two Nikaj men as guides.

The track up the mountain was good enough for Marko to ride all the way. We reached a fine grassy plateau—the source of the Lumi Zi, a tributary of the Nikaj River—hidden in a great beech forest. Here our Nikaj guides, who were dull-witted, let the mules escape while watering them, and lost much time. Then on, always mounting through miles of forest till we came to its edge, and saw the peak of the mountain rising up beside us with startling abruptness, a glaring razzle-dazzle of raw white limestone, no leaf nor twig upon it. The people call it Mal-i-bardh, the White Mountain. We were on the top of the pass—Chafa Nermandjesh—some five thousand feet high, the frontier of Nikaj and Shala. The descent to Abate is easy. Our guides delivered us safely at the church-house, but rather late, as one of them was an important Head, and, with the engaging Nikaj peculiarity of doing just as he pleased when there was no one to force him, he sat down and held long parleys with every one we met on the way, taking no more notice of us than if we had not been there.

Shala is lucky in its young Franciscan, a keen, active man, who has for eight years been working hard to amend the law of blood; and has succeeded in restricting it so that now only a member of the house actually concerned may be shot, and that house only burnt. Previously any relative however distant was liable, and four or five innocent houses were sometimes burnt, merely because they were related. So far, this new law has been kept — a step, though small, in the right direction.

But for blood, and the awful destruction of property following, Shala would be rich. When I was there, it had been at once in blood with Shoshi, Plani, Nikaj,

Skreli, Krasnich, and Gashi—not to speak of blood
within the tribe—but had just sworn *besa* with the
Christian ones as a protective alliance against the
Moslems.

Shala, like Nikaj, is very fond of Turkish names, but
forbids the selling of daughters to the Moslems, and
burns the house of any one doing so. It steals girls freely
from Nikaj, founding many blood feuds. And though
honest within, the tribe enjoys of all things raiding across
its borders. A Vuthaj man had just been in search of a
"lost" cow. Shala, having eaten it, denied all knowledge of its whereabouts.

Now Shala was all agog to go to the feast of St.
Bonaventura, at Shoshi. The tribes do nothing by
halves; their hospitality is lavish beyond belief. One
man near the church had killed two oxen, five sheep, and
three goats, and expected guests enough to eat the lot.
By early dawn nearly all the male population, and very
many women, were off to Shoshi in their best clothes.
If Krasnich had made a raid, there would have been no
men to oppose them.

They returned on the fourth day, having enjoyed
themselves hugely, fired a fabulous number of cartridges—
we had heard the rattle as of a small war—and eaten roast
meat for two solid days. Shoshi had been eaten out of
house and home; had spent on powder, *rakia*, and food
some 30,000 francs, it was said, in entertaining some
fifteen hundred guests. A yearly affair on that scale is
more than a tribe can stand. Shala promised not to go
to the feast of St. Bonaventura next year, on condition
Shoshi does not come to the feast of Shala's patron saint,
St. John Evangelist.

Wild yells suddenly announced that the Archbishop
was in sight. He, too, had been celebrating St.
Bonaventura at Shoshi. Out we rushed to greet his
Grace with the hail of bullets the occasion required,

as he rode uphill, followed by my gay young friend, the Padre of Thethi, firing return volleys.

How we all fitted into the small house I do not know, but it was managed, and the party was most lively.

We were all, as is the national custom, drinking *rakia* before supper, and I was being taught the correct complimentary phrases to accompany each glass, when the servant dashed in to say a man had been shot just outside. The Padre seized his bag and dashed out to give absolution if there were yet time, but the man was dead—shot from the back, right through the left breast and the leg.

Not one of us had noticed the two rifle-shots, though quite near the house, for there had been a fusillade all day, on and off.

The man was dead. We went back to supper, and talked of blood and sudden death, of the miserable state of the mountain tribes, owing to the prolonged drought; the hopelessness of remedying social and material conditions under the then existing Government. And over all the poverty, crime, and ignorance hung the shadow of a greater horror—the dread of a combined Moslem attack on the Christians. A doleful evening enough.

Next morn brought the details of last night's murder. The youth had been shot by his own second cousin, with whom he lived in a communal family house, for his own house had been burned for blood, but he had some fields. He was twenty-three years old, had shot two men—one only the year before—and had not confessed for five years, so could not have Christian burial. His relatives, however, came at once to the church-house to beg the Padre for sugar for the funeral feast.

The two had quarrelled over irrigation rights. The deceased had, that day, rightly claimed the water for his fields. The other diverted the stream to his own lands, and as his cousin stooped over the channel to reopen it, shot him twice from behind.

Torrents of rain fell next day—water enough for all. Judged from the lowest standpoint, the slaughter of the youth was totally unnecessary. I waited with interest the judgment of the tribe.

The development of the case was amazing. As the blood had been taken within the family, there was no outsider to avenge it. It was a crime only against the head of the house, and he alone had the judging of it. As he decided to publicly forgive the murderer, the tribe had no power to inflict any punishment. So the murderer dwelt as usual with the rest of the family in the communal house. He, as well as his victim, had had his own house burnt for blood previously.

As a member of the family, he was present all day at the funeral feast, and looked at his victim's corpse in the grave apparently quite unmoved, while the death-wails of the mourners echoed round.

Public opinion by no means wholly approved of the affair. But it was *eghel*—it had to be. God must have meant him to die, or why should only two bullets have killed him? Many men recover even from ten—if it be *eghel*.

I urged that the case was a disgrace to the tribe, and a law to deal with such should be passed; but was told that no law interfering with the rights of a man in his own house would ever be obeyed, even though passed. The mountains do not approve of " grandmotherly legislation." Nevertheless, there was a feeling that the murderer had acted scurvily. The best way for him to reinstate himself would be for him to shoot some one else—not a near relative. His ground could then be confiscated for a time, and his goods destroyed. He would be liable to be shot, and in this new feud could clean his honour.

News of the murder was sent at once to Scutari, and

the officials there would duly claim some forty napoleons as their fee.

The majority of blood-takers, said the Padre, die quite impenitent, saying they would rather go to hell with their honour clean than to heaven dishonourably.

As at Nikaj, I found they declared that their souls were not responsible for the deeds of their bodies.

Shala, like the other tribes, declared that, in spite of shooting, it had a large excess of males. The excess of females in England always astonished them. One man ingeniously explained it. "England does not need so many fighting men. Very many women prefer to be virgins, whereas very few men do. Therefore God has arranged to satisfy all tastes!"

On July 18th came great news from the outer world. The Vali of Scutari had been dismissed, with all his *entourage*—the soldiers had again struck for pay—he had been in office but six months. Hot on this came rumours that the same had happened in Prizren and Salonika. A planned and prearranged revolution in Turkey was an almost unknown thing. The wildest hopes flew through the mountains. Something was going to happen. Who knows? Perhaps the Turks will be driven out!

Life went on as before. I spent my time with the children. Some were in charge of beasts. Most merely killed time by fooling aimlessly about, till one punched another and a general squabble took place. They rarely, if ever, played an organised game, and, if they did, never stuck to it long. When I asked for children's games I was told, "They have never been to school. How can they know games?" In truth, from childhood upward, the chief topic of talk and interest is the family blood, and who has killed whom.

In all the mountains I saw but four games, and two of them only once. One is an elaborate form of Cat's

Cradle called Kamb-e-Pulat (Hen's Foot). It ends with a three-toed figure like a bird's foot. The string is wound round the feet as well as round the hands. The second is Knucklebones, played with pebbles.

The other two were played only by boys. A boy stands on all-fours with his back well arched, while one boy dodges over, and a second under, him. The object of the upper boy is to butt the under one "behind" with his head. If he hit this mark he wins, and the butted boy has to form an arch. If he miss, he strikes the top of his head violently on the ground, which causes roars of laughter. I had seen this game previously in Montenegro. But it was quite new to Marko, though he is Albanian and has travelled much in the mountains.

In the fourth game a boy guards a ball within certain limits, while the others try to kick it out. When kicked out, the defender of the ball must throw it at the kicker, who, if hit before he reaches a place of safety, becomes guardian of the ball. The ball was made of a tight bundle of fern, so gave little sport.

A cheeky boy of fifteen suggested that I should buy him a wife. Wouldn't he make her work! Now he lived with his grandfather, and they had no woman—he had to make all the bread himself.

He pointed out a girl near who, he said, was sold to an ugly old man. She threw stones at him indignantly, but he persisted. She knew only that she was sold, and would be sent next year—to whom she had no idea. She and her sister lived with their widowed mother. Her father and uncle had both been lately shot. Her mother had gone to the Shoshi feast, and had not yet returned.

She went back to her hut, and presently the most pitiful sobs and wails recommenced. Her sister had taken their only goat to graze on the hillside. A viper had bitten it in the tongue, and it was dead. The two

sang death-wails. " Oh, my goat, my goat, my only one !
Some have so many goats—why has the serpent taken
our only one?" Their weird cries resounded till they
sobbed themselves exhausted. Not only was the goat's
milk an important part of their living, but they dreaded
that their mother would beat them on her return.

This was easily remedied. I sent the price of a milch
goat. The relief, coming unexpectedly after a night of
despair, produced torrents of tears. And the gratitude of
both girls and mother was touching in the extreme.

This people is a strange mixture of violent emotion
and apparent insensibility. The way in which women
will weep on the grave of a brother killed years ago is
heartrending to witness. Men speak with deep feeling
of a murdered son—but the shooting continues.

A hideously raw version of the Pot of Basil story was
told me by a Franciscan in whose parish it took place.
A widow had one son. He was shot in her presence and
his skull shivered. She collected his scattered brains and
kept them in a box to weep over—all she had left of him.

We left Shala for Thethi, where I met again the fine
fellow who had piloted us to Vuthaj. He had been there
since to buy maize, and reported, had it not been for the
old Moslem whose guest we were, we should have been
caught. He had purposely kept us shut up, as a spy was
seeking us from Gusinje. After we left he was asked by
the authorities why he had not at once reported our
arrival, for he knew no strangers were wanted in the
district. He gallantly replied that it had never been the
custom of his house to betray a guest. That he knew I
was a foreigner, but that I had behaved perfectly well.
He took what guests he pleased, and would shelter me
again if I required it.

To all my hosts, Christian and Moslem, I owe more
than I can ever repay. I can only hope to show the line
of pure gold that lies beneath an outward rugged nature.

There was difficulty in finding mules for our journey, as all Thethi was going to the high pastures to celebrate St. Veneranda. We started finally with the two men and mules that had taken us before—we undertaking to halt at Skreli for the feast.

The track over Chafa Shtegut is exceedingly steep, but so well made that, except for the very top, which is cut in steps, it is rideable the whole way. The lower slopes are fine pasture. Above is rock and scrub. The descent on the Boga side is easy. I was glad, when I saw how very precipitous this pass is, that I had not attempted it when full of snow. A slip might mean a fall of a thousand feet.

Passing through Boga, where the priest offered us all possible hospitality, and upbraided us for not stopping the night, we reached Skreli by the same track as before. It was my third visit there, so I felt quite at home.

We celebrated St. Veneranda next day. The church was packed with all Skreli in its best, for no outsiders were present. They come only for the patron saint of the tribe.

Coming straight from the heart of Pulati, I was much struck with the difference in the physical type of the people—finer, better built, and a very much larger proportion with grey eyes and fair hair. We were in the priest's house after service, when a fierce quarrel took place outside, between two men. The most awful noise ensued. One man dashed up into the room with us. The other howled insults from below. Our man, who had a Mauser, rushed to the window, and was just about to fire when two women, who were on the landing outside, hurled themselves on to him and struck up the rifle. The man below aimed up with a Martini.

Women may not be shot, so one hung on to the Mauser man, while the other leaned out of window, as also did I. The priest ran in, and made him give up the

Mauser. The man below was running wildly up and down, aiming upwards at the windows, yelling and threatening to shoot, while the priest, seated cross-legged right out on a window-sill, commanded him to stop. Two men threw themselves upon him and tried to disarm him by force. It was an exciting moment—the three locked tightly together fighting like hell-hounds for a loaded rifle, its owner livid with rage, his eyes glaring madly as he yelled like a wild beast. They mastered him. He rose snarling and impotent.

The priest descended, and gave him a severe talking to. He consented at last to go home, and slunk off, two others going with him—he, reluctant, turning back often, and vowing loudly he would return soon and shoot.

Our mules were waiting, saddled and ready. We left for Rechi, meeting its priest on the way. He was bursting with news, fresh from Scutari.

There was a rising all over Turkey: Shemsi Pasha shot at Monastir—Osman Pasha captured—rumours of a new Government. We roared with laughter at an Austrian newspaper, which described Shemsi as an " unblemished character," but contained little more definite news ; and we opined that now the ultimatum which Maltsia e madhe was about to send in for the removal of the detested Shahir Bey, from the post of Sergherdé of the mountains, was likely to be listened to. The bitter plaint of all the tribesmen, their urgent appeals for help against the Turk, still rang in my ears. It seemed that the "something" that "must happen some day" was upon us—that the psychological moment, as the novelists call it, had arrived. We were in the saddle early next morning, and soon at Scutari. It was the 27th of July. Scutari was all astir with the news of the Constitution. What? when? how? where? why?—no one knew. No Consulate had any official details. All that was known was " Constitution."

CHAPTER VIII

THE COMING OF THE CONSTITUTION

"For euery Wight that lovede Chyvalrye,
It were a lusty Sighté for to see."

It was not till August 2nd that Scutari formally accepted
the Constitution. We began early in the morning, troop-
ing to the great drill-ground in front of the Government
House, under a blazing sun, in a cloud of white dust.
The crowd was largely Moslem; tentatively at first came
town Christians, then more. A Turkish official on a
platform read an inaudible proclamation in Turkish (a
tongue understood by very few), a Hodja followed with
another. Then a Catholic Albanian, a schoolmaster,
leapt up and spoke in Albanian—an impromptu address
—and the people found voice.

To the Christians, especially, the moment was
supreme. "We are free! We are free!" cried an old
man. "All my life I have waited for this moment.
Now, thank God, I shall die happy!"

The impossible had happened. Albania's day had
dawned. The pent-up emotions of centuries burst
forth, and the child-people was whirled away in a
torrent of joy and hope.

There is but one way in which joy can be expressed. That is by firing ball cartridge. Every
one had weapons: every one fired. The dazzling
white cotton and crimson fezzes of the Moslems, the
orange barrack walls, the scarlet Turkish standards,
the two bands that glared brass and blared different
tunes at once, the shrieking pipe and throbbing tomtom

223

of four black gypsies, the clouds of smoke and the showers of sparks from bad powder, and the heavy, cloudless, blue sky over all, were swept into one gorgeous, unforgettable whole.

There is an extraordinary exhilaration in the sound and concussion of continuous firing when you are in the thick of it. It was impossible not to be carried away by the general enthusiasm. By the light of history and experience, the thing was incredible. "The leopard does not change his spots nor the Ethiop his skin," said Reason—"the Turk is always a Turk." But Hope cried, "Albania is free!" And Hope prevailed.

We trooped back through the streets. The artillery that suddenly clattered by showed that the authorities were not, as yet, certain of the effect of the proclamation. But it was not needed. Scutari saw sights it had never seen before. The Moslem band played outside the Cathedral, and Christian and Moslem swore brotherhood on the Koran and a revolver—a sinister combination.

"Ah, la bella cosa, la Liberta!" cried a Christian. "We are united! Albania is free!" But the older Christians mostly kept aloof. "Thirty years ago we rejoiced for this same Constitution," said one, "and what came of it?" Another prayed me not to go into the streets at night. "The massacre will begin. I know it will. It is a Turkish trick to kill us all."

Songs and shots went on till two in the morning. Bullets whistled continuously over every roof—we picked up plenty next day—but there were no fatalities, nor any street fighting nor drunkenness. Without any police force, perfect order was maintained.

After more than fourteen hours' solid firing, Scutari fell asleep, and slept till midday, when it awoke to rejoice and fire again, till not a cartridge was left in any gunshop.

The moment found its poet, and the hymn of the

Constitution, written by a native Franciscan, brief and to the point, caught the populace at once. Scarcely printed, it rang down the streets.

There was but one black spot in the general joy. Amnesty of prisoners had been granted. Those of other towns, we heard, were already freed. But Scutari gaol remained grimly closed, and the white-faced prisoners crowded at the windows, vainly waved their hands, and cried to the friends below, who awaited their release.

Next day came the men of the Serb village of Vraka. That they, who never pretend to wish for anything but union with Montenegro, should hurry to hail Turkish rule, caused some surprise. They swung in, in fine style, firing a salute before the Russian Vice-Consulate as they passed, with cries of "Zhivio!" (Long live!) And they heard the incomprehensible proclamation read with cries of "Zhivio!"

"To whom are they wishing long life?—to Turkey or Russia?" asked some one. It did not matter. They were free to fire guns in Scutari, and they did so to their hearts' content, and wound up by building a human tower—six men standing on the shoulders of twelve— and perambulating the drill-ground; then they danced the Montenegrin *kolo*, and retired happy, after again saluting Russia. Afterwards, they explained that they had come in obedience to Turkish Government orders. They did not know why—but had enjoyed themselves very much.

They had come when called. Would the mountain tribes? Scutari waited. The tribes sent in a strongly-worded ultimatum. The Sergherdé must be dismissed, or those responsible for his retention take the consequences. At this crucial moment it was necessary to buy the tribes at almost any price. The Young Turks dismissed Shachir Bey at once. Then, and then only, the tribes thought Constitution meant a new era of justice.

The first to come were the Postripa men, on August 6th, under four bariaks, great banners with a hand, a sword, a crescent, and star on a red ground with a green border—Suma, Ura Strengit, and Drishti. Scutari had by now gone crazy. Business was at a standstill. The hitherto-forbidden national song, "*Shcyptarii*" (Albania), heard formerly only in the mountains or in strict seclusion, rang through the streets, till we wished it again forbidden. And if firing ever ceased, we wondered what was the matter.

I was in the thick of everything. Every one knew me. Such was the whirl of Liberty, Fraternity, and Equality, that I was invited to visit the oldest mosque in Scutari, *Dzamija Plumbit* (Mosque of Lead), and went, to the surprise of some of the foreign consulates, who had tried, in past times, to obtain permission and failed.

It was an amazing visit. I was told—I know not with what truth—that I was the first Giaour female that had been inside it, that I need not put off my boots (of course I did though), that I might photograph, that now we were all free and equal.

It is said to have formerly been a church of St. Mark, and, though much altered, possibly was. It is square, with a big dome, and its square courtyard is surrounded with columns whose capitals are certainly pre-Turkish. The cloister walk that they form round the court is roofed by the many little leaden domes that give the mosque its name. And I was invited into the other small mosques in the neighbourhood—buildings of no interest. The point was that they were open to a female Giaour with boots on.

August 10th was the climax. All else was as naught compared to the Coming of the Christian tribesmen.

It was unrehearsed, undrilled, but no preparation

could have made it more magnificent. Summoned by their chiefs, they came—chosen representatives of all the big tribes—one thousand five hundred strong, each tribe headed by its Bariaktar with the bullet-riven banner, and led by its priest or Franciscan—sons of the Church militant (a revolver peeped from the habit of more than one)—riding or marching in front of their men, and marshalling them with a precision that called forth general admiration. Keeping neither line nor step, but in perfect order, they swung down the street with the peculiar stride of the sandal-shod mountaineer.

It was a day of days for the missionaries. For the first time in the land's history they were entering the capital triumphant, with their flocks, to hail the Constitution that was to give equal rights to all nationalities, and to Christian and Moslem alike. Through a cloud of dust, sweltering heat—to the continuous roar of fifteen hundred rifles and the applause and revolvers of the onlookers—singing and shouting, the mass swept into the drill-ground.

Each well-known figure was hailed as he passed. There was the "tiny but terrible" priest of Skreli, a black bundle of energy, looking minute among his men; the priest of Rechi, soldierly, erect on his white horse, with his big hound following; the Bishop of Pulati, in Franciscan habit, but wearing a fez, to the joy of the Moslems; the fighting men of Shala-Shoshi, led by Padre Cirillo, happy and excited; Kastrati, Grudi, Hoti, Boga, Rioli, Plani—all with their priests, and brave in their best array, aglitter with silver chains and weapons.

They swung round in a great circle, in perfect order, and stood expectant. The Hodja and two Turkish officials read the inaudible Turkish proclamations that meant nothing to the tribesmen. But the priest of Rechi sprang to the platform, and, in a stentorian voice that rang clear everywhere, roared an impromptu speech, and cried, "Rrnoft Constitution! Rrnoft Padishah! Rrnoft Schyptarii!" (Long live the Constitution, &c.).

The tribesmen and their rifles roared applause, and, firing and shouting, the whole army rushed off to be fed, Christian Scutari "standing treat."

The addition next day of Dushmani, Shlaku, and Toplana, five hundred strong, taxed the lavish hospitality of the Christian townsfolk to its furthest limits. The Cathedral grounds were one vast picnic. No such sight had been seen in Scutari before. For two whole days and nights over two thousand heavily-armed men were loose in the town—nor was there either military or police force sufficient to have coped with an outbreak,—but not one incident occurred to mar the general joy. They rejoiced like children, too happy to be naughty. Even the representatives of two Consulates, who frankly detested the Albanians, said, "*Mon Dieu*, under a decent Government, what a people this would be!"

The tribesmen hailed me with joy, pressed weapons into my hands, and swept me away. Down the main street I went, blazing ball-cartridge from a Martini, and ran about the Cathedral grounds, firing any revolver handed me, while the populace applauded and the Archbishop laughed.

It came on me with a great crash that the simple mountaineers believed largely that I had worked this marvel—the dismissal of the Sergherdé and the change of Government. They had begged me to do it, and no sooner had I returned to Scutari than it was done! Some even declared that they would follow me and obey my King. I denied it vainly. Never before have I been so popular; never in my life shall I be so again.

The feasts were over. It was time to return to the mountains. Then came the dramatic climax. The prisoners still stared pitifully from the bars—daily expecting release, daily disappointed. I went to the governor of the prison for news; there was none. The mountain men began to leave the town. The prisoners were in despair. Two were Shala men, and they yelled to their tribe, "Shala, save us!" And all the two hundred prisoners took up the cry. Shala swore promptly not to leave the town till all were freed, and the remaining tribesmen swore to support Shala.

Scutari was anxious. Shala calmly drew up an ultimatum in the terms of "Forgive us our trespasses," saying: "We have been ordered to swear *besa* among ourselves, to pacify our blood fends, and forgive those that have broken our tribe-law. We obey. *But you too must forgive.* If the prison doors are not open by noon to-morrow—we force them!"

This was sent to the new Vali. We waited and asked, "Is it peace?" The tribesmen, quite calm, behaved as though nothing were happening. Only their priests, as go-betweens, hurried to and fro, from tribe to Vali, anxious, but conscious that they held the trump cards.

Finally, late in the evening I met a well-known priest coming from the Government House. "What news?" "We are sworn to tell nothing," said he. He looked at me with victory twinkling in his eyes, and burst out laughing. "Thank you!" said I, "I understand." And at midnight quietly the two hundred prisoners were freed.

At seven next morning was a final feast outside the Cathedral before an admiring crowd. The two released Shala men, clad in festal attire that had been brought for the purpose, and already fully armed, ran about madly embracing all their friends. Decked with a scarlet and white tie—the colours of the Constitution—I went round as madly, distributing cigarettes to all.

Shala then started a wondrous dance, the only mountain dance I have seen. Four men pranced grotesquely, stepping high and waving their arms, yelling the while, but unaccompanied with any music. One old boy, in a crimson *djemadan*, had lost one arm and brandished a sword with the other to make up. Prancing like a maniac, and uttering loud howls, he arrived opposite me. For the time being, at any rate, I belonged to the mountains. I yelled too. He yelled louder, pranced higher, and slashed wildly. I pranced, waved my arms, and shrieked. He shouted me down again. I screwed all my strength into one appalling scream, pitched high enough to carry over the general roar. The crowd of onlookers, including the assembled Churchmen, roared with laughter and applause. The old boy's delight was unbounded. He considered he had made the star performance. The nearest men handed me up bottles of *rakia;* quite a number thanked me for the beautiful addition I had made to the entertainment. I fired every revolver offered me.

The band played, and triumphant Shala returned to the wilderness. The last of the tribesmen disappeared in a cloud of dust, and Scutari sank into silence.

Twelve days had gone in a wild whirl. Constitution was a fact. It remained to see what it would do.

It blundered from the beginning in Scutari. On the day on which the tribes' representatives were swearing universal *besa* in Scutari, a tribesman up in Shoshi, unaware of what was taking place, shot another for blood. The tribe had accepted Constitution—so the Young Turk authorities, regardless of the fact that the deed had been done in ignorance of the *besa*—ordered the slayer to be given up to justice. But he had fled straight to Shala and thence to a Moslem tribe. They then ordered the Shala men who had sheltered him to come down. And they, loyal to Constitution, came down voluntarily at once. To shelter a man that flies from blood, in tribe law, is not merely no crime, it is a sacred duty. But instead of explaining to these men that in future it was punishable to shelter a murderer, and dismissing them with a caution or small fine—the Young Turks cast them all (fifteen) untried into prison.

Nothing more foolish could have been conceived. The revulsion of feeling was immediate. Tactfully handled, the tribesmen would have been a bulwark of the Constitution. But from their own, quite reasonable, point of view they were betrayed the first week. " Cursed be he that putteth his faith in the Turk " was once more the watchword.

Christian Scutari still hoped. And in the new freedom opened a club for the promotion of the hitherto forbidden Albanian language.

As for the Consulates, not one appeared to have the faintest belief in Constitution. Some openly derided it, and intimated that as it did not suit their national plans it would not be allowed to succeed. It had foes without, and was making foes within.

CHAPTER IX

IN THE DEBATABLE LANDS—DJAKOVA—DEVICH

"For thrones and peoples are but waifs that swing,
And float or fall in endless ebb and flow."

A UNIVERSAL *besa* had been sworn till St. Dimitri (Nov. 6). I leapt at the chance of being the first foreigner to enter the "closed" districts under the new state of affairs, and applied properly, through the Consulate, for a *teskereh* to travel to Prizren. Djakova was my object. The Young Turk authorities, pleased to find a British female willing to test the new régime in her own person, gave permission at once. Personally, I put all my faith on the inviolability of the *besa*.

We were going to a Moslem land, so Marko arranged that we should travel with two Moslem *kirijees* bound for Prizren with a caravan. Leaving Scutari at 3 P.M. with one *kirijee*, Ren, a Djakova man, we crossed the plain by a fair road to the Drin, followed its right bank as far as Vaudys, and ferried over in the *trappa*. Vaudys is the frontier of Mirdita and the legendary capital of Paul Dukaghin, who, it is said, ruled from Vaudys to Djakova. But these tales are vague.

We rode up the valley of the Drin, fertile, rich in maize and grass, wood and water, caught up the caravan of ten packhorses heavily laden with bales of stinking goats' hides, and halted at dusk at Gomshiche, on a tributary of the Drin, Ljumi Gomshichet. The caravan camped in a field; Marko and I were put up at the church-house. Pack-saddling next morning was not done till 7 A.M.

We were on the old Prizren-Scutari trade-route—a right-of-way when nobody sees fit to close it—so were without local escort. It was therefore thought fit that, for safety, I should ride last of all the caravan. It was a hot day, and such air as there was bore the concentrated reek of all the ten packs of goat-hide straight at me. I objected. "It is very healthy," said Marko. "It stinks," said I. "With respect," said Marko, "it is not a stink. It is the smell caused by the way they are prepared."

I infinitely preferred to take the risk—which was *nil* —of being shot at by Mirdites, but my guardian angels insisted on at least two horses being ahead of me. We followed up the right bank of the Gomshiche River to the church of Dushaj, near which a tributary enters the main stream, and rode up the right bank of this tributary high on the hillside above the water, making many detours to head the streams that flowed to join it.

The wretched packbeasts were overladen. One hundred *okas* (over two hundred pounds) is a packload, without counting the heavy wooden saddle. They staggered downhill, had to be shoved and pulled up the worst places, and if they stumbled could with difficulty recover. Descending a stony track, one fell and would have turned a complete somersault downhill had not the pack jammed between the rocks of the narrow track. Tightly fixed, with its head twisted under it between its forelegs, it was in danger of strangulation, and was extricated with great difficulty. The men were stupid at the job, nor did they see, till I pointed it out, that the luckless brute could not possibly rise till a rock that jammed one hindleg was moved. It was badly cut on head and knee, but was reloaded, and we started again.

The track was rough. I walked, and was well ahead at the bottom of one of the narrow valleys, when a second packhorse, forced by the size of its pack to go on the very edge, crashed over, rolling over and over with its legs

tucked tightly under it, and fell some thirty feet into the
stream below, the heavy pack and saddle saving it from
many blows. There it lay helpless and terrified, wedged
in a pool among rocks. It was a three-quarters of an
hour job to raise and reload it. The dry hides absorbed
a lot of water, and were so heavy the loads had to be
redistributed.

We crawled slowly on—a wearisome drag. Every
pack shifted, and had to be readjusted after every descent.
About 4.30 we arrived at a *han* not far from Puka, men
and beasts all tired out, and camped for the night in a
field. There was plenty of water. The horses, freed
from their packs, were turned out to graze at twopence
a head.

Two time-expired soldiers had joined our caravan, one
a Moslem Serb from Plevlje, and the other an Albanian
from Mitrovitza, both homeward bound. The Serb, a
civil fellow, spoke little Albanian and kept quite apart
from the others. He was deathly tired, groaned at the
thought of the week's tramp yet before him, and rolled
over fast asleep upon the ground as soon as we halted.

The *hanjee* provided hay for my bed and a stewed
fowl for my supper. The hides were piled high, the
horses picketed in line. We sat round a fire on the
ground—the two beaky-nosed, grey-eyed Djakova men
and the two soldiers. The Serb—though a Turkish subject and a Moslem—appeared to be considered as much
a foreigner as myself. There was a red glow of firelight
and a crackling shower of sparks as dry brushwood was
piled on. The picketed horses munched steadily at a
feed of maize. Over all was the intense blue depths of
the cloudless night sky, ablaze with a myriad stars. I
wondered why people ever lived in houses as I rolled up
in my rug on the hay bed.

Two faithful dogs guarded us all night, and had they
not chosen my hay as the most comfortable place to sleep

in, and barked loudly close to my ear whenever an imaginary danger threatened, I should have slept very well. But to lie awake under the stars is not the misery of sleeplessness in a room—rather it is pure joy. I saw them fade slowly as the dawn crept up—the crescent moon hung low—there came a dash of brilliant yellow over the hills—another day had begun. We rose and shook ourselves, and those that wished went and dipped their hands and face in the stream.

The weary task of pack-saddling began again. I walked with Marko to the brow of one hill and saw over to the land of Berisha.

Puka is a very large tribe of seven bariaks—Puka, Komani, Dushaj, Cheriti, Chiri, Berisha and Merturi-Gurit, and Kabashi. It is partly Moslem and partly Christian. Puka is the gathering-place for all. Three days before they had celebrated " Constitution," and enjoyed themselves immensely, said the *hanjee*. Now they would like to know what Constitution was.

By six the caravan started ; we swallowed the usual dose of black coffee by way of breakfast, and rode up the hill to Puka proper—a mere bunch of hovels, the Kaimmakam's little better than the rest. A few Nizams hung about it, but let us pass unquestioned.

We entered into a desolate wilderness of sandhills— or rather hills of earth so friable that it disintegrates at every shower, and no blade nor leaf can find a hold upon it. Nor was there any living creature—nothing but round bare hills, fantastically water-hewn, and dead as the mountains in the moon. Part of the track had to be taken very carefully—a narrow, friable ledge high along the mountain-side.

We got down into Arshi—a fertile valley, an arm of Mirdite land, the bariak of Spachi, that runs into Puka —and pulled up at midday at Han Arshit.

Han Arshit provided nothing—not even coffee.

Marko and I ate the remains of last night's fowl which we had saved. The wretched horse that had fallen over the cliff the day before was dead lame, and had to be left at the *han*.

Trade, said the *hanjee*, was not what it was in the old days. Then a hundred horses at a time were often put up at the *han*. The railway to Salonika had ruined Albania by diverting all the traffic that used to go to Scutari and Durazzo. They were all being starved out; nothing but the long-talked-of railway to the Adriatic could save the land — let the Constitution hurry up with it.

Arshi lies on a river—Ljumi Gojanit. We followed it up a stony valley, steeper and steeper, to its source at the top of the pass, Chafa Malit.

There is a joy that never palls—the first glimpse into the unknown land. On the other side of the pass, a magnificent valley lay below us, thickly wooded with beech, and beyond were the lands which two rival races each claim as their birthright—one of the least-known corners of Europe.

I hurried eagerly down the steep descent on foot, by a rough track to Flet. Flet is Moslem, save for six families, all large; one, consisting of fifty members, showed quite an imposing group of stone houses. A church, but three years old, served occasionally by the priest of Dartha, showed trim and white.

We pushed on to Han Zaa. The *han* was shut up. The *hanjee*, on being summoned, said he could supply nothing—nothing at all, and that there were neither fowls nor eggs in the neighbourhood. He gave us leave, however, to pick as many beans as we liked from his field for twopence. The two soldiers started bean-picking, and I shucked industriously. Marko sent a child foraging for a fowl, and went to borrow a caldron. An ancient hen was produced, and Marko, who is a perfect camp cook, had it simmering in a huge pot of beans within half-an-hour. The *hanjee* volunteered two wooden ladles and a large bowl, and in due time we fed the entire company off beans stewed with hen. As they would otherwise have had nothing but the remains of the day before yesterday's maize bread, this put all in high good humour. I declined a kind offer that I should sleep in the lee of the pile of odoriferous hides, lay down on a heap of hay about 10 P.M., and slept right through till half-past five next morning, when I was surprised to find I had rolled into a dry ditch, and had slept on top of Marko's thick walking stick and a large stone.

We were bound for Djakova, and the rest of the party for Prizren, so started at once with one *kirijee*. Free of the pack train, we pushed on quickly down the valley of the Goska, past Han Sakati, and by a steep descent to the Drin, which we successfully forded, led by a native who stripped and carried my saddlebags on his head. It was a ticklish job, and can only be crossed thus in very dry weather.

Following Drin down a short way to its junction with the Kruma, we struck up the valley of the Kruma, and were in the land of the Hashi. A great wall-like cliff, rising on the stream's left bank, is known as the fortress of Lek Dukaghin.

Hashi is a large tribe, variously reckoned at 600 to 1000 houses, the large majority of which are Moslem. It is separated by the White Drin from the Moslem tribe of Ljuma on the one side, and on the other marches with the Moslem Krasnich. Hashi land includes the Pestriku Mountains, which the Mirdites state to be their own ancestral home. They migrated to their present home, and the land was subsequently occupied by Hashi, which is no relation to Mirdita.

We left the Kruma, and rode on to a high undulating plateau of loose, friable soil, covered with stunted oak-scrub, parched and sun-scorched. There was neither shade nor spring. A Moslem friend of the *kirijee's* hailed him, and invited us all to take our midday rest at his place. The nearest spring on the track, he said, was two hours' distant, but he had plenty of water. We accepted gratefully, and followed him uphill. He had two houses side by side—ramshackle shanties made entirely of wood, save for the large chimney and fireplace of clay built up at the side.

He did not ask us in, but spread mats under a tree. His women—not veiled—stared at us from the doorstep of the farther house, and fetched a large jar of fresh water, but sent it to us by a boy. Several men joined us, and were very civil.

Our hosts had never seen a foreign woman dressed *alla franga* before in their land, and thought my coming rather a joke; for a Giaour to be riding openly through Hashi to Djakova unarmed was unusual, to say the least of it—only the *besa* made it possible. Had heard of " Constitution," but did not know what it was, only that there was a *besa* about it.

They were all of the same type as the Gusinje men— very tall, thin, and narrow-built, with large beaky nose and almost no chin, an odd bird-like pattern that seems to be wholly Moslem. They told us the land had once been all Christian, and that under the ruins of a church not far off was a vast treasure, but that it was impossible to find it—it was *amanet*.

They owned plenty of land, but it lay high, and lacked water. This year was a drought, and the pasture was all burnt up. The place they said was called Puka Zarisha. It is not marked in the Austrian staff map, which for all this neighbourhood is very faulty.

Returning to our track, we rode for over an hour through dull, dusty oak-scrub, then into a wood, where we watered the horses at the two-hour spring, and pushed on, as it

was absolutely necessary to arrive before nightfall—passed
a few wooden houses at Helshani, and met scarce a soul
upon the road. It was a deserted wilderness. A long
ascent brought us to the top of the pass, Chafa Prushit,
and there lay Djakova on the plain below, with a long
descent of rolling hill between us and it—red roofs
glowing among green trees, slim white minarets twinkling delicate like lilies. Djakova—as are all Turkish
towns—is beautiful from a distance. And when it is
civilised and black factory-chimneys arise in place of
white minarets, it will be lovely neither within nor
without. You cannot have everything.

I beheld it as a dream city—thought of the aching
days of toil I had gone through vainly five years before,
only to be turned back. The pleasing sensation of attain-
ment wiped out temporarily the fatigue of a long, hot day
in the saddle, and two scrappy nights' rest, and I hurried
down the stony track—too steep for riding—on foot, a
painful job enough, as I had started in new *opanke*, and
had foolishly neglected to soak them in oil. The heat
of the sun had shrunk the raw hide tight on to my feet
and made it hard as iron. But it is only when you fail
to reach the goal you set out for that raws really count.

Finally, we came down to the banks of the Erenik
and a great seven-arched stone bridge, the usual parapet-
less, steep, narrow Turkish bridge, whose bold elegance
of design makes one pardon the fact that it can be used
only by foot passengers, and is very inconvenient even
for them. The majestic height of the middle arch raises
it high above the wild floods of winter.

On the farther bank lay Djakova, golden in the
evening glow. We rode up to the priest's house, where
Marko, an old friend, was greeted heartily. Marko's
cousin, the schoolmaster, turned up at once.

After twelve hours' almost continuous travel and very
little food, I accepted gladly the orthodox cognac and

black coffee, and contemplated a rest till supper-time. But there is no coping with Albanian hospitality; the schoolmaster had flown home as soon as he had greeted us, and I was told he was ready to receive us at once. I was plastered with dust and sweat—had not washed for three days, let alone had my clothes or even my footgear off—and begged to be excused. Marko insisted that I was perfectly clean and looked beautiful. The priest humanely gave me a bowl of water and a towel, and they allowed me five minutes.

I crawled wearily over the *kaldrmi* to the schoolhouse. *Kaldrmi* is large irregular stones jammed together to make a roadway. You cannot call it pavement. There is no word in any other European language to express it. It is *kaldrmi*. When a stone is missing—I do not know how it gets out, but it does—a hole is left deep enough to break the leg of man or beast that trips into it. *Kaldrmi* is a cheap way of making a road, it never wears out, for no one ever thinks of driving or walking on it if there is any way of dodging it, but when it wanders beyond a town it is apt to be removed by folk, who build houses with it.

Luckily the schoolhouse was near. A large company was assembled, very smartly dressed, all most kindly eager to welcome me. A daughter of the house, married in Prizren, was making her first visit home since marriage, and was in full Prizren bridal dress—quite wonderful.

Her hair was parted across the back of her head, and plaited into two plaits, one upward and one downward. The lower hung down as a pigtail and was ornamented with a few coins. The upper was made into a solid block on the top of her head, standing in a point over the forehead. (This is probably the origin of the pointed headdress of the Scutarene Catholic women.) On this foundation was a mass of sham gold coins—three bands of them and a big central gold medal. The side hair was cut short in two different lengths, and greased into two solid slabs, that hung on either side of the face. Over all were seven rows of pearl beads and coins that hung in loops to the shoulders.

A zouave, a solid mass of gold embroidery, an embroidered fine white silk shirt, yards and yards of a thick silk sash, striped green and orange, wound round her till she was a huge unwieldy lump, and big white bloomers with gold ankle-pieces, made up her costume. The other ladies, in Scutari dress, laughed at her. And the schoolmaster's wife—who was *alla franga* and looked quite out of place in the picture—was held up to her as a shining example. But the Prizren bride outshone them all. Bizarre and glittering, her many dingle-dangles forced her to sit stiff and still like a Byzantine ikon, and her pallid face and dead black hair gave decorative effect to the blaze of gold and colour.

It was not till I saw her next day that I realised her costume. Then I was too tired. The hospitable *sofra* was spread with the usual chopped hard eggs, sliced melon, cheese, grapes, sweetmeats, all their best, with true Albanian liberality. And the usual spirit-drinking and snack-nibbling began, a process most painful when one is tired and wants real food. I struggled to speak Italian with the bride and the schoolmaster, and to air my weak Albanian on every one, with aching limbs and a splitting head and an empty stomach, into which politeness demanded that I should pour *rakia*. The room was suffocating. *Meze* (titbits) and *rakia* were Marko's great delight. Many Albanians indeed prefer this part of an entertainment to the meal that it precedes. And all were happy. We returned at last to the priest's house, supped, and slept.

Djakova, like most Turkish towns that are not in a stone district, is built of mud. Two or three of the lowest courses of a wall only are of stone, then follows a beam, then eight or ten courses of sun-dried bricks (*chepchi*) and another beam—all quite haphazard. If the beam be crooked, mud is bunged into the hole and the bricks are humped over all irregularities, regardless of the fact that the wall bulges. If it be too crooked to stand alone, extra supports are shoved against it. All houses are surrounded by walls, the tops of which are tiled to prevent the rain from melting them, and the eaves of all the houses project widely for a similar reason. The streets, *kaldrmi* in the middle, and a sea of mud or a bed of dust on either side, according to weather, are incomparably filthy and stinking. All the muck from the privies, and every sort of refuse, are thrown out on to any open spot—street corners and cross roads, and the river bank—and left to fester. The carcase of a dead horse rotted in the sun, while the hooded crows—the only scavengers—tore at its gaunt ribs. No windows look upon the streets, which are flanked with blank mud walls, the doors in whose gateways are often plated with iron and dinted with bullets.

Djakova was founded about four hundred years ago by two stocks from Bitush Merturi—Vula and Merturi. Of these two the Vula stock still flourishes ; our *kirijee* belonged to it. Merturi is reputed one of the oldest Albanian tribes, known in Roman times as Merituri. It is fair in type, and fair men seemed not uncommon in Djakova.

Djakova was all Christian at first, but the Vula stock perverted early. The Merturi remained Christian, but have now no representatives left in the town. Many of the neighbouring villages perverted in a block one Easter, when an Italian priest foolishly celebrated mass so early that when the villagers arrived at the town it was over. As he could not comply with their angry demand to repeat it for them, they went over to the nearest mosque.

In the town the number of Catholics has been

steadily diminishing. Twenty years ago there were still a hundred Catholic families in Djakova. Little more than twenty now remain, and of these many are not of old town stock, but recent refugees from neighbouring villages. Sixty villages still remain Catholic in the district, but have few churches and no priests. Three priests and one Franciscan, resident in Djakova, ride—often at very great personal risk—from one village to another, doing their best to aid their scattered flock. These villages are offshoots of various Christian tribes that came at different dates—from Berisha, Shala, Mirdita, &c. As the Serbs weakened in power, the Albanians surged back again over the plains from which tradition tells that they had originally come.

As I was the first traveller that had come to Djakova with Government permission for a long while, I decided to report myself and Marko, in person, at the Konak at once.

There was no Kaimmakam. The late one had belonged to the Young Turk party, but the cheery Moslems of Djakova—hearing that other towns were deposing their governors—promptly chivied him, Constitution having, to their minds, done away with the necessity of any Turkish representative. The Kaimmakam was temporarily replaced by a Bimbashi (Colonel).

The small Catholic population keeps mainly to its own quarters, and my wish to go through the town to the Konak caused much nervousness. The day after the Constitution had proclaimed a general amnesty, and it was announced that Christians were henceforth to be justly treated, a Christian had been shot dead in the bazar by a Moslem zaptieh (policeman) for no offence. His relatives had not obtained redress, and the zaptieh was unpunished. It was dreaded that Constitution was a trick for allaying the fears of the Christians and then massacring them.

A Catholic consented to guide Marko and me to the Konak, but he put on a loaded revolver before he ventured out. A crowd of Moslem boys gathered at once, and followed shouting and howling at us. Nor was it surprising, if it be true that (as I was afterwards told) I was the first quite unveiled woman that had walked through the town within any one's recollection, if ever. Marko and our guide were both horribly nervous. The latter kept his hand on the butt of his revolver all the time—to my annoyance, for under such circumstances fear should never be shown, whatever happens. I explained that lots of little London boys would jeer just as much at an Albanian woman in full dress. But this they would not believe, and hurried me along through narrow back streets, avoiding the bazar.

The Konak, a ramshackle, wood and mud building, stood in a big yard, through one of the walls of which an extra gateway had been made by simply smashing a hole. We passed through a ragged crowd of zaptiehs, suvarris. and their horses, and a general rag-tag and bobtail, and were shown up into a dingy room, where the Bimbashi, in uniform, sat *alla franga* on a chair, and the rest of the company, in native dress, squatted cross-legged on a wide seat that went all round the room. The most important—the head of the Moslem faith in Djakova— an old man in a white turban, with a long, white beard and immense white penthouse eyebrows, sat at the Bimbashi's right hand, and eyed me with marked displeasure.

The Bimbashi was very civil, but spoke no language I know. My remarks had, therefore, to be translated by Marko for the benefit of the whole company. They were all ears at once.

I showed my *teskereh*, and answered the usual questions. The Bimbashi who, as is the wont of Turkish officials, continued signing documents and giving instructions aside to various persons all the time he was conversing—(I have often wondered whether this is why Turkish affairs are always in a muddle)—expressed himself as delighted to see an English visitor. Of Djakova and neighbourhood he knew little. He reckoned that there were between two and three thousand houses in the town, but the number of inhabitants was quite unknown—a census must be taken under the new law. He was anxious to know how the conversion of England to Islam was proceeding, and regretted that press of business prevented his entertaining me at his house to discuss this question, but the laying of blood feuds, under the new *besa*, occupied him from dawn to dark. He hoped, however, to establish peace shortly.

Meaning to be polite, I wished all success to this beneficent work, and that the Constitution might spread peace and prosperity through the land.

At this the old white-beard, his eyes glaring stonily from their deep caverns, shouted something in a hoarse, deep voice. There was a general murmur. Marko looked uneasy, and interpreted: "Tell that Giaour woman it is no affair of hers. She is not to interfere in the Sultan's business. It is the Sultan's business alone. We want no Giaours."

Marko replied we had no wish to interfere; we had but agreed with what the Bimbashi said. Some one coming in on business, I rose and said good-bye to the Bimbashi, who very politely called up a zaptieh and told him to escort me back.

We passed through a crowd at the gate, who growled angrily, "We have only had this Constitution a month, and the Giaours have already begun to come."

The zaptieh hurried us back, this time through the bazar. I noticed that the numerous gunshops were heaped with Mauser cartridges. My escort was too nervous to allow me to stay—unnecessarily, I believe, for I doubt if any one would have really molested me—and we arrived back safely. The native Catholic took off his revolver with a sigh of relief, and swore that not for five pounds would he again cross the town with me.

For the past ten months things had been going from bad to worse, and the worst was now feared to be imminent.

In the previous October (1907) an Albanian Franciscan, Frate Luigi, resident in Djakova, started to ride from Djakova to Ipek, with a Moslem *kirijee*. He was captured when not far from Djakova by a large party of armed Moslems, taken to Smolitza, a Moslem village, and there imprisoned in the room of a house. No ransom was asked, but he was held as hostage for the release of a brother of one of his captors, who had been imprisoned by the Turkish Government.

The Turkish Government was at once informed, but took no step whatever. The Catholic Church in Albania is under the protection of Austria, and the Austrian Consulate at Prizren was applied to also, without result. The Frate was several times threatened with death if he would not turn Turk, to which he replied, they might kill him as soon as they liked. He was not otherwise molested, and was given enough to eat. The Catholics in the neighbourhood, exasperated, called on the Catholic mountain tribes to come to their help. A dead pig was then found in the mosque of Smolitza (this is the usual Christian way of declaring war on the Moslems), and Fra Luigi was suddenly released, after ten weeks' detention, though the man for whom he was hostage was not. No explanation of the affair has ever been forthcoming,

There was more in the affair than meets the eye, but by whom engineered we shall never know. The report, widely current in the Sanjak and Slavonic borderlands, that so soon as Austria was ready to move she would cause to be got up a massacre of Christians of sufficient magnitude to compel her to go to the rescue, and make Europe give her another mandate to "civilise" Balkan lands, occurred to my mind; more especially as in 1906 many Austrians in Bosnia had boasted to me that they meant to be in Saloniki, under the Austrian flag, by November 1909.

The pig in the mosque aroused at once an attack on the Christians. The village of Ramotzi was accused of the deed; but to this day the doer of it is not known. Nevertheless, Ramotzi was attacked, and thirty-one houses burned, with all their goods. One house was forced to surrender after forty-eight hours' siege. The defenders were promised safe-conduct, but were fired on when coming out—four killed, five wounded. In all, fourteen villages were attacked, and eighty-six houses burnt and plundered. Each contained from twenty to fifty inhabitants. When I was there, all were destitute and houseless. This went on through the spring of 1908. The Catholics were given till Ramazan (September) to turn Turk or be killed.

In Prizren also it was reported that a pig had been found in a mosque. This is believed to have been false. Even Hilmi Pasha said he did not believe it. The two men who said they had found it, declared they had at once thrown it in the river. On account of this alleged pig, a severe boycott was then started against all Catholics, who were almost reduced to starvation, and very many had to leave the town.

The worst case of persecution was that of the Bibez family at Bretkotzi. They had a group of very large houses, and great store of food and cattle. The head, though he had no quarrel with the Moslems, was told it was not seemly for a Christian to have such a large house, and that he must pull down a storey or it should be burnt. He asked the Kaimmakam for protection, and was given a hundred soldiers and some zaptiehs. He also appealed to the Austrian Consulate at Prizren.

After an anxious month, he received an ultimatum from the Moslems. He must turn Turk, or they would burn him out.

He hurried to Djakova, where the Kadi (the Kaimmakam being absent) swore to him that the soldiers should not be withdrawn, and that his goods were safe. He therefore did not remove any of them. A few days later the soldiers were suddenly all withdrawn by order of Shemsi Pasha (afterwards shot dead at Monastir), and a crowd of armed Moslems at once attacked. No lives were taken, but the entire group of houses, with the possessions of the whole family, were utterly destroyed. I made a vain attempt to draw the attention of the charitable in England to the piteous plight of these Catholic villages. The papers that had always space for the sufferings of the Orthodox in Macedonia had no corner to spare.

The people themselves thought their plight due to the European intervention in Macedonia, which had incensed the Moslems against Christians in other parts.

The aforesaid intervention did no good at all in Macedonia, and seems to have made matters worse elsewhere. It is possible that the Powers most interested intended that it should. At any rate, the English officers were carefully shoved into a corner where they could do least harm to other people's plans.

Djakova is in Kosovo vilayet. Kosovo vilayet was a most important part of the great Servian Empire of the Middle Ages. The Serb of to-day looks at it as part of his birthright, and of its recapture the young men see visions and the old men dream dreams,

Djakova, having been founded by Albanians after the fall of the Servian Empire, is naturally an Albanian town.

Of its two thousand and odd houses, but one hundred are
Serb Orthodox. These are segregated on the opposite
side of the town from the Catholics, and have little or no
communication with them. A Catholic actually told me
he had never been in the Serb quarter. The two Churches
distrust one another more than they do the Moslems.

There are no Serb villages near Djakova. But I
heard that the feast of the Assumption would be celebrated by a great concourse of people at the Serb
monastery of Devich, some twelve hours away, and
arranged to go on pilgrimage with a Serb family of
Djakova, and travel as they did, without escort, in a
native cart—a *strema*. At 3.30 A.M. it clattered into
the yard. I was asleep. It was pitch-dark. They could
not wait, I was told. "Be quick, be quick!" I
scrambled into my clothes, gulped a cup of black coffee,
threw myself unwashen and uncombed into the cart, and
we were off.

It was pouring with rain. The dawn had not yet
broken as we plunged through Djakova in the dark. I
braced my feet hard against one side of the cart, and my
back against the other. Save a little hay, it was un-
cushioned, and rocked, reeled, and rebounded over
boulders of *kaldrmi*, into yawning holes, almost falling
over on one side, only to recover and stagger on to one
wheel or the other.

Marko and I bumped together like dried peas in a
pod. We drew rein at the door of the Servian school.
Two *stremas*, full of men, women, and children awaited
us, well wedged and padded in with cushions, *dusheks*,
and *yorgans*, and heaps of coloured bundles—their best
clothes and provisions.

The chill, grey dawn broke as we drove through the
iron-plated, bullet-marked gate of the town, past stinking
heaps of refuse, unutterable filth—horses' bones—black
mud—a forlorn graveyard—the dismal barracks, with the

great wall of a dismantled building alongside melting into mud—where half-clad Nizams wandered drenched and miserable, like damnèd souls forlorn in a circle of the Inferno.

The rain cleared as we came out on to the plain—the road, as usual in these lands, bad, but considered good—boulders, mudholes, gullies, which were taken at a canter and "switchbacked." Our driver was a Serb of the heavily-built, fair, very broad-headed type, that one finds in Bosnia but never in the mountains of High Albania. He, as indeed did my travelling companions, spoke a mixture of Serb and Albanian, even to each other, and when I questioned him in Serb replied sometimes wholly in Albanian. I noticed that they never inflected their adjectives, but said " dobro, po dobro, mnogo dobro," *i.e.* good, more good, much good, for " good," " better," " best," as do the Slavs of Macedonia.

At first the plain was mostly covered with oak-scrub. Farther on were a few houses and maize-fields. It is very sparsely inhabited. It was impossible to follow our route in the Austrian staff map, it being very faulty, which is not surprising if it be true, as I was assured, that no European had been before by this track. Roughly speaking, we followed up the right bank of the White Drin to its junction with the Dechanski Bistritza, which we crossed, crossing also the Drin rather higher up. We then followed up Drin's left bank on a narrow road some ten feet above the river. Here we pulled up to ask the way of some men, and one of the *stremas* at once fell over the bank. The driver left it at the very edge ; the horses backed, and the whole thing capsized and rolled clean over, the horses and the front wheels remaining on the road above. The women screamed loudly, but as the tilt was very strong and they were well wedged in with cushions they were luckily not thrown out. Half-an-hour's repairing put all right. We left the river and struck uphill.

On the plateau on the top we found typical Servian *zadrugas*, family groups of houses enclosed in huge palisades (*palanka*). Thick stakes, some nine or ten feet high, cut into spikes at the top, are driven into the ground about eighteen inches apart. These are wattled together, not with simple withies but with twisted ropes of branches, very thick and solid. Outside, this dense wall is buttressed at short intervals with small tree trunks. The top is roofed with thick masses of blackthorn, which project so widely as to make it quite impossible for any one to climb the fence from without. Above the blackthorn project the spiked stakes. The whole mighty wooden wall is one of the most primitive types of fortification. So, in all probability, did the ancient inhabitants of Britain defend their hill encampments—as do the Serbs now—against both men and wolves.

We saw but one church and no mosque, but were told there were many Moslem families. The ruins of one old church were pointed out. Money enough had been collected to rebuild it, but the Sultan had refused permission. The families in this part mostly owned and worked the land they lived on. Further on were, for the most part, Moslem *chiftliks*. The track in many places was really good, and a proper road could easily be made.

After six hours' travel, we halted for an hour and a half at Han Zaimit, a wretched clay-built shanty which I did not enter. A scattered village not far off was called Zaimit Pes. A crowd of gypsies made their lair near the *han*. The real wild Balkan gypsies rarely bother about a tent, but crouch in the lee of any bush or bank that is near a water and fuel supply. Swarthy, scarlet-lipped, with black brilliant eyes, long heavy elf-locks of dead black hair, and unspeakably filthy, they are scorned alike by Serb and Albanian. The scorn they

return tenfold, for they hold that they are the chosen
of all races, and that none other knows how to enjoy
the gift of life. One came up and boasted that he was
the father of thirty-two children. The Serbs, not to be
outdone, told of a Serb near Ipek who is father of twenty-
four sons all by one mother, and that all are grown up and
pod oruzhja (bearing arms). To cap this we were told of
a Moslem with forty-two children, but by how many wives
was unknown. After these cheerful proofs that the
country was not depopulating, we proceeded, and lost
the way several times and were much delayed. Passing
through a village, Kopilich, we crossed a stream, Reka
Devichit, and got up into a plateau, all scrub-oak, and
topped one hummock after another without ever seeming to get any farther. On slopes below were many
palisaded *zadrugas*, some with very large houses within
them. Many were said to be Moslem. Others had
crosses on them.

The descent was awful; the driver lashed up his
horses, and, once off, we had either to smash or come to
the bottom whole, plunging at a break-neck pace down
a narrow gully over loose boulders. The terrified horses
kept their legs somehow, and landed trembling and
drenched with sweat at the bottom. As for me, I was
pitched violently across and across the *strema*. Giddy
with concussion I alighted, joined the stream of pilgrims,
and ascended on foot to the monastery in the oak forest
above—a mass of irregular white buildings that scrambled
at different heights haphazard round three yards.

We passed through the lower yard with a seething
mass of pilgrims, and went straight into the church on
one side of it. It was about 5 P.M. The tiny church
was dark, and crammed with people. My appearance
created the greatest excitement. As I passed the side
where all flocked to light tapers, the glare fell on me,
and I was at once surrounded, seized upon, and fingered

all over by an eager crowd.   My hat, my kodak, my bag
all were examined; how much money was in it? from
what vilayet was I? who was I? my name?—all regardless of the service which was in full swing.   A man in
European dress—the monastery secretary—hurried to the
centre of hubbub, learnt that I was English, and dashed
off to inform the officiating priests.

The heat was suffocating, and the fingering and pulling about more than I wanted after the twelve hours'
jolting drive.

I left the church.   Opposite it stood the house of the
Archimandrite, or Hagi as they called him here.   A steep
flight of wooden steps led to a perfect rabbit-warren of
pilgrims' rooms which were reached through a narrow door
about four feet high.   Beyond, a huge, white-washed,
three-storeyed hospitium—with the usual big wooden balcony to each floor—surrounded two sides of a large yard.
Below, on one side, was a smaller yard surrounded by
stables.   The whole was an indescribable confusion—a
seething mass of pilgrims, babies, bundles, sacks, and
rugs filled the entire space of the two yards, and each
balcony and staircase, some seeking rooms, others camp-
ing where they were, all in search of some one or something—a deafening babel of voices.   The third yard was
a struggling tangle of packhorses, carts, draught-oxen,
and buffaloes, and their owners.   And no matter what
any one was doing, they left off to come and examine me.
The monastery servants, who preserved their wits wonderfully in the confusion, allotted a tiny room to our
party, and I crowded into it with my Serb fellow-travel-
lers, who proceeded to furnish it with their cushions and
coverlets.

The Hagi himself visited me, so soon as he had
concluded service in the church.

He was a tall, fair, handsome man, very friendly,
and much relieved to find I understood Serb.   Marko,

who knows but little, asked him if he understood Albanian.

He laughed heartily, and replied, " I am an Albanian." Born of Albanian parents, he explained he had spoken Albanian only as a child. But having joined the Ortho- dox Church, he was now a Servian, and Servian was more familiar to him than his mother tongue.

So is it in the Debatable Lands. The Serbs have a converted Albanian as head of their monastery, and conversely, one of the most patriotic Albanian priests at Djakova was a Serb by birth—had spoken Serb only as a child, and now had almost forgotten it.

The Hagi at once said I was to be his guest. The Metropolitan of Prizren was there with some Servian schoolmistresses from Prishtina, and we should all be a party together. No foreigner, so far as he knew, had ever been to Devich with the exception of one Russian Consul—the good man was almost as excited over me as were the pilgrims. I came forth from the very temporary rest in the little room, and was introduced. To my amaze- ment I found I was celebrated. Some one recognised me as having been in Dechani five years ago. " Ah, it is the Balkan Englishwoman, the friend of the Monte- negrins ! " The Metropolitan knew all about me — a schoolmistress, lately from Saloniki, retailed my Mace- donian career. We had supper on the terrace under a pergola. Fast day—but an excellent meal of river-trout, tomato salad, balls of rice and herbs rolled in vine leaves (*japrak*), and green paprikas stuffed with rice and fright- fully hot. Plenty of *kaimak* (clotted cream), sheep- cheese, and fruit. It was the merriest party. You reached out and helped yourself to whatever was handy, and made the same plate do. And above, around, and beneath us was one vast picnic.

Rations were served out all hot from the kitchen, the air was heavy with the fumes of roast and baked, all food was gratis, and each had as much as he liked. People ran hither and thither with steaming bowls and trays. Save ourselves at the high table, every one fed off vessels of solid copper, tinned, of which the monastery had enough for the two thousand and more pilgrims.

It is characteristic of the Balkan man, be he Slav or Albanian, that he can enjoy himself thoroughly and whole-heartedly, without ever becoming rowdy or losing his self-respect. There was no one to keep order among this vast concourse of happy people, nor was any one required. It is to be hoped that what is called civilisation may never reduce them to the barbarous level of 'Arry and 'Arriet on Bank holiday. I was told off to sleep with the schoolmistresses, and we retired at 10.30, for which—having been on a pretty constant strain since 3 A.M., and having finished up with talking Servian all the evening, having had no practice for over a year—I was not sorry.

It was a small room, the floor entirely covered with mattresses. There were a great many of us. They kindly gave me the only bedstead. Unfortunately, however, one of the ladies was married, and her son and husband shared our room. So though I had a bedstead, it was impossible to go to bed in it properly. Fortunately, the only window was just above me, and I opened it surreptitiously.

The schoolmarms, declaring sleep was impossible, began to dance the *kolo*, but I was asleep from sheer exhaustion before they had done.

It was but a short sleep, for, suddenly, in plunged the *djakon*, telling us to get up and come to church. I wearily looked at my watch. It was 1 A.M. Only three ladies went. I slept again. In came the *djakon* again, this time to get medicine out of a drawer near my head. The floor being covered with sleepers, this made no end of commotion. At five, again the *djakon*—this time to do his hair! And then the Hagi for something or other. Further sleep was impossible.

My stable companions used a common comb. I was the proud possessor of a private one. I went out dirty, sticky, and staggering with sleep, and asked if it were possible to wash. When the Metropolitan was up, I could have his basin. Not before.

The great man having emerged, I was conducted to his washstand, and a serving-man poured two table-spoonfuls of water over my hands, which I rubbed on my face in the approved style — and my toilet was complete.

Outside, coffee was being served at the kitchen door (no food, of course). It waked me at once. I turned to the marvellous scene.

And it was truly marvellous—such costumes as I had never seen before and may never see again—many of them indeed museum pieces, all the best of every district.

The finest of all were from Ipek Caza. Ipek itself is almost entirely Moslem Albanian, the Serbs and Catholics form but a small minority; the villages around, however, are very largely Serb, and form a Serb island in an otherwise Albanian land.

The women's shirts are a mass of the very finest cross-stitch embroidery in dull red, blue, and green, the colours all native dyes. Cross-stitch (very common in Russia) is Slavonic and does not occur on Albanian costume. It makes, of necessity, angular patterns. Albanian patterns are all of flowing lines adapted for braiding and gold thread. The flowing line is similarly found on old Albanian carved chests and ceilings.

Over the richly-embroidered shirt is a very short petti-coat—a mere waist-frill some 12 inches deep—of striped material, the stripes being almost always all hand-work in the finest stitches. A very broad binder is bound round the lower part of the body like an abdominal support.

Over this is a heavy, leathern belt, with brass plaques on it studded with red and green "jewels" of glass, the workmanship poor. On the shoulders is a zouave of various colours, usually black, with scarlet or yellow braid. The breast is quite covered with a mass of large silver coins—Maria Theresas—and numbers of glass bead and coral necklaces and crosses, and hearts of glass like those popular in Bosnia. Some wore triangular leather amulet-cases on a string slung over one shoulder.

The married women wear a peaked head-dress, similar to that of mediæval ladies, but smaller. It is of white linen, with a finely embroidered edge in various colours, the ends hang down to the shoulders; over the top of the head, and hanging either side to the ear, is a broad band of turquoise-blue beads ending in a triangular dingle-dangle.

The hair is parted in the middle, and again lower down. The top section is twisted round a solid foundation to make a huge curl, a great sausage of hair stiff with grease, which curves forward on each side of the face, framing

Serb woman of Ipek Caza carrying cradle on her back.

it completely. The end of the curl is sewn with coins—it is a head-dress that is made to last—sometimes as many as five Maria Theresas on each, and to make all firm both curls are sewn down to a leather band which goes under the chin, and is thickly covered with blue beads. Such of the hair as is not used for the curl is plaited and used as a support behind the curl to which it is fastened. The whole makes a solid block of hair—grotesque and extraordinary; at least so I thought till I came back to England and found every one's head swollen to double its size with stuffings, frizettes, and "transformations."

I had just started drawing, and was getting on well, when one of the schoolmarms espied me. With the best of intentions in the world she summoned everybody to see what I was doing, and all my chances were over. I was the centre of a mob all striving to see me do it again, and attention being turned on me, I was hunted all day. Every peasant wanted to speak to me, and most of them did; I was questioned till I was on the point of exhaustion, and all the time I had a ridiculous feeling that it was a case of the biter bit. For months I had been incessantly questioning about manners and customs, now I was myself the victim. I was asked about all that I did, and then "why?" The thing that bothered everybody was my straw hat; they had never seen one before; "Why do you wear wheat on your head?" Every one broke a little bit off the brim to make sure it really was "wheat."

"Do you wear it in the house?" "Do you sleep in it?" "Do you wear it to show you are married?" "To show you are not married?" "Did you make it?" "Are all the women in your vilayet (province) obliged to wear wheat on their heads?" "Is there a law about it?" "Or do you wear it *per chef* (for pleasure)?"

"I wear it because of the sun," said I desperately. "Why because of the sun?" "It is hot," said I. "No, it isn't," said they. They did not wear wheat because of the sun. Would I tell them the real reason? It occurred to me that if there was a Devich Anthropological Society it might report that it had found traces of sun-worship in the English, and mysterious rites connected with it that no questioning could elicit. I fell back on the answer that has so often tried me in others: "I wear it because I do. It is *nash obichaj* (our custom)."

This satisfied them wholly, for there is a proverb which says: "It is better that a village should fall than a custom." The brim of my hat looked as though it had been gnawed by rats all round, and I felt justified in pulling every one about mercilessly in return, and examining all their ornaments; but it was very fatiguing—on an empty stomach.

Two gypsy bands played incessantly, both at once. One instrument was a cylinder of earthenware with a piece of hide strained on the top, and slapped with the hand; another was a big drum. The sun was nearly at full strength, the air was thick with the dust of many dancing feet; the perpetual pom-pom-pom, rhythmical, insistent, throbbed like a fever pulse in the sizzling heat. Only for one half-hour, when a service was held in the yard outside the church (it was far too small to hold the congregation), did the band stop, and then there was singing.

Midday brought the much-needed dinner in the Metropolitan's room. I sat next to him, and was excellently well fed. But even the meal was a long and stiff *viva voce* examination in Servian. His Grace was pleased to express his admiration for the physical strength of the English. He himself, for example, though he had not had such a long and exhausting journey as I had, and accustomed to the country, was quite tired out!

After dinner all went to rest. I had two hours' heavy sleep in the crowded room of the night before. Then we were all poked up. Tumblers of water were passed round; Serbs are always water-thirsty. I amused every one highly by pouring mine over my head and neck.

Thus roused I went out again, and, as the first excitement about me had somewhat subsided, managed to get some photographs and drawings made.

Then a long strip of mats and carpets was laid right across the yard. The Hagi, his secretary, and some monks sat on cushions at one end, and I was invited to join them. A number of heads of families then sat in a long row, cross-legged, on either side the carpet. *Rakia* and the usual snacks were served all round. Each man in turn came up, kissed the Hagi's hand, and made an offering to the church—from a few piastres to a pound Turk, and the secretary inscribed each in a book. They were nearly all townsfolk from Prizren, Prishtina, Ipek, and Mitrovitza. The peasants had already left or were leaving. It was a very long job; about a hundred and fifty napoleons were collected.

Then came gifts in kind, brought for the most part by women—shirts, drawers, towels, and sheets, and handkerchiefs, many finely embroidered in colours and gold.

Almost all these town women were dressed *alla Turka*, had their hair dyed black, and their eyebrows joined by paint in the middle. One in particular wore a magnificent white satin overcoat (*koret*) brocaded with silver and stiff with raised silver embroidery—another, an equally fine one, of crimson velvet and gold. The apron, usually worn over the large bloomers, was of wonderfully fine silk tissue, embroidered in colour and gold. Native eye for colour, when let alone, rarely goes wrong, but alas, "civilisation" is working sad havoc, and hideous parrots and bunches of flowers in Berlin wool-work (as taught in the schools) were among the most admired of the offerings to the Church. The curse of "made in Germany" is already withering the land. The bad beginning, may be, of a bad end.

Supper was late. I was dog-tired, nor was there any corner where I could sit at peace. By this time two women from Andrijevitza, in Montenegro, two from Berani, a man from Ipek, and a young monk from the monastery of Miloshevo, in the *sanjak* of Novi-bazar, had

all recognised and claimed acquaintance with me, and I
sent greetings to all friends in each place.

It was strange, in the heart of the wilderness, to find
so many that knew me.

The *djakon* took me to see the monastery library of
old Slavonic church-books, both in print, from early
presses, and in manuscript. They had been shockingly
neglected, and, unluckily, no perfect copies remained of
books that, even in their battered state, are of considerable value. It is possible that among the litter missing
pages might be found. I begged that all that remained
should be carefully preserved.

When it got quite dark, I sat on a stone by the wall,
and got a rest for a few minutes. Then I was poked up
to drink cognac with the Metropolitan. I would, by that
time, gladly have drunk a quart. It kept me up till
supper. Then we turned out again to see the *kolo*
danced round bonfires, and sing national songs. We
turned in at 11.30, I with orders to be ready to start
at 3.30 A.M.

I seemed scarcely to have fallen asleep when the head
of the Serb party I had come with knocked at the door.
The carts were ready.

I collected my coat, belt, and boots, and crawled out
over the sleeping schoolmarms into the chilly night air,
reeling with sleep.

We swallowed our ration of coffee, and were soon off.
The Serbs kindly lent us two sacks, which we stuffed full
of hay, so that we were not so badly shaken on the
return journey. The women of the Serb party reproached
me with not having come to sit with them in their room
in the monastery. I was sorry, for I felt that I had not
been polite to them, and they meant most kindly. But
all spare time—and it was not much—I had used in
getting the opinion of as many different people as
possible on the Constitution.

We arrived safely at Djakova about 6 P.M., said good-bye to our Serb friends at the entrance, and drove through the town, followed by a hooting, howling mob of Moslem boys, who hung on to the cart and poked up the cover with sticks—Marko and the driver very vexed and nervous, but bad words break no bones.

We found the priests as tired as we were. They had been out in the villages all the time we had been away. Typhoid had broken out in them. Water, on account of the drought, was scarce and bad, and all provisions short as a result of the recent persecutions. I could only prescribe complete rest, cleanliness, and a slop diet, and vainly strove to prevent the administering of the filthy local remedy—dogs' dung that has been dropped on a stone in the sun, powdered and given in water. Marko and one of the priests had absolute faith in it. They each knew cases which had survived it, and were reckoned as cures.

And I learnt that the only emetic known to the Albanian pharmacopœia is human excrement and water— given in all cases of supposed poisoning ; and that the remedy for dipsomania is the same, mixed with rakia.

So ended a weary day.

The Moslems of Djakova did not seem pleased with the Constitution, did not desire Turkish interference, and certainly objected to the visit of a Giaour. Subsequently I heard that there had been much talk about me, and that the Catholics were told that it was a good thing they had not harboured me a day longer.

The Christians, both Orthodox and Catholic, had not the smallest hope or faith in the Constitution.

Devich Monastery was founded after the great defeat of the Serb nation at Kosovo, and dates from the time of George of Smederevo (*ob.* 1457), who ruled a restricted Servia under Turkish suzerainty.

At that time the great emigration of Serbs to

Hungary had not taken place, and the population must have been mainly Serb. The gathering at the monastery was unusually large, owing to the temporary peace. The very large majority were from Ipek caza, more than half of the whole gathering. And there, I was assured, was the largest Serb population. Near Djakova there was none. Those I questioned were much disappointed that the Government was to remain Turkish—had hoped for foreign intervention. They did not want a Turkish Government, because then the land would never be theirs. They wanted to own the land themselves, and not work on chiftliks. All Turkish Governments had been bad, and this would be also.

The Moslems of Ipek had not accepted the Constitution, and vowed they would accept no law that would interfere with their rights. The Serbs round Berana (part of the Vasojevich tribe) were very much disappointed about the Constitution. They did not want to be any more under any Turkish Government.

The report that in future they were all to be called Ottomans enraged Serb and Albanian alike. It was all another trick to keep them under the Turks. The Christian Powers ought not to permit it. At present all agreed it "was like a dream," but they expected a rude awakening, and the Serbs, regardless of the fact that in most places they are much in the minority, still had visions of the expulsion of all Moslems, and the reconstruction of the great Servian Empire.

I passed the rest of my time in the Catholic quarter. Djakova has always been renowned for its silver-workers. It is an interesting fact that throughout North Albania almost all silver-work is by Christians, and the trade is hereditary in families. The designs are therefore in all probability genuine Albanian, deriving from pre-Turkish times. In Djakova, Prizren, Prishtina, and Mitrovitza, I found all silver-workers Christians.

As might be expected, Djakova revels in the supernatural, and miraculous happenings are frequent. In a mountain-side hard by, on the left of the road to Prizren, is a magic cavern. For miles does it go underground; none knows how far, some say even beneath the Drin. In it is a large and ancient city where no man now lives; but the bazar, to this very day, is stocked with all that is finest and best—fruit, flesh, fish, jewels, and fair raiment. But should any man venture to touch one single thing, his torch at once goes out, serpents spring up and devour him in the darkness. And these are no serpents; they are *oras* (spirits) that guard the cavern. No man has ventured in for many years.

I said I would, and asked to be guided to the spot, but none dared take me. Nor is this the sole spot that is miraculously guarded.

Not far from Djakova, on a hill, are the ruins of a chapel. A Moslem tried to dig there for treasure, but was at once struck dead by lightning out of a cloudless sky. Not sufficiently warned, some men went to remove stones for building purposes, but a crowd of serpents at once leapt from the ground, and the intruders only just escaped. For *oras* can take what form they please—birds, beasts, women, or serpents.

Quite recently a man was driving past with an ox-cart, when both the oxen fell on their knees before the ruins; and the holiness of the spot being now proved beyond all doubt, none dare meddle with it in future.

As for tales of adventure, enough could be collected to fill a volume. Here is the tale of a wedding that took place some thirty years ago :—

THE TALE OF THE UGLY BRIDE.

There was a young man in a village near Djakova. His father was dead. He lived with his mother and

sister. Oh, how ugly his sister was! She was not engaged as a baby—town customs differ from mountain
ones—and they really did not know how to get her
married. Of course they never showed her; but somehow, when a girl is very ugly, every one knows.

One day the young man went to Prizren on business.
There he met a Prizren youth, They made great friends
at once, and each confided to the other that he was fairly
well-to-do and wished to marry shortly.

" I will give you my sister ! " cried he of Prizren.

The family lived in a village near Prizren, and was a
desirable one to be connected with, so the Djakovan
accepted at once. " And I," said he, " will give you my
own dear sister in exchange ! "

It was settled. Away went each home, highly pleased.
But the Prizren mother was no fool.

" What do you know about this girl? " she asked.
" Wait a while. I will go and see her."

Off went the old lady on a horse. When the Djakovan
mother saw her, she knew quite well what brought her.
" Leave it to me," she said to her son. Quickly she ran
next door, and invited her neighbour's pretty daughter to
come into the garden.

In came Mother Prizren. Mother Djakova received
her nobly, with coffee and sweetmeats. They exchanged
compliments, but the rules of good society prevented
Mother Prizren from asking to see her future daughter-
in-law. Finally, she was shown the garden and saw the
pretty girl in it. Home she went and reported favourably. The bride was duly fetched and the wedding celebrated. When all was over, the expectant bridegroom
raised the veil and saw his ugly bride. Furious, he
vowed that he would never give his own pretty sister to
the Djakovan in return. But that wedding also was
fixed, and on the appointed day the Djakovan's bride
leaders—thirty gallant men, armed and in their best—

rode to the river half-way between the two villages to meet and fetch the bride. And no bride was there. They waited. Time was passing. If the bride did not come soon, it would be too late to get home that night. Two of the elders of the bridegroom's family crossed the river, and hastened to the bride's house. Arrived at the door, the chief drew his yataghan, and hammered on it with the hilt.

" What do you want ? "

" I've come for the bride."

" Go away. There is no bride here."

" You give me that bride, or I'll cut your heart out."

"There's no bride here, I tell you ! "

"There is."

"There isn't."

"They called down curses on one another and hurled insults : "*Ken e bir kenit*" (Dog and son of a dog).

The Djakovan thundered blows upon the door and delivered his ultimatum :

" I'll burn your house—I'll cut your liver out. You give me that bride, or I'll fetch up thirty men and we'll burn the whole village down."

The Prizren youth escaped by the back door and hurried to the head of the village. "Two men have come, and want to steal my sister," he said.

" Two ! Drive them away."

" But they say thirty will come and burn down the village."

" Thirty ! Have you promised her ? "

" Yes ; but——" He tried to explain.

" Can't help that. I can't have the village burnt because of your sister. You promised her. Hand her over at once."

Back he went.

" Look here, you shall have her all right, but not

to-day. She isn't ready. Her hair isn't dyed black yet.
She——"

"Oh, you go along! There is plenty of hair-dye in
our place. Bring her out, or I'll fetch up the others!"

And brought out she was. And so the Djakovan
acquired a beautiful bride and got rid of his ugly sister.

Serb Women of Ipek Caza.

CHAPTER X

PRIZREN

" Onamo, onamo,
Da vidju Przren ! "

(Onward, onward, let me see Prizren.)

—H.R.H. Nikola, of Montenegro.

THE first *strema* we had engaged to take us to Prizren was requisitioned by a Moslem Bey at the last moment. We got off, finally, one morning at 8.30 A.M.

The road, quite a decent one, followed up the left bank of the Erenik as far as Ura Terzijit (the Tailors' Bridge)—a grand stone bridge of eleven arches—said to have been built three hundred years ago by the tailors of Djakova and Prizren.

Fording the river, we drove up the right bank, and struck across to the White Drin. Erenik joins Drin through a narrow gully, where a hill arises from the plain, and is spanned by a lofty bridge of one large arch, Ura Fshait. Our driver suddenly loaded his Martini, and rushed off to shoot at two wild-geese on the river. It proved a wild-goose chase.

We drove along the plain, on Drin's right bank, passing on our left a Moslem village, Djurtha, and on our right another, Ragova, both with mosques. Fording Drin, we halted at midday at Han Krusha, a newly-built inn of mud bricks, whose Moslem owners were most civil. Then on over land that was fairly cultivated and looked fertile—maize, corn, and tobacco—and through Pirona, a large Moslem village, up over rising ground, and there lay Prizren in the valley below, with the ruins of an old castle and the white walls of modern barracks on the height beyond.

Fortune was favouring me beyond my deserts. Prizren was another of my dream cities, and I beheld it with my waking eyes.

Prince Nicholas' song—the song that enshrines in a few verses the Great Servian Idea—the song that every Serb school-child knows, "Onward, onward, let me see Prizren," rang in my memory. I had seen the tribesmen of Montenegro sing it with tears in their eyes. I had heard it secretly sung in Bosnia, where it is forbidden by the Austrian Government.

After the Russian-Turkish war, when the beaten Turk had to yield to Europe's demands, the dearest hope of the Serb people was that Prizren, the heart of the old Servian Empire, the capital of Tsar Dushan, would shortly again be theirs.

Pondering all these things, we clattered into the town.

Prizren is a large town, and highly picturesque. It lies both sides of the Prizrenski Bistritza (a tributary of the Drin), and sprawls up the mountain-side, from which spirt and gush numberless streams of clear, cold water. The water supply is quite amazing, and the river would be a considerable size were it not diverted into three channels at different levels, which supply the town and work mills.

The streets are very fairly clean, and the town full of life and activity.

But even the best friend of the Serbs must admit that it is a Moslem Albanian town. The Servian Metropolitan had already lamented to me that the Serbs were in a considerable minority, but I had not expected to find them such a mere drop in the ocean.

The census just made under the Constitution gives:

Moslem houses	3500
Servian houses (with 4320 inhabitants) . .	950
Catholic Albanian houses	180
Vlah houses	180

In the case of the Christians, I believe these figures
to be fairly correct. The Prizren Moslems, already
alarmed at the rumour that Constitution meant loss of
privilege to them, and determined not to be compelled
to give military service, were said to have understated
the number of their houses and to have refused to give
the number of inhabitants. It could be reckoned, I was
told, at ten to a house.

Of the Moslems, some are genuine Ottoman Turks,
settled since early days, but the bulk are Albanian.

Each nation that designs to pick up the pieces, when
Turkey in Europe bursts up, keeps a Consul on the spot.
A Russian represents Slav interests, to claim the land as
Old Servia.   An acute Austrian is posted there to forward
his country's plan of " Advance, Austria," and Italy has
had to plant a man to see what he is doing. The Moslem
Albanian objects to the presence of all of them, and the
Turkish Government impartially gives them all armed
escort. There is something truly pathetic about the way
Turkey, everywhere, carefully protects the gentlemen
whose only *raison d'être* is to hasten the dismemberment
of the land.

Servia sent a Consul some years ago; but he was
almost immediately forced to withdraw by the populace.

Of one thing the populace is determined: that is,
that never again shall the land be Serb.

The Moslem Albanian's game, here as elsewhere, had
been to support the Turkish Government in order to keep
out others, and he was already growling sullenly at the
Constitution, as offering equality to Christian Slavs, and
therefore threatening Albanian power.

The leading Serbs of the town kindly invited me to stay at a private house, but, as I did not wish to be attached to any political party, and meant to see life in general, I stayed at an inn, where folk of all sorts came to drink.

September 1st saw all the streets gay with flags, tissue-paper chains and fans, for the Sultan's accession day. I called, at the correct hour, at the Seralio. Over the entrance gate is a great wooden star, the rays of varying length, with tiny crescent moons on their tips (is it really the sun and moon?). The yard was full of Nizams, gendarmes, and officials in their best. Upstairs, the Vali-Pasha, gorgeous with medals and decorations, was receiving in state.

The Consuls were present in uniform. The police officer, who showed dirty ragged me in, said that the Vali-Pasha spoke Serb. He turned out to be a Herzegovinian from Trebinje. We got on beautifully. He had expected me before. Scutari had warned him of my approach. Had heard of me from Djakova, and sent suvarris to meet me, but I had disappeared. I explained I had been to Devich in a cart, without escort. I relied on the *besa*, and wanted no escorts. He hastened to say that peace and prosperity were established for evermore. I congratulated the Sultan, and was given a glass of pink syrup.

The Vali-Pasha was amazed at the route I had chosen. I could have come in comfort, he said, by steamer from Scutari to Saloniki, thence by rail, quite *alla franga*, to Ferizovich, and driven in a carriage to Prizren. For himself, he never went up country unless obliged—I never found a Turkish governor that did. The wild-cat methods of the English were beyond him. I might go where I pleased, but "sooner you than I" was his attitude.

Having thus advertised to authority the confidence

which the British Empire put in the new order of things,
I did not expound my private opinion, which was then,
that the Turkish Empire was playing possibly the first
scene of the last act of its tragic existence, but withdrew.
And unluckily just missed a farcical interlude, for the
chief accountant, accused of embezzling public funds,
was attacked and chivied from the town with a petroleum
can on his head.

It was a general holiday, bands pom-pommed all
night. The heat was intense, and sleep impossible. I
did not get to the bazar till 7.30 A.M. next morning, a
scandalously late hour in these lands.

It is a grand bazar. Worth all the journey, for as
yet it is but little spoiled with *alla franga*. The gold
embroidery is not to be surpassed anywhere; the tailors'
shops are a blaze of gorgeous colour and design. Had it
not been for the difficulties of transport, I should have
ruined myself. As for the carved walnut-wood frames
inlaid with silver, they are the finest work of the kind I
have seen anywhere. It was in Prizren in the olden
days that the finest artists in gold and silver inlay
flourished, and turned out yataghans and gunbarrels fit
for fairy princes, and from thence they spread into
Bosnia. The so-called Bosnian inlay is mainly of
Albanian origin, and much of it actually Albanian
handicraft.

The demand for very fine work is now slight—*alla
franga* will maybe soon kill it—but there are still in
Prizren workmen who can execute it.

The main trade is in rough and cheap ornaments for
the peasants. The silver-workers are all Christian.

I wandered up and down and in and out the long
wooden tunnels of the bazar streets, dark with hot, rich
shadow, glowing with goods.

Gentian root and iris root are heaped at the herbalists',
black nuts for the black hair-dye of the Christians and

logwood for the red of the Moslems, henna for the palms and finger-nails. Three-cornered amulets sewn up in velvet, strings of dried bamias for stewing, *jeleks* and *djemadans* richly embroidered with thick orange silk cord, horse-trappings with scarlet tassels, and gay saddle-bags.

Out in the big open spaces, in a glory of golden light, were piled tons of grapes, peaches, melons, pumpkins, gourds, glowing heaps of scarlet and orange tomatoes, shiny paprikas, yellow, green, and red, black purple patajans (aubergines), long green bamias, cabbage, lettuces, beans, in Arabian Nights profusion. Then I heard the East a-calling, and cried in my heart, as I thought of the Powers that crouched like beasts of prey upon the frontier ready to spring and shatter this world :—

> "Confound their politics,
> Frustrate their knavish tricks."

I remembered the words of an old Albanian, spoken long before Constitution days : "The Turkish Empire is an old house, decayed and crumbling. It is propped within and without, and will stand for who knows how long. But if any one tries to repair it, and moves but one prop —but one brick even—it will fall about his ears. It is too late to repair it." And the peace that reigned in the bazar seemed the hush before the storm.

"Constitution justice" was much discussed. On one of the festival days to celebrate the Constitution, a Moslem zaptieh had made an attempt on a Christian maiden for which he had been condemned to be flogged so severely that he died the next day. Encouraged by this, a Serb zaptieh had then arrested a Moslem for theft, and had been expelled from the town and the service. Serb zaptiehs were only to arrest Christians. A Moslem who had shot a man at Mitrovitza had been hanged at once without trial. This afforded satisfaction to the

Christians, until it transpired that the shooting was really a pure accident, then the Moslems were enraged. The Young Turks were suffering from *trop de zèle*.

Next day I was to dine at the Servian Bogoslovia (Theological School) at noon. At 10.30 in rushed Marko, "You will not be able to dine with the Serbs. There is a revolution!" I rushed out to see. The alarm had already been given. In ten minutes every shop was shut and barred, and all the Moslems fully armed were rushing down the street to the Seralio, led by Sherrif Effendi, a very popular Hodja, acclaimed as their head by the Moslems of Prizren and Ljuma.

The armed crowd swung down the street in a pack, like wolves on the trail—a far finer show than the few ragged Nizams that followed. The air was full of rumours. Sherrif was said to be responsible for the expulsion of the Serb zaptieh. He and his were prepared to defend the Sheriat (Turkish law) at any price, and would tolerate no privileges for the Christians. They returned shortly, satisfied that no immediate attempt would be made on it.

The fact that the whole population can turn out under arms within ten minutes gives an idea of the possibilities of the town. Like a couchant tiger, brilliant, bizarre, and beautiful, it is ever ready to spring. Unlike the tiger, it is industrious. Having decided not to revolute further, for the time being, the whole crowd was at work again at the various primitive manufactures of the place, shops reopened, and eating-houses in full swing in another hour's time.

I went off to the Servian Bogoslovia. The Director, his wife, and three children were recently arrived from Belgrade. They received me with the greatest hospitality; were afraid the revolution would prevent my coming. The poor lady, terrified of the Albanians, was amazed to hear I had been out to see it.

The school, a fine building, recently enlarged and repaired, holds a hundred students. Many come from Montenegro even. I went over it sadly. It seemed sheer folly to make a large and costly Serb theological school in a Moslem Albanian town, and to import masters and students, when funds are so urgently needed to develop free Serb lands.

The white castle of Tsar Lazar was but a dream in the night of the past. Around us in the daylight was the Albanian population, waiting, under arms, to defend the land that had been theirs in the beginning of time.

An old Bariaktar, eighty years of age, in the mountains, had, but a few weeks before, told me how Prince Nikola, flushed with victory, at the close of the war in 1877, had said to him: "You and I will live to see my flag float over Prizren!" "And neither he nor I will ever live to see it," said the old man.

We sat down to a regular Serb dinner, the first I had eaten for more than a year—*kiselo chorba* (sour soup), fried chicken paprika, *kiselo mleko* (sour milk), all excellent of its kind. The Director knew all about me, and regarded me as the champion of the Serbs in England. I accepted his hospitality unhappily, for I felt that, so far as Prizren and its neighbourhood were concerned, the cause was lost, dead and gone—as lost as is Calais to England, and the English claim to Normandy. And the mere terror of his wife showed how completely she felt herself a stranger in an unknown land. Yet I could not but admire the imaginative nature of the Serb, who will lead a forlorn hope and face death for an idea.

And—for I do not know the how manyeth time—I cursed the Berlin Treaty, which did not award to this people the truly Serb lands of Bosnia and the Herzegovina, where they could have gathered their scattered forces and developed, but gave them to be crushed under Austria.

I left the poor little Serb quarter—the houses clustered on the hillside around the two churches (for there is an old and a new one), and the school—and found Marko waiting me without. He is the worthiest and kindliest of souls, but race instinct, that strongest of all human passions, prevails—he does not like the Shkia (Slav).

The real policy of Serb and Albanian should be to unite, and keep the foreign intruders from the Balkan Peninsula. But this will never be.

Poor Marko would never admit to me that there were any Serbs in Prizren. "What is that man?" I would ask.

"A native."

"What do you mean by a native?"

"He was born here."

"Yes, but is he a Serb or Albanian?"

"Lady, there are no Serbs here. This is an Albanian town."

Further pressed, he would admit: "Perhaps he belongs to that schismatic Church. I know nothing about his religion." And this, though Serb costume and speech were unmistakable.

Of early Servian days, naught now remains but the ruins said to be those of Tsar Dushan's white tower. I went in search of them up the valley of the Prizrenski Bistritza (called also Kara Potok), along the foot of the hill on which the fortress stands, and through a suburb (Kirch Bonar). We left the town behind us, and followed the lonely valley. Below us, men were collecting stones for building—poking them out of the half-dried bed of the stream with crowbars, and loading them on packhorses, which filed off to the town. The stones, I was told, were thus obtained "ready made," and all trouble of blasting and hewing saved. But the time spent in levering up one stone, and the impossibility of loading up more than about a dozen large ones on a pack-saddle, made the labour and loss of time quite appalling.

About half-an-hour up the valley, it turns suddenly, and the rocky crag on which stand the remains of Dushan's castle comes into view, rising isolated in a ring of mountains, the great Shar Planina rising up behind. Lonely and ruined, only a wall or two and some frag-ments remain of the white tower of the ballads—as wrecked as his Empire. Here he sat, and drank red wine with his Voyvodas. Hence he rode with a great army to sway the fortunes of the Balkans.

I turned from the desolate "*sic transit*" spot, and, returning down the valley, found the women of Prizren on the river bank, bleaching hand-woven linen in the sun, and sprinkling it with fresh spring water, as they have done doubtless since the days of Dushan.

I decided that the best way of seeing Kosovo plain would be to drive over it with a Serb driver, the man that drove us to Devich. Leaving most of my scanty possessions with the *hanjee* till I returned, we left Prizren at 4.20 A.M., in a cold dawn—a lemon-yellow gash above the horizon marking where the sleepy sun would soon arise, as we drove through a large Moslem graveyard that lay desolate on either hand.

The first village of any size was Korisha, all Christian, consisting partly of Serbs and partly of Roman Catholic Albanians from Fandi. Above it, up a valley on the right, is a large Serb church, Sveti Marko.

On, past scattered groups of houses within stockades, land cultivated with maize and tobacco, across the little river Sofina, and over a low range of hills, we went, and descended to Suha Reka (*lit.* dry river), a large village which, in spite of its Serb name, is now, according to the Serb driver, all Moslem Albanian. A black and white mass of magpies was feasting on the stinking carcase of a horse at the entrance, and rose screaming as we passed.

We crossed the stream (by no means a dry river) on a wooden bridge. Then we ascended again, and drove over a great plateau of scrub-oak. On the left, we passed Pechanj, a Moslem village, and Dulje, consisting of stockaded groups on either side of the road. The road was actually being re-made ; men were working on it in three places, and new stone bridges were being built. What was done was really very good ; of the rest, the less said the better. We passed over Chafa Duljash, and descended into the beautiful wooded valley of the Crnoleva, and halted for midday at Han Crnoleva, an Albanian house. The place-names, it will be noted, are all Serb. The driver, himself a Serb, said regretfully that everywhere the majority of the population is Albanian.

We descended the valley, rich with beech forests on either side, to Stimlje, a very large village, whence the main road leads to Ferizovich and the railway. There spread out, burnt, and parched before us for miles and miles, was Kosovo-polje, the fatal field on which the Turks gained the victory that established them, even to this day, in Europe—the Armageddon of the Servian people.

"Kosovo-polje," said the Serb briefly. It summed up all the fate of his race. In the spring every year, he added, all the unploughed land is covered with blood-red flowers that grow in memory of the fight ; they are sent by God.

We struck across the great plain, uncultivated, desolate, and undulating ; the parched turf was split into yawning cracks by the drought, the scrub hawthorn burnt brown, the track dusty, and we reached the Sitnitza, crawling shrivelled between banks of cracked mud—the river that once ran red with the blood of heroes.

" Thy Milosh, O lady, fell by the cold waters of the Sitnitza, where many Turks perished. He left a name to the Servian people that will be sung so long as there are

men and Kosovo field "—runs the ballad. Over this
dreary plain spread the Turkish army, " steed by steed,
warrior by warrior ; the spears were like unto a black
forest ; the banners like the clouds, their tents like the
snows ; had rain fallen from the heavens it would have
dropped, not upon the earth, but upon goodly steeds and
warriors."

After Sitnitza we passed several stockaded villages—
all Moslem—and the earth looked black and fat, but the
plain as a whole lacks water. We plodded ceaselessly
on through heat and dust, seeming to get no farther.
Suddenly there was the iron track of the railway—an
impossible anachronism—stretching as far as the eye
could see on either hand across our path. " The railway ! " I cried. " There is no railway here, lady," said
the dozing Marko solemnly. Our *strema* bumped over
the rails ; he gazed at them : " Dear God ! " he cried, and
could scarce believe his eyes. We reached Lipanj, the
station, which was crowded with buffalo-carts loaded with
sacks of maize, waiting for the next train to Saloniki.
Three trains run up and three down every week, and none
on Sundays. Marko mourned the days when all goods
came down on packbeasts to Scutari. This rail had
killed Scutari, and indeed all the transport trade of North
Albania. We left it and all sign of the twentieth century, and reached the borders of the plain—up over low,
parched, dusty hills, and at last saw the cupolas of the
Monastery of Grachanitza rising from the valley below.
We arrived there at 5 P.M.

The imposing red and white church towered above
us as we drove through a ramshackle wooden gateway
into the monastery grounds, round which stood two old
buildings, and one new and unfinished.

The old Stareshina, a jeromonah, and a young djakon,
surprised and hospitable, came out to greet me, and we
were soon sitting in the monastery balcony opposite the

church, whose mellow tones glowed in the afternoon light. My companions had had one foreign visitor before. They thought he was French, but "he could not talk." I could, and their joy was great. They asked of the great world beyond the Turkish frontiers ; if it were true that there was a railway that went underground, and another that was on the roofs of houses—of electricity and motor cars. And we talked of Great Servia and Kosovo-polje. For from the Monastery of Grachanitza came forth the monks who gave the Communion to all the army of Tsar Lazar before the fatal fight, and the great church is a monument of pre-Turkish days.

It was founded by King Milutin (1275–1321), who planted his victorious standard even on Mount Athos— father of Stefan Dechanski, and grandfather of the great Stefan Dushan, said the Stareshina. Built of large stone blocks, with two courses of narrow red-tile bricks between each horizontal course and one between each upright, the red and white effect is original and beautiful ; the wide mouldings are all of bricks in patterns ; the narrow, round-headed windows have herring-boned brickwork above them ; there is a high central dome, and a small one at each of the four corners.

The original building was nearly square, with an apse, but a large narthex was added two hundred years later, which somewhat spoils the appearance of the building, as it is inferior in style.

The interior is frescoed with saints, gaunt and Byzantine, on a ground which is now nearly black. The central dome is borne on four large square piers, on the right hand one of which is King Milutin, and on the left his Queen, sister of a Byzantine Emperor, stiff and gorgeous in their royal robes—the Queen with a huge jewelled gold crown and large round pendants (or ear-rings), recalling those of the Herzegovinian peasant women—the King long-faced, with a pointed beard. One of the piers is

hollow, and a steep and narrow staircase inside it leads
up to a small chapel in the roof, with a window giving
into the church—said to have been made for the royal
family to hear Mass from, though how they managed to
climb on a stool and squeeze through that door and up
that staircase in those royal robes I do not know.

The lower parts of all the frescoes are much damaged,
as the Turks used the church as a stable, and until a
hundred years ago it was several feet deep with mud
and manure. The upper ones are fairly preserved and are
said, probably with truth, to be contemporary with the
building of the church—at any rate they are pre-Kosovo
(1389), and have not suffered restoration.

The tall slits of windows admit little light. The
interior is dim, with faded colour and embrowned gold
—old-world, barbaric, decorative. Art to be decorative
must be barbaric. When it becomes "civilised" it
becomes anæmic, and crawls feebly in pallid mauves
and greens, with long spindle stalks that lack vitality to
throw out more than one or two atrophied leaves. It has
lost red blood and the joy of life.

In the more recent narthex are frescoes of St. Sava
and his father St. Simeon, the first of the Nemanja line
of Kings that led Servia to glory ; it ended with Tsar
Dushan. Servia rose with the Nemanjas—and fell with
them.

St. Simeon is pictured not as king, but in a grey
cloak as monk of Mount Athos, whither he retired. He is
hooded, and wears a moustache and a beard in two
points. St. Sava, first Bishop of Servia, is in his bishop's
robes. Unlike the present Bishops of the Orthodox
Church, his head is tonsured, the whole crown shaven,
but the locks below left long and curling to the shoulders.
He, too, wears moustache and beard. Both have long
faces, and the long aquiline nose with the drooping tip
so characteristic of the fair Albanian. This is a curious

fact, as the paintings are undoubtedly very old, and though not contemporary portraits (St. Sava died in 1237), yet Byzantine art is so extraordinarily conservative that it is possible they are traditional likenesses. For the Nemanja stem sprang from the Zeta (Montenegro, the district where the mingling of Serb and Albanian blood seems most marked). Is it too fanciful

St Sava   St Simeone.

Frescoes in the Narthex of the Monastery Church, Gracanica, Kosovo Vilayet.

to suggest that it was to a dash of Albanian blood that the victorious Nemanjas owed their success and the Montenegrins their independence? The now dwindled and poverty-stricken monastery formerly possessed a printing-press, and printed many church books, a few of which it still preserves.

The three ecclesiasts mourned the past and were hopeless of the future. They, and the young school-

master who had joined us, took me out to see the village
that adjoins the monastery. It consists of about seventy
stockaded "houses," fifteen of which have recently been
taken by Moslem Albanians, the rest all Orthodox Serbs.
Many of these "houses" are *zadrugas* (communal groups).
I asked to see one. The Stareshina, having first shouted
to an old woman feeding pigs from a petroleum can to
call off the dogs, we entered and were heartily welcomed.
The main house, recently rebuilt, was fairly smart, with a
new tiled roof which projected far in front, and formed a
verandah under which we sat. It, like most of the houses
where stone is scarce, was a frame-house of mud and
wattle. I take this to be one of the earliest types; that
of *chepchis* (mud bricks) seems a later development.

On the left a house just begun showed the method
of construction. The house is merely a large frame of
unshaped beams, resting on a base of three courses of
unhewn stones. The uprights are roughly mortised into
the horizontals. The cross-beams between the main uprights are quite childishly placed, with no science of
how to support and strengthen the building. On to this
frame are fastened the wattle walls, and the whole is
thickly smeared with mud, and smoothly finished. In
quite small sheds the uprights are driven straight into
the ground, and the wattle wound round them.

On the right of the main house (A) were three small
and much rougher houses (B), the sleeping rooms of the
three married sons. C was a hut of wattle not mudded,
as it was the dairy, and a through draught needed. D, D
were two cattlesheds, and E, E the usual Balkan wattled
maize barn. Near the cattlesheds were some straw ricks
and the usual round wattled henhouse (F), and the whole
was surrounded by a high stockade, as before described.

The old lady wore her black hair in a very thick plait
on either side of the face, doubled back so as to make a
solid block, which, with a flat drapery on the top of the

head, gave an odd, square, Egyptian effect. Her shirt-sleeves were most beautifully embroidered ; she wore a little black kilted frill round her waist and a scarlet apron. The daughters-in-law appeared and her one unmarried daughter, who, we were proudly told, was betrothed. They all kissed me heartily, and insisted on making me coffee. Their interest in me was extreme. Never before had they seen a foreigner, and they had not the faintest idea whence I came, for the name of England and the

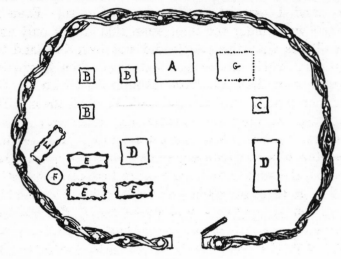

Plan of Servian Zadruga—Grachanitza.

British Empire were unknown to them. But the fact that it would take more than three weeks to ride to my vilayet on a horse was enough for them.

My unmarried condition bothered them horribly. They discussed it eagerly, to the great interest of the churchmen, who were equally curious but too polite to ask. We had arrived at questions which—even in Servian —were most embarrassingly personal and physiological, when luckily one of the pigs got its head jammed in the petroleum can, rushed thus bonneted shrieking through the yard, and diverted the conversation. A number of children came out of the three huts, all unusually clean and neat, well-grown and healthy. They were very markedly broad-headed at the temples, and some were almost blue-eyed. All were learning to read, write, and reckon, and were given very good characters by the schoolmaster.

The land was all worked on the *chiftlik* system, the workers getting three-quarters of the profits, the owner supplying the implements. This seemed to me liberal pay, and I astonished them by saying so. Even the priests were under the impression that it was only under the Turks that the people did not own the land they worked. Their amazement was great when I explained roughly how the agricultural labourer lived with us. The idea of paying rent amazed and shocked them. They regarded working for another as, under any circumstances, "*veliki zalum*" (great tyranny). I asked what was the objection supposing one was well paid. They replied, the master told them to go here and fetch straw, and to go there and sell hay when they did not want to do it—when to-morrow would do as well. Perhaps for a Christian master it might be all right, but it was always very hard to work for another. Their master forced them to work on Sunday.

About the Constitution they were hopeful. Since it had been started they had lived without fear. Previously they had always feared robbery and assault. If the beasts were not shut inside the stockade at night they would certainly be stolen. Only they feared lest Constitution meant that the land would always belong to the Turks. Many people had left the neighbourhood because of the great tyranny and had gone to America. Many others had been shot. There were much fewer Serbs here than formerly.

I very heartily wished good luck to this kindly hard-working family, and left their tidy homestead, when great herds of buffaloes, sheep, and goats were plodding into the village in a blinding cloud of dust which the setting sun turned to a golden glory. I was glad to turn in early that night, for it had been a long day crammed with new experiences. The jeromonah and the serving-man woke me at five next morning by hammering respectively on the slung wooden and iron bar, that served as bells, a rude rhythm.

The coachman had bargained to take us on to Prishtina, provided we left early. So about eight we said adieu. I wrote my name in Servian in the monastery book, and we drove off. It was bitterly cold. Up till yesterday the summer heat had been nearly intolerable. Even driving in the *strema* I had sweated through all my scanty attire. Now autumn had come at a blow, and a most bitter wind swept hill and plain. After barely an hour's drive over two low hills, we saw Prishtina below us, gay with red roofs, green trees, and white minarets. Within, it is frowsy, dirty, tumbledown—a shade better than Djakova, and that is all that can be said.

I marvelled that the Metropolitan should choose to reside here rather than at Prizren.

The population is mixed, and the statistics impossible to obtain, as every one gave different figures. There are about 2500 houses, of which about a quarter are Orthodox. Of these many are Vlahs, not Serbs. There are also a considerable number of Spanish Jews—some said as many as two hundred houses, and there are no Roman Catholics at all. The bulk of the population is Moslem, mostly Albanian; probably also some Moslem Serbs.

The bazar, partly roofed, but the roof all to pieces, was full of foreign rubbish of the cheapest description— one of the benefits brought by the railway. There was a sickening display of diseased meat in the butcher's quarter. The silver-workers here, as elsewhere, were all Christian. Of one—a Vlah from Monastir—I bought a charming little amulet, made of a mole's foot.

We lodged at an inn kept by a Vlah, who, as I was such a rare bird, most kindly invited me to visit his private house. And all his family in their best—the ladies dressed *alla Turka*—received me with great hospitality, and the very strongest *rakia* it has ever been my fate to sample. Marko was quite happy here. The Albanian and the Vlah meet as brothers. "Vlahs have sweet blood," said Marko; "not like Slavs." "Vlahs are like us," said an Albanian to me once; "a man will marry his daughter to a Vlah; but a Slav is different—sour through and through."

The Vlah is believed by some to be the descendant of the Roman colonist and original inhabitant. It is possible that both Vlah and Albanian are unconsciously aware that "blood is thicker than water."

According to promise, I called on his Grace, the Servian Metropolitan. And the same night he sent two schoolmasters to invite and escort both Marko and myself to sup with him.

Off we went, and found a large party—the Metropolitan, his secretary the Archimandrite, and all the schoolmistresses who had been at Devich. The Metropolitan, in the highest spirits and most festive, received us with bottled beer, jam, and water. The whole party had only just recovered from the results of Devich. The schoolmistresses had all been violently sick, or had bad colds, and the Metropolitan completely knocked up. I was the only one who had got off scot-free. When the beer was done we adjourned to the supper-room. I was placed at the right of the Metropolitan. The Archimandrite, a most kindly man, took Marko under his wing. He spoke a little German, and, trying to be very friendly, said: "Ach, my dear Marko! You are an Albanian, and you have come to see our Old Servia. Ach, but that is very beautiful!"

Poor Marko was paralysed with horror. To the genuine Albanian the mere name Old Servia is as "a red rag to a bull."

We had a grand "spread." The Metropolitan insisted that, *alla franga*, it was correct to begin with a *hors d'œuvre*. There ensued a great search in the dining-room cupboard, and the Metropolitan discussed which of many mysterious tins should be opened. His final selection turned out to be potted ham. We emptied the tin, and then started on a vast dinner of five courses, all good and extremely "filling," washed down with some good Servian white wine. And the Metropolitan enlivened the meal with humorous tales. It was late before I turned in at the *han*.

On the plain, just below Prishtina, on that fatal June day in 1389, fell Sultan Murad, slain by that best-beloved of Servian heroes, Milosh Obilich.

I drove down over the plain to Sultan Murad's tomb, passing, on the hill above, the turba of his standard-bearer, buried on the spot where he fell.

Murad's turba—or, rather, small mosque—stands in a walled-in ground, containing several graves, with a guardian's house at the entrance.

Rather to my surprise, I was at once admitted, and even invited to walk in with my boots on. Everything was changed now since "Constitution." If a female Giaour could come without escort to Kosovo-polje, God alone knew what would happen next. Nor did any one seem to mind.

As there were two Turks praying in the building, I refrained from desecrating it with Giaour boots ("Constitution"—if it is to mean anything—requiring, at any rate, respect for everybody's beliefs), and stood in the doorway.

In the centre, on a very fine Turkey carpet, stands the large coffin, covered with black cloth, and over it several coloured silk draperies—one, of crimson and silver, very handsome. At the head of the coffin is a great white turban of the old pattern, covered with a dark green and silver scarf. The decorations of the room are appalling. The walls are stencilled in crude colours to look like the cheapest wall-paper. Shiny *alla franga* wooden curtain-poles and red curtains of the lodging-house type adorn the windows; and over the coffin hangs a large glass chandelier.

The whole place had recently, said the guardian, been beautified. I stared at the hopeless incongruity of the adornment.

The nation that had done this had just dressed itself up in an imitation *alla franga* Constitution. Would it be any more suitable? I thought of the Daw in borrowed plumes, the Wolf in sheep's clothing, and of the Old, old Man who "madly thrust a left-hand foot into a right-hand shoe."

It was bitterly cold; an icy wind swept the plain. I left the spot on which the Turk had established himself in Europe and wondered whether the fact that he proposed now to take a new lease of life and remain was one to rejoice over.

I myself was the first visible sign of "Constitution" from the outer world, and, as such, of interest to the populace; so a Turkish officer travelling through Prishtina — an Ottoman Turk (not Moslem Slav or Albanian) — most kindly insisted on my visiting his family—temporarily established in a Moslem house— while Marko was entertained by officers below, in which company I too should have felt more at home. I was taken upstairs and shot into an apartment full of stout, pallid, collopy females, and a heap of children. There were nine women. I never discovered which belonged to whom. Door and windows were tightly shut; a *mangal* of hot charcoal burnt in the midst. The atmosphere was monkey-house.

Two of the women spoke Serb fluently, so I was thoroughly and effectively interviewed amid shrieks of laughter. The idea of an unmarried woman travelling with a man was new to them, and their conversation quite unprintable. They all sat on the floor smoking and eating oddments—roasted maize-cobs, bits of melon, sticky lumps of rahat-lakum, sugar-sticks. These people nibble all day. The floor was messy with seeds and bits. Heaps of soiled, crumpled garments were strewn around. Every one was touzled and dressed, half or wholly, *alla franga*, but wore their European clothes in Oriental manner—unbuttoned, crumpled, torn, and impossible. One, in European *dishabille*, had hitched up her white petticoats for greater convenience in squatting cross-legged. She was a handsome young woman, but her appearance with dangling pink stocking suspenders, of which she was very proud, and unbuttoned bodice, was unlovely.

The oldest lady had almost scarlet hair. Another, not so successful, had come out streaky, and, as the natural colour of her hair was black, the effect was comically tigerish. The eyebrows of all were painted black as broad as the finger, and joined in the middle, and their toe- as well as finger-nails were red with henna. All looked most unwholesome, and one had a row of burst glands oozing down the side of her neck. Only one was an effective colour arrangement. She was partly *alla Turka*, had scarlet hair with an orange handkerchief on it, and a striped white and yellow shirt. But she was as broad as she was long—and bulgy.

Being kept mainly for breeding purposes, their conversation was much like what that of a cow might be,

could it talk. They were most friendly, plied me with
coffee and pieces of all the eatables, and pressed me to stay
the night—there was plenty of room for another—or come
to-morrow. And I tore myself away with difficulty.

I give the above details because I invariably find that
gentlemen of all nations are consumed with curiosity
about the secrets of the harem. I thought of the bright,
tidy Vlah women, of the civilised Serbs, of the poor
Catholic women in Djakova, their clean rooms and
intelligent questions; and I asked myself if they were
not after all right when they said, "The Young Turk is
the son of the Old Turk." Islam has, so far, done nothing
but evil in Europe.

Having come so far, I decided to go on to Mitrovitza
by rail to save time, and learnt the day, but not the hour,
at which the one train ran—only that the station was a
very long way off; that I must start early, and that if
I went with some others who were going it would be
all right. We got seats in a carriage with another man,
a Moslem Slav. I was eating soup, not knowing when
I should again see food, when the carriage arrived, and,
urgently requested, left it, jumped into the carriage, and
off we went over the hills at a hand-gallop in company
with three other carriages—one filled with young men with
tambourines and a fiddle, who played and sang loudly all
the way; for a railway journey in these parts is a great
event.

We arrived at 10.30 A.M. to learn that the train—
which was generally late—was not even due till 12.30.
" God be praised !" cried every one; " we are in time !"
There were plenty of people already there—buffalo-carts
—baggage—a regular hurly-burly, and a man had already
lighted a fire on the platform and was cooking kebabs and
vegetables for such as desired refreshment. Even Marko
was surprised that I thought we were too early, and looked
on a railway journey as " not by any to be enterprised nor

taken in hand unadvisedly, lightly, or wantonly." The inspection, however, of *teskerehs* and the entering of the name (especially mine) and destination of each of us into the police book whiled away much time.

Moslem women, as fast as they arrived, were hastily driven into a separate waiting-room with opaque windows. I talked to our Moslem travelling companion, a native of Prishtina. There were very many more people than usual travelling, he said, because it was safe. Till now the railway had been of little use. It was three-quarters of an hour from the town, and the road was too dangerous —could never be ventured on unarmed ; as for the plain, till now it had been most dangerous. "Look at me," he said, tapping his sash. "This is the first time in my life I have ever come out so far without a revolver. I have no weapon at all, and am not afraid."

I asked if it had been as dangerous for Moslems as Christians, and he replied that robbers did not mind what you were so long as you were worth robbing. He was so astonished at the present calm that he knew not what to make of it. It was "like a dream, and could not last." A female Giaour from abroad (myself) had crossed the plain without escort—after that, anything amazing might happen. He himself wanted peace and a good government.

The train was punctual. Its smooth motion after the jolting *strema* made Marko cry delightedly, "It is like swimming in oil!" I went third-class, and luckily travelled with a Spanish Jew and his wife, so sampled all the mixed races of Prishtina.

He, a splendid old man of seventy years with a patriarchal beard, was saying farewell for ever to Prishtina, for he meant to die in Jerusalem, whither he was now bound. His poor old wife wept most bitterly at parting with her relations, who clung to the carriage door till the train started. He looked on stoically, moved only by the elemental passion — earth-hunger, the desire of a man for the land of his forebears. With all their worldly goods contained in a large basket and a sack, the aged couple were going to Sarajevo, where he would say good-bye to his old brother—and then to Jerusalem. I trust he has found peace in the Promised Land of his dreams.

The train ran through fertile land, cultivated fairly well, passing only one town, or rather village, of any size, Vuchitrn (wolf's thorn)—said to be largely Serb.

Mitrovitza, on rising ground at the very end of Kosovo plain, is small, but cleaner and less hopeless-looking than Prishtina. It is a new town made mainly since the railway; and, as it is on the junction of the Sitnitza and the Ibar, has a good and ample water supply, and fine vegetable gardens.

I strolled through the bazar, and was promptly hailed by a silversmith. " That foreign woman. Where does she come from?" " From London." " From London! Do you know my brother-in-law, X ? " " I do." The world is very small. I had found a friend in a far country. We drank coffee, and I departed laden with messages for his people.

There are but ten Roman Catholic families in Mitrovitza, and one priest. The number of Orthodox I failed to learn; they are building a large new church. The large majority of the town are Moslems, who were not going to make census returns though ordered by " Constitution "—the news having just come in that Ipek and Djakova had flatly refused; and that certain villages which had made a return had made a false one to dodge possible conscription.

We found quarters at the *han* of a friendly little Vlah, who said that he woke up every day surprised to still find peace. " We were living like snakes in holes, and now here we are all out in the sun ! " And we fed at a restaurant newly opened by some Italians from Fiume, who had hurried to be first on the spot when Baron

Aehrenthal announced that the railway from Mitrovitza to Uvatz was about to be made—the railway which was to be the last link in the chain, and to convey Austrian troops to Saloniki. The plans for Austrian advance had for the time being been completely upset by that " bolt from the blue," Constitution. But Mitrovitza, though it looked so peaceful, is tinder waiting for a spark.

Here we come to the crucial race question.

Exact figures are unattainable, but of the general facts there can be no doubt. Kosovo plain is now, by a very large majority, Moslem Albanian. What proportion of Slav blood there may be (one should perhaps say, is) in these Albanians is of purely ethnographical interest and politically of no importance. Albanian predominance is proved by the fact that — so far as my experience goes, and I tried repeatedly—the Albanians are almost solely Albanophone, whereas the scattered Serbs usually speak both languages, and when addressed in Serb often replied at first in Albanian. Were it not for the support and instruction that has for long been supplied from without it is probable that the Serb element would have been almost, if not quite, absorbed or suppressed by this time. It has been an elemental struggle for existence and survival of the strongest, carried out in relentless obedience to Nature's law, which says, " There is not place for you both. You must kill—or be killed." Ineradicably fixed in the breast of the Albanian—of the primitive man of the mountain and of the plain—is the belief that the land has been his rightly for all time. The Serb conquered him, held him for a few passing centuries, was swept out and shall never return again. He has but done to the Serb as he was done by.

The celebrated Canon of Tsar Stefan Dushan throws light on the means employed to crush the conquered, when Great Servia was at its greatest. " Tsar Dushan, the Macedonian, Autocrat of Servia, Bulgaria, Hungary,

Wallachia, and other countries. . . . Laws established by the grace of God in the year 1349 at a meeting of the Patriarchs, &c.

" Law 6. As to the Latin heresy, and those that draw true believers to its faith. The ecclesiastical authorities must strive to convert such to the true faith. If such a one will not be converted . . . he shall be punished by death. The Orthodox Tsar must eradicate all heresy from his state. The property of all such as refuse conversion shall be confiscate. . . . Heretical priests of other communions who try to make proselytes will be sent to the mines or expelled the country. Heretical churches will be consecrated and opened for priests of the Orthodox faith.

" Law 8. If a Latin priest be found trying to convert a Christian to the Latin faith he shall be punished by death.

" Law 10. If a heretic be found dwelling with Christians he shall be marked on the face and expelled. Any sheltering him shall be treated the same way."

It appears also that certain pagan rites were still observed. Law 45 enacts that : " If there be heretics that burn the bodies of the dead, or dig them up for the purpose of burning them, the village where this takes place is to pay a fine, and the criminals be handed over to justice."

The fact that the whole " village " is fined (just as the whole " house " is excommunicated to-day, for the sin of concubinage with a sister-in-law), indicates that the whole village, if not wholly pagan, had pagan sympathies.

These laws imply no worse religious persecution than the whole of Europe has enjoyed at various times. On other subjects Dushan's laws are often good, and even in advance of their time.

But history shows that the Latins in the districts we are considering must have been mainly Albanians.

The persecution was therefore not merely religious but racial. And that special legislation was needed against the Latins, and the express mention of what is to be done with their churches, tends to show that even in the strongest Servian days they were numerous enough to have to be reckoned with as a danger. The Serb strove to stamp out—or, shall we say, Slavise—the Albanian. The Albanian, circumstances being changed, has done as he was done by. He has employed mediæval methods, for this is the land of the Living Past, and he has forced back the Serb tide. Kosovo-polje is Albanian.

Its borders, however, are still largely Serb. Roughly speaking, the territory between the railway and the Servian frontier is Serb. It at any rate has a large Servian majority, but there is a remarkable Catholic island in and around Janjitza, not far from the monastery of Gra-chanitza. In this district were silver mines worked, it is said, with much success, from the beginning of the thirteenth century. The present Catholic inhabitants are reported to be the descendants of the Italian colony settled there as miners. They now call themselves Albanian. I do not know enough of the district to offer an opinion on the subject. But it is an odd fact that, before hearing this tradition, I met a man whom I took, beyond doubt, to be an Italian, and he proved to be a Janjitza man.

From Mitrovitza to the Servian frontier is also mainly Servian, though the town and environs of Novi-bazar is largely Albanian. Beyond Novi-bazar the *sanjak* is prac-tically solid Serb, Moslem, and Christian—no other race has any justifiable claim to it.

The Albanian has swept the centre of Kosovo vilayet. The Serbs are thick only along the Servian frontier and near the Montenegrin frontier, especially around Berana and Ipek. East of Prizren they begin to predominate. The land becomes more and more Slavonic. At which

point Serbs turn into Bulgars is beyond the scope of
this book. It is, I think, the fashion to draw the line
too far westward.

Mitrovitza may be called a " frontier " town. Albanians and Serbs alike claim it jealously. Austria (to
gain her private ends) wins Albanian support by promising that never, never will she allow the *sanjak* to
become Serb.

The town looked so peaceful that it was hard to
believe that but six years ago it had been the scene of
fierce fighting, in which Shtcherbina, the Russian Consul
forced into the place in the teeth of Albanian opposition,
was killed. Of his gallantry on behalf of the Slav
interests that he was sent to protect there can be no
question, nor of the indiscretion, alas! with which he set
to work. Austria at once planted a consul to watch her
own interests; and there the two most interested Powers
watch to this day.

Just outside the town is a relic of the Serb empire—
the fine ruins of the castle of Zvechana. Here, in 1336,
was strangled King Stefan Dechanski, son of Milutin,
the founder of Grachanitza. Stefan was Milutin's eldest
son, but the young Byzantine Princess, his second wife,
bore him another son and plotted to make him heir. In
a fight that ensued Stefan was taken prisoner, and his
stepmother prevailed upon his father to cast him into
prison, where, to make matters sure, she ordered him to
be blinded with red-hot irons. When freed after many
years, behold he was not blind at all! The tale spread
that he had been miraculously cured. He came to the
throne with a great reputation for piety, and was the
builder of many churches, notably the very beautiful
white and pink marble church of Dechani—a thank-
offering for the subjugation of the Bulgarians, whom he
defeated in 1330.

His death is said by some to have been brought about

by his son and heir, the great Stefan Dushan, but the patriotic Serb denies this. He was canonised as St. Stefan Dechanski, and his wonder-working shrine, pictured with his strangulation, draws many pious pilgrims still to the marble church of Dechani. Moslem and Catholic are in awe of it. Even the wild Catholic tribesmen of Nikaj tramp thither for the little round loaves of holy bread there distributed, and consider " By the bread of Dechani" a binding oath.

Mitrovitza has little else to show. To leave it, I had to have my *teskereh* stamped. The official at the *konak*, in order to make a good job of it, licked the stamp three times and licked off all the gum. As it would not stick, he licked it four more times. As it still would not, he put it in his mouth and sucked it patiently. It then showed signs of melting altogether, so he called a colleague to advise. He suggested the gum-pot. They searched for it high and low, and called in a third official —luckily that day there was no press of business in that department. The gum was found and the stamp stuck. It took half-an-hour, but was thoroughly done in the end. And we left by rail for Ferizovich, where we arrived at 10.15 A.M. A Serb fellow-passenger pointed out, on the right of the line just before Prishtina, the hill to which Vuk Brankovich, Tsar Lazar's traitorous son-in-law, withdrew with his men and gave the victory to the Turk. " What askest thou of Vuk the accursed ! Curséd be he, and curst be he that begat him. Curséd be his stem and his seed. He betrayed his Tsar at Kosovo. He deserted with twelve thousand men."

Ferizovich, till lately, had been of importance merely as a railway station. Now it is of historic interest as being the spot upon which the casting vote was thrown —the spot from which the voice came, " Let there be a Constitution." And there was a Constitution, and all Europe was shaken.

" Constantinople is the key of the Near East; Albania is the key of Constantinople," say the Albanians. European plans for tinkering and "reforming" the Turkish empire have all ignored the Albanian, his rights, and his aspirations—and they have all failed. Outsiders might make this mistake. Those within the empire knew that, so far as Turkey in Europe is concerned, the side that could enlist the Albanians, solid, must "come out top."

The Young Turks' secret was well kept; but it would appear that certain Old Turks suspected something was brewing. One of these, Shemshi Pasha, sent mounted messengers through the Moslem tribes, summoning them at once to repel the attack of an expected enemy. One of the many men from whom I heard the tale persisted that the advance-guard of the Austrian army, forty battalions, ready on the frontier, had actually been seen, and that Austrian annexation had been imminent. The tribesmen flew to arms and hurried—some nine thousand strong—to the appointed spot, Ferizovich, where they were to receive orders. And there they fired on a train—reported to contain " enemies."

But Shemsi Pasha was "a day behind the fair." The Young Turks outwitted him. They shot him at Monastir; skilfully took advantage of the fact that the tribesmen were at Ferizovich; called on them to save the country, and explained that something called Constitution was the only way by which it could be done. The fierce, ignorant tribesmen, jealous only of their privileges and territorial rights, and absolutely unaware that this was not the job for which they had been originally summoned, loudly and unanimously demanded this unknown amulet, " Constitution," that was to keep their land intact, and save the Padishah.

The Sultan heard that the Moslem tribesmen—the men upon whom, above all others, he had always reckoned—were with the army. The game was up; he

succumbed at once, and the Constitution was granted.
That the main outline of this tale, which I found widely
spread and believed, is correct, I believe is beyond all
reasonable doubt. The tribes were tricked, and many
folk had already found this out when I arrived in
Djakova.

Such freedom as they had retained under the Old
Turk, they did not mean to be swindled out of by the
Young.

We arrived at Prizren to find it smiling sardonically.
Four Frenchmen had come to report on "the Constitution"—had come and gone.

"What did they see here?" I asked. "Nothing.
They only dined, and left next morning for Djakova.
One is in the Diplomatic Service, so of course they will
not be allowed to see anything. The Young Turks have
arranged it all. An escort of twenty-four suvarris, as a
guard of honour, is with them, to prevent them talking
to the wrong people, and a suvarri has been sent ahead
to prepare a deputation of 'Christians rejoicing under
the Constitution,' in case they wish to make inquiries.
The escort will 'protect' them all the way. They will
think they have done something very brave, and will
report most favourably in the French newspapers." And
they did.

CHAPTER XI

LURIA—MIRDITA

I LEFT Prizren finally with the same Moslem *kirijee* I had come with, planned no route, and left all to luck. Towns are hotbeds of gossip. If you do not know yourself where you are going, nobody else can. Once off, we decided to make for Han Brutit, and learn further possibilities there.

The plain was dusty, the track fair. We crossed the Prizren river, went on over the plain, passed two fine springs that joined and made a fair stream, on which was a mill and a group of houses—Vrmitza—and soon reached the White Drin (Drin i bardh). On the farther bank were a village, Selchan, and the ruins of a great kula, the former home of a powerful Moslem family that had recently, after twenty-four hours' heavy fighting, been conquered by soldiery from Prizren. We were now in purely Albanian territory, and halted at midday at Han Lachit, farther down on Drin's left bank. Following Drin down its lonely and most beautiful valley, we came to its junction with Lumi Ljums (the river of Ljuma), and crossed it by a slim and elegant stone bridge, guarded on the farther side by a kula. We were in Ljuma, the land of the most notoriously independent of all the Moslem tribes.

As we were watering the horses, up rode a fine old man, who leapt from his saddle and greeted us hilariously—shook hands with me and rubbed cheeks with Marko. My presence struck him as a huge joke. No strangers were allowed in his land, he said, but, as they had given *besa*, I could go where I liked. He wished us

"Tun ghiat tjeter," and rode off. The men at the kula roared with laughter. He and his whole house were the most notorious " holders-up " of wayfarers in the district. Our *kirijee* told with glee how this very man and his party had " held him up" on this very track two years ago, when he was travelling with a priest, to whom he had promised safe-conduct. " ' Stand aside,' they said ; ' you are a Moslem. Our business is with the Giaour.' I said : ' Those I convoy are my business. If this is a joke, it is a silly one. I am a Vula. If you shoot me you will have to settle with all my people.' They let me through. Not many people care to quarrel with all the Vulas."

Following down the White Drin, we crossed it by the Ura Nermienies (middle bridge), one of many arches built by the Vezir who built Ura Vezirit, and came to where White Drin meets Black Drin.

A little below this stands Han Brutit, by a stream that flows to the river. The *han* is a large stable, with a small house attached. The *hanjee* and two wayfarers were hobnobbing outside.

"You can have a room up there," he pointed, " if you like. But I am an honest man, and tell you plainly it is swarming with bugs. I wouldn't sleep in it myself. You had better sleep in the stable." The rest of the company corroborated this—from experience. I decided on the stable. There was hay to sleep on; three eggs each for supper. Board and lodging were secured.

Route was the next question. I did not want to go through to the Christian tribes by the Ura Vezirit, like other travellers. What I wanted was something new— through Moslem lands, which, perhaps, when the *besa* was over, would again be closed.

Fortune favoured. Our stable companions were a very pleasant Catholic and his servant, bound for Arnji, in the heart of the Moslem land, to start a shop. He was travelling under the *besa* of Arnji, with two packbeasts laden with salt, sugar, and coffee. We should be safe with him, he said, under the double *besa*—the general one and the private and particular one of Arnji ; and Arnji would give us safe-conduct on.

It was night. The full moon rose majestic, flooding the vale with mystic splendour. Somewhere out in "that faeryland forlorn" lay Arnji. I did not stop to ask in which direction, but accepted the salt-and-sugar man's offer at once.

We retired to the stable, lit a fire in the middle, and I slumbered peacefully on hay, till waked by a horse, that had broken loose, eating it from under me.

We started very early. After this for three days the Austrian staff was useless. Its makers, I learnt afterwards, had not been through here, and had relied on imagination. I made such notes as I could, but even had I had the means of making a survey, it would have been too dangerous in a land where all strangers are suspect.

In order to cross the Drin we went down to Ura Vezirit, a majestic bridge of seven arches, no two the same size, but the effect of the whole quite admirable. It is the work of a great artist, for nothing more in harmony with the landscape could be imagined.

Unfortunately a great tree-trunk, brought down by last winter's flood, has shattered the last arch badly and lies jammed against a buttress, blocking the stream.

Having crossed, we went back up the river to a point opposite Han Brutit. And I saw that there were two, not one, tributary streams by the *han*, and that Bruti, the village, lay high on the hill between them, not on the river-brink as in the map.

Striking uphill from the Drin, we reached a fine grassy plateau and village, Kolchi, and then came to a tributary of the Drin that flows into it, opposite to and rather above Han Brutit.

We rode up its right bank till it forked in two, then followed its right branch, bore to the left away from it, and came out on the top of the watershed. Here, on a grassy plateau, is the village of Mal i zi. The whole district is called Mal i zi (Black Mountain). According to the map we should then have been on the mountain-side above the Drin ; but the men assured me that Drin was far, and we were on the other side of the mountain.

We continued through beech-wood, passing an un-mapped village, Chinimak (? Chin i madh) and dropped down to Sroji, a village in a valley. Some one at once welcomed us. We sat in the shade of a doorway and ate our lunch. An old man lay in the full glare of the midday sun, shivering in the cold fit of an intermittent fever.

Two men—one a very fine young fellow—swaggered up and demanded what right we had to come, and who had given us leave. He was the nephew of the old brigand we had met at the bridge. He and his family had hitherto occupied such leisure as their other profession left them, in selling salt, sugar, and coffee in Sroji, and the Arnji people had had to come and fetch it. Now, Arnji meant to have a shop of its own, and, what was worse, had invited a Catholic to keep it. The nephew, furious, prowled round the packbeasts, growling.

Marko told him sweetly that we had the pleasure of his uncle's acquaintance. The salt-and-sugar man said he had brought us; the Government was now in Prizren ; we all had permission to travel, and had all Arnji on our side.

The nephew grumbled that if Constitution meant the arrival of Giaours, and that any one could come and sell what he pleased, he would have no more of it. He eyed the packbeasts covetously. He cared not a rap for Constitution ; but—as the plunder was not worth the wrath of Arnji and the vengeance of all the Vulas—he withdrew, saying many things, without molesting us.

Our hosts pointed out the rocky crest of the mountain, south of the village, as the "fortress of Lek Dukaghin," and told that Lek, to show his strength, had cleft a rock in twain with one blow of his yataghan. Otherwise all they knew of Lek was that he was a great hero and made the Canon a long while ago.

Sroji gave us an old man as safe-conduct, and we started up the Lek Dukaghin range, a long and steep ascent through fine beech forest to the pass, Chafa Benks, at the top. This is unmapped, as is indeed the whole route. We descended a steep slope on the other side (rough above, and studded with bushes of sweet yellow plums, and cultivated below), and reached Arnji, a wide level, covered with well-irrigated maize fields, and scattered with good stone kulas.

Our Salt-and-Sugar friend led us straight to one of the largest, which stood in an enclosure with a second smaller house within it. Out came the whole household of staring, wondering people. The Head welcomed the Sugar man warmly, and looked at us with doubtful astonishment. I had been instructed to hold my tongue, and did so.

After explanations, he laughed at our coming, and said, had we not been brought by his good friend here, he would certainly not have admitted us, as the tribe wanted no strangers. As it was, we were his guests, and very welcome.

The women were sent in to make ready, and Marko and I were left alone, sitting on the ground outside. Time passed. Marko was depressed. It was not till the light was fading that we were summoned within to a large, very clean room, with an earthen floor and a low ceiling. A pile of logs blazed on the hearth. I lay on sheepskins, and stretched blissfully in the grateful warmth, for evening brought a touch of autumn chill to the air. A dozen or so of men came in—fairish, with grey or hazel eyes—all friendly. Talk and tales went round.

The Salt-and-Sugar man told

The Story of the Bravest Man.

Some forty years ago a Djakovan and a Scutarene were each known in his own town as the bravest man in all the land. The Djakovan, in anger, swore to kill the Scutarene; there could be but one bravest man.

So he journeyed over the mountains to Scutari, where he knew no one, and in the streets he asked, "Which of you is the bravest man in this town?" And the people said, "He is yonder, in the bazar." And showed him the man's shop.

The Djakovan stood without and looked at the goods. The Scutarene asked him whence he came and what he wanted.

"I come from Djakova, and I want nothing," he said.

"Have you friends in the town?" asked the Scutarene.

"Not one," said the Djakovan.

"If you have come so far," said the Scutarene, "you must be very weary and thirsty. Come in and rest."

And the Djakovan entered and sat down.

The Scutarene gave him cold water, and then coffee, and spoke to him kindly. The Djakovan drank it, and said nothing. Thrice did the Scutarene serve him with coffee as is meet for an honoured guest. Then he said to him, "You have drunk and have rested. Now tell me your business here. In all the town you have no friend; it will be hard for you—let me help you."

The Djakovan sat silent, and bitterly repented of the vow that bound him to slay a man so kind to a friendless stranger. The Scutarene urged him to speak.

"I cannot trouble you with my business," he said.

"But you have come so far," said the Scutarene, "to you it must be important."

"I have come to shoot you," said the Djakovan at last, and told him the whole.

"Shoot me, then," answered the Scutarene. "Here am I. It were a pity that you should take so long a journey for nothing."

"We cannot fight here," said the Djakovan, reluctant.

The Scutarene arose, and thrust his pistols into his sash. "Come out on to the plain if you wish," he said.

The Djakovan followed him till they came to a lonely spot.

"Now shoot me," said the Scutarene; "here is my heart."

"But you must shoot too!" cried the Djakovan.

"I have made no vow," smiled the Scutarene. "Shoot, lest when you go back men laugh at you."

The Djakovan drew a pistol, fired, and it flashed in the pan.

"I have lost. It is your turn," he cried, much relieved.

"Nay," said the Scutarene. "There is one thing I can never do, and that is kill a guest from under my roof. You have your second pistol; remember your vow. Try again."

The Djakovan, reluctant, drew his second pistol; fired, and grazed the Scutarene's coat. Then, throwing down his weapons, he embraced the Scutarene warmly: "I could not stand up to be shot at without defending myself!" he cried. "You are the bravest man in all the world." They swore brotherhood, and remained fast friends ever afterwards.

Our Djakovan *kirijee* heartily confirmed the tale, which shows indeed the noble traits of the Albanian character—the duty of hospitality—the sacredness of the guest—and courage. It was much applauded.

The women spread supper—a large bowl of cheese melted in butter, into which we dipped our maize bread, and very good it was. Then came the inevitable sour *kos*, followed by hand-washing, mouth-rinsing, and sweeping up of the crumbs. The whole was over in twenty minutes. Large stones were then set in the two loopholes that were the only windows, to make all safe for the night.

We lay down and slept on sheepskins. The women slept in another room. They were not veiled, and wore, like the Mirdite women, long cotton drawers, with knitted ankle pieces in red and white patterns, which show beneath the skirt; also Mirdite pattern earrings, and four or five large silver coins on a black cord round the neck.

Arnji is a small independent tribe that goes with Debra. I am told it is au offshoot of Berisha, but my men were fearful of arousing suspicion by asking questions for me. It is all Moslem now, but crosses stood in many maize fields.

The other Moslem villages we passed belong to Prizren district, and are offshoots of various Christian tribes—Shala and Fandi among others—dating, I believe, from about two hundred years ago. At five next morning our host made us each a cup of black coffee, and sent us on our way with a dark, surly-looking man as safe-conduct to Katun i veter in Luria.

We left Arnji by a good track along the hillside, high above the Mola (Mala), a tributary of the Drin. Three-quarters of an hour after starting, we headed a small tributary stream, and saw three villages not on the map. —Djur on the opposite side of the Mola, and Mars and Domi on the tributary. We continued on the high level for an hour, passing from Arnji land into Rechi, another small tribe, and then descended into the valley by a long steep track by a very large " house "—a group of three houses (one a large kula), and a number of sheds and out-houses—the house of the Dedas, the mightiest in the neighbourhood—seventy - two in family. Thirty-three are armed men; they have twelve serving - men, and live in great state. There are three brothers, each has his own house, and all goods are shared in common. They are said to possess vast flocks and rich lands. At the be-ginning of each year each reckons what he will require for household expenses and takes it. The remainder, which is said to be large, is almost all used for hospitality. A whole flock of sheep and

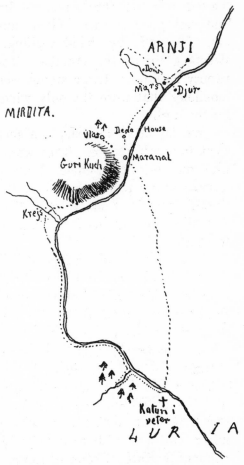

Sketch Map—Arnji to Luria (see page 319).

one of cattle is set aside yearly for guests, and any one who comes to the house, be it never so early, must stay and be feasted till next morning. I was strongly tempted to call but was advised not, and regret now that I took the advice.

We zigzagged down a very rough track on foot for over an hour. The guide then, though it was quite early, insisted that he could go no farther without resting, and stopped at a group of houses on the brink of the Mola, called Naramal (? Maranal), just beyond which rose a great cliff - like mountain, Guri kuch. Really he had relatives there, and wished to give information about us.

We were inspected. A long parley took place. We appeared to be most unwelcome, but were told to come in. I was hastily instructed to walk last and keep quiet.

The house was very large. We went up a pitch-dark ladder staircase that stunk, and into a clean and decent room on the first floor, very low-ceiled, dark, save for two loopholes, and full of men who seemed angry. I went and sat in a far corner which was pointed out to me, and looked modestly at the floor. "Now we are in a wasps' nest," murmured Marko uneasily.

A great noise went on, but we were served with coffee. I suggested to Marko on the first chance that as we were so unwelcome we had better leave, but our guide meant to stay for dinner, and refused to go. Dinner was ready at ten o'clock. I was invited to the *sofra*, on which was a bowl of *kos* (so sour that it drew the mouth), with lumps of sheep-cheese in it, and maize bread steaming hot. I could tackle neither *kos* nor cheese, but they gobbled so fast that it was all done before I had decided how to avoid it politely. A jar of honey followed and a cold heavy pancake apiece, with which to scoop it up and carry it to the mouth—eating honey with one's fingers is very difficult. More kos, even sourer, followed, and a very unsatisfactory meal was concluded. Our guide then announced it was too late to get to Luria that night, and we must stay where we were till to-morrow. That he wished to delay us seemed clear. Marko appealed to me. I was convinced that our host at Arnji did not mean to betray us, and he had said we should reach Katun i veter in Luria early.

All the time the general attitude and conversation had seemed most uncomfortable, so I said, very decidedly, that I meant to go, and that there was plenty of time. We got off at last. Once outside, I asked what all the row had been about.

One of the men had asked the *kirijee* how things were going in Prizren under the new rule. "Quite quietly," said he. They then all asked if the news had yet come when they were to begin expelling the Giaours. Constitution was not going to tolerate Giaours any more; the land was to be swept clean of them. They were only waiting orders to kill the lot, and hoped it would be soon. That was what the new rule was made for.

And, as they knew we were Giaours, this was not a polite thing to say.

We crossed the Mola, and went up a very steep ascent away from the stream, through oak and beech wood, then through a fir wood of splendid trees. Here the guide halted and quarrelled badly with the *kirijee*. He demanded pay for the corn the horses had eaten. The *kirijee* said I had already paid enough there. He retorted by calling the *kirijee* dirty names. An awful row ensued. As soon as I knew what was the matter, I settled matters by paying. It was only sixpence. But the *kirijee's* honour had been wounded by the names, and he lamented loudly that he was unarmed. For the first time in his life he was without his revolver—every one had said under Constitution all was safe—and this was the result! If he had but had his revolver, he would have shot the beast dead through the forehead so soon as the words had left his lips. He should feel the vengeance of the Vulas later.

The guide pocketed the piastres, and then sat down

and said he would go no farther till he had been paid for the whole job.

This I flatly refused. I fancy he had been told at the house we had left to delay us or leave us in the lurch. After a lot of shouting, we got under way again. According to the map, we were going quite in the wrong direction. Luckily, the map was wholly incorrect.

We came out of the wood, and dropped down over grass land to the river. We were in a splendid and most fertile plain, ringed round with lofty mountain and lordly forest—quite the finest spot I know in all Albania. Beyond the river stood the wretched half-ruined church and house of Katun i veter, where a luckless young Franciscan—a solitary outpost in a Moslem land— wrestles vainly with his first parish.

Luria tribe is of great interest, as here one sees Christianity disintegrating and giving way before advancing Islam, as history shows it has been slowly doing for the last four hundred years in these parts.

Luria consists of two hundred houses (average ten to a house). Of these now only twenty are Christian at all, and scarcely one wholly Christian—some, indeed, mainly Moslem, with a few Christian members.

Within the last five-and-thirty years, eleven whole houses have turned Turk, and members of very many others. A mosque is being built, and a Hodja had already arrived. The Franciscan was in despair. The Church, with curious apathy, let the whole district slip without making an effort till too late. Luria is in the diocese of Durazzo. The former Bishop, an Italian, had only Italian friars. By the time one knew the language, he was changed for another. And, till lately, there was no priest at all in Luria, save in the summer.

Islam all the time has kept on a steady propaganda. No persecution of any kind has taken place. All has been done by persuasion and heavy bribes. The beggarly methods of Christianity, compared with the open-handed liberality of Islam—the wretched hovel of the church and the new mosque—were enough alone to convince a quite ignorant people that the one was a dying, the other a living, cause.

The ground fact is this. The North Albanian tribesman is an Albanian first. He has never absorbed the higher teaching of either Christianity or Islam (I speak of the masses only). Christ and Mohammed are to him two supernatural "magic dickies," each able, if propitiated, to work wonders. Looked at, impartially, through the eyes of a tribesman, which has succeeded better? As a Christian, the tribesman was trampled by that hated unbeliever, the Slav (he has never called the Slav a Christian). With the help of Islam, on the contrary, the Slav has been beaten back. The Albanian has regained much territory. But for foreign intervention, he would have regained much more. The magic of Mohammed has given him fat lands, ruling posts in the Government, has not exacted compulsory military service, has paid him well when he chose to fight, and has never troubled to teach him Mohammedanism properly, but has left him free to keep his old customs.

He does not veil his women, nor seclude them more than do many Christians, and rarely has more than one wife, save a sister-in-law. He pays no more attention to his Hodja than to his priest. Except at a mosque, I have never seen him perform either the proper prayers or ablutions. If he be an earnest believer, he belongs to some Dervish sect—preferably the Bektashes—which love the Orthodox Mohammedans as do the Dissenters the Church of England. Briefly, he has had all the advantages of Islam, and gone his own way. As a counter-attraction, Christianity offers him the position of underdog, problematic advantages in another world, and, mark this, probable foreign domination in this one.

Roman Catholicism, to-day, in Albania is, as the Moslem knows well, an Austrian propaganda, worked for purely (or shall we say impurely?) political reasons, caring, so far as Austria is concerned, neither for the moral nor mental development of the people—desiring, indeed, to retard it—for a Bishop, an Austrian subject, has been known to refuse permission for a school in a tribe anxious to have one.

Till recently, fights between Moslem and Catholic have been all either intertribal or "blood," just as between Christian and Christian or Moslem and Moslem. Religion has not been more of an excuse for fighting than have other things. Only quite lately have Moslems persecuted Christians as Christians. This is because the Moslem sees that Catholicism is the thin end of the wedge for a foreign invader—to wit, Austria. He has no particular quarrel with Catholicism as such, but foreign rule, disguised as Catholicism, he will resist as long as he can stand and see. From his own point of view, he is reasonable. And those who have seen and understood the results of Austrian rule in Bosnia, cannot but sympathise with him, even though they may deplore his methods.

I was a Giaour—a being from the outside world, that plots annexation—therefore, and reasonably, Luria was not at all pleased to see me. Moreover, I was the guest of the Franciscan.

Katun i veter turned out in some force to inspect me. I sat on the grass, and the heads sat around in a circle.

To me, personally, I do not believe that anywhere the Moslems had any objection. Were it not that I was suspected of being the forerunner of Giaour interference, they would have regarded my tour as rather sporting, which some of them indeed did, and myself as quite as amusing and welcome as is a dancing bear or an organ-grinder's monkey in an English village.

The tale had gone round that I was sister to the King of England. My appearance, however, justified them in believing my statement that I was of low degree. The Bariaktar's son said they did not want the King of England, or any king, interfering in Luria. Luria is a free country. If he thought I was really the King's sister, he would cut off my head at once. He asked if I were afraid. I, entering into his pleasantry, replied that if some one would lend me a revolver I should be very pleased to shoot him. This is the sort of joke they like. He became quite affable, and suggested showing us what sort of a shot he was himself. They started shooting at a white stone—a long shot, across the valley—which he hit every time he tried, to our admiration and his great satisfaction.

I had not been many hours in Katun i veter when a good-looking Greek turned up, and asked the Franciscan's hospitality for the night. He was a serving-man from the great house of Deda, had come on foot as fast as he could, in order to attend Mass to-morrow, so he said. But really, beyond doubt, to see and report on me.

He chatted of the wealth of the Dedas—was in a comfortable berth there, but had had a bad time before. Had knocked about eleven years in Albania—horrible country—worked his way up from the South. Would be jolly glad to get back home again.

I asked him how many men he had killed there— guessing at once that he had fled from blood. "Two," he replied at once, and he told us of his escape over the border, under cover of night and a thunderstorm. It was an affair of honour. He was no vulgar criminal— was indeed, as I learnt later, a skilled craftsman, and could find work anywhere. In four years he would be free to return home—murder charge would then have lapsed. Fifteen years' exile had been a long price to pay for his honour, but there was no other way. In a like case he would do the same again.

He joked freely about Islam; said his present employers wanted him to turn Turk, but it wasn't good enough. Had eaten and smoked even in Ramazan. Had lived much with Moslems.

Which shows that it is not so much the religious views of the Giaour that these most exclusive of the Moslem tribes object to as the political results that may come in his train. A Giaour that comes for reasons with which all can sympathise is a man and a brother. Yarns spread by imaginative newspaper correspondents to the effect that the Moslem tribes—which they have not visited—have been known to capture foreigners and hold them as slaves, are wholly imaginary.

Mass was early on Sunday, and the congregation strangely mixed. Besides Marko, who assisted at the altar, and a Catholic woman and child, were the Greek —who stood all the time and crossed himself, in the manner of his Church—and myself. After service had begun, came four women and two men, all Moslem, crawled up on their hands and knees, lifted the altar cloth, and all crowded in under the altar, the women taking three babies in wooden cradles with them. The space was packed tight, and the babies' muffled squalls disturbed the service.

When it was over the party came crawling out, and wanted to be blessed. The Frate complied; it was the only way they would come, he said, sadly. The three babies were not well, so their mothers had brought them, and the three other adults were all ill. Moslem charms had not succeeded, so they were trying Christian ones. It was a most difficult parish. They explained to him that they were pleased to receive him in their houses, but he must not talk about religion.

Lately, a young Catholic had married a Moslem girl,

who had turned Christian and been baptized. The
Moslems, much annoyed, then bribed the youth, who
was barely twenty, to turn Turk. He had just done
so. Now his wife is very unhappy, and came to the
Franciscan to know if she could have her marriage
dissolved, and has refused to live with her husband.

The Greek said he had come expressly to hear Mass,
and should leave directly after; but, when he found I was
staying, said he was rather tired, and stayed too.

The Bariaktar—a fine old man—and several others
flocked in. Talk ran entirely on "Konstitutzioon," the
mysterious unknown something that had come upon the
land. What it was, said the old man, no one knew.
That it meant war against Giaours was certain, but
whether with the Russians, Austrians, or Italians remained to be seen. They were ready in any case. "We
are a free people," said the old boy, with a grin; "we
do not obey Abdul Hamid except when we choose. But
wherever he makes a war we flock like butterflies."

The Greek said there would be a big war. He had
seen it a few days ago in a glass of wine. I wondered if
it were a case of *in vino veritas*, and noted that wine
was drunk in the Moslem strongholds of the Dedas.

Luria is the head bariak of the redoubtable Debra
group—the "tigers of Debra," as some even of their
Moslem compatriots call them—Luria, Matija, Debra.
Matija is a very large tribe of some 1200 houses.
The three tribes are intermarriageable, and claim Lek
Dukaghin as former lord of the land. Their law, so they
said at Luria, is the Canon of Lek. But they do not
compound feuds by blood-gelt. Unless the families con-
cerned choose to make peace, it continues indefinitely.
I need scarcely say they pay no fine to the Turkish
Government, nor, indeed, recognise it, except as an ally
against the Giaour in general and the Slav in particular.

The Bariaktar said he must know where I was going

and what I was doing. I asked permission to visit certain lakes in Luria of which I had heard. He did not smile on the notion. An Austrian Consul had been there; they wanted no more Giaours. It would have to be referred to a *medjliss* of the whole tribe. That would take some days. I found I should have to pay a heavy fee for this legal opinion—if it were to be in my favour —and decided it was not worth while; also a bad precedent for the next traveller.

When they had gone to their midday meal, and I thought the coast clear, I went out and drew a

Kulas. Katun i vieter
Luria 1905.

characteristic kula. (By special request of my companions, my camera had been hidden since we left Prizren.) A boy of nine, swaggering up, said, "You are not to write about our houses," and went off to report. Back came stringent orders that nothing was to be written in Luria. Luckily I had finished.

What I really wanted to find out was where I was and the lie of the land. According to the map, the river Mola ran quite straight from Guri Kuch to the church of Luria, and we should have followed the stream up. Instead of this we had left it, crossed a mountain, and come straight down on to what I took for another river— but it was the Mola after all.

I was bound for Mirdita, to see the reception of the

Hereditary Prince of Mirdita, Prenk Bib Doda, whose return from exile was, in the eyes of both Moslem and Christian tribesmen, far more important than the Constitution. News came in that night that Prenk had been shot by the Young Turks at Saloniki. Luria was excited, for Prenk represents the blood of Lek Dukaghin, and Prenk's mother is from Luria. I hastened to start for Mirdita. A guide was easily found, and we started along the mysterious river. We followed down the left bank, high above the stream, through fir wood, making a detour to head a tributary. The track was good. We came round a big bend, and soon I saw the unmistakable Guri Kuch rising, a great cliff, from the stream. The land lay below me in bird's-eye view, and I saw where the map had gone wrong. The church was marked in the straight of the river instead of on the other side of the great bend, and the names were wrong. We crossed two tributary streams, on which stands Krejs, a fair-sized village, on the left bank of the river (not the right as marked on the staff map). Passing round Guri Kuch by a track high above the water, we saw Naramal below us, rather farther down stream, and farther still, high on the valley side, the house of the Dedas. Leaving the river's course we struck straight inland a steep ascent by the side of Guri Kuch to Vlas, a high-lying village. Vlas is all Moslem, and goes with Ljuma (see sketch map, p. 309).

Shortly after this we reached Mirdita territory. The fir woods around Vlas were a sad sight, hundreds of big trees had been felled and left to rot, with the mistaken idea that pasture would grow in their place. But denudation and desolation follows speedily, and the people do not learn by experience. I spoke vainly. They said it was the custom, and must be. Grass, it was true, had not grown in this spot. That was no reason why it should not in another. Then they would have flocks and be rich.

We rode through more forests, when entering Mir-dita, of huge fir trees, quite magnificent, and came out on a large plain with rude wooden huts—the summer quarters of the herd folk—dotted about. Out came the people, running to welcome us, bringing a wooden vessel full of buttermilk and a large sheep-cheese, which they insisted on our taking as a gift. "Thank God!" cried Marko; "now we are in a Christian land!"

By a stony track we went on till the summit of Mal i shaint (the Holy Mountain), with the Abbate's summer residence upon it, rose before us against the sky, and pulled up by the ruins of the old church and Benedictine monastery, from which the mountain takes its name and the Abbate his title. We ascended on foot to the little wooden house and chapel. The Abbate knows many things; among others, how to place his summer quarters on one of the finest spots in Europe. A wondrous, wild scene lay below. All Albania glowing in golden light, cleft by great blue shadows—Rumia beyond Scutari Lake in the dim distance—the ragged, jagged Shala range—far on the other side Guri Kuch, with the Debra Mountains beyond.

From the men in charge we learnt that the rumour of Prenk Pasha's assassination was false, and started down through woods by a good track to Oroshi, that lies some 2000 feet below. Kapetan Marko Ghoanni, Prenk Pasha's cousin, had kindly told me to come to his house if I went to Oroshi, and thither, finding it was no house of mourning, we went. He was absent, but his brother Kapetan Nue and his cousin received us with the greatest hospitality.

The great stone house, high on a shelf on the moun-tain-side, its big, airy, white-washed rooms, the great hooded hearth, the solid native-made furniture, chip-carved in old Albanian style (alas, that it should ever be replaced by commonplace machine-made European stuff!)

is the fitting home of a mountain chief, and harmonises with the simple dignity of its owners.

We dined and supped excellently well with our two hosts. The younger men of the family waited on us, stately and mediæval, in the fine dress of the Mirdites. I thought of Chaucer's " Yonge Squire,"

> " Of his stature he was of even length,
>   And wonderly delyver and great of strength . . .
>   Curteys he was, lowly and servysable,
>   And carve beforn his fader atte table,"

and hoped that Constitution would not entail the loss of what was good and beautiful in the old life—old lamps for new.

Mirdita numbers some three thousand houses, said my host, all Christian, and consists of five bariaks, of which Oroshi, Spachi, and Kushneni are of the same blood as Shala-Shoshi, and not intermarriageable either among themselves or with Shala-Shosi. They came from the Pestriku Mountains, near Djakova, when the Turks first oppressed the land. Lek Dukaghin, they said, was one of their own ancestors, and ruled all the mountains in the time of Skenderbeg; Luria was part of his lands. Skenderbeg ruled farther south. Lek was followed by his nephew, Paul i bardh (White Paul), and it is from his house that the Montenegrin tribe Bijelopavlich (son of White Paul) descends, though it is now Serbophone and Orthodox. Skenderbeg and Lek, they said, were related, therefore Mirdite women wear the black *gjurdin* in mourning for Skenderbeg, which in all other tribes is a man's garment only. But no authentic pedigree exists, nor could I from tradition compile one that fits.

Before their migration the Mirdites say that they belonged to the Ipek group, which was then all Christian. This statement is not easy to reconcile with history, as in the first days of the Turkish conquest, Ipek must have been almost wholly Serb and Orthodox. Was Mirdita one of those tribes of mixed blood that became Serb or Albanian, according to the Church with which it threw in its lot?—as has undoubtedly been often the case.

Or is the further tradition true that the Mirdites, after the death of Skenderbeg, when the Turks took Scutari, and were harrying the land, fled from Mirdita, and returned again to Pestriku, and came back once more to Mirdita two hundred and fifty years ago? The tale of a double shifting is complicated, but I incline to believe it, as it accounts not only for the connection with Ipek (which by that time was already almost overwhelmed by Albanians), but accounts also for the fact, commented on by many writers, that previous to the latter half of the seventeenth century there is no historical reference to the Mirdites. Probably before their second shifting they were known only as Dukaghini.

The other two bariaks, Fandi and Dibri (not to be confounded with the Moslem tribe of Debra) are not related by blood, but only adopted by Mirdita. Fandi used to belong to the Ljuma group, but left it when Ljuma turned Moslem and joined Catholic Mirdita. In battle Kthela, the border tribe, goes with Mirdita. Kthela in several particulars resembles Mirdita, but is not blood-related.

Mirdita had not yet decided to accept Constitution, till it knew more about it. It had sworn *besa* when the others had. Otherwise, by now it would have declared war on the Moslem tribes of Djakova, and have gone to avenge the wrong done to the Frate and the Christian villages. I gathered that something like a " Cross and Crescent" war had been contemplated—and relinquished with regret. It feared that by accepting Constitution— unless with special conditions—it would lose status. It had never from the beginning accepted Turkish rule, nor paid a tax.

My hosts were astonished at the taxes we pay in

England, and thought it showed very bad management.
I daresay they are right. But they admitted that for
blood alone, a very considerable tax is paid in Mirdita.

A regular outbreak of shooting was going on. It
was rumoured that blood-vengeance was to come to an
end, so all were paying off old scores while yet there was
time. Mirdita has special blood laws of its own. Immediately on the death of a man, the slayer must pay the
Kapetan an ox and £T.5. A *medjliss* is then called to
decide what more fine he pays. His house is not burnt.
The fine varies from ten to twenty sheep or goats according to his means. To make peace blood-gelt is paid.
The whole expense, including fee to the *medjliss*, is
about £60. After the first twenty-four hours, when a
man may be expected to act in hot blood, vengeance may
be taken only on the guilty party, and not on any relative.
This is an emendation of the old law.

On a point of honour Mirdita can and has shed blood
in torrents. The Mirdites are famed of old as cattle-
lifters, going a-raiding joyfully, as did the clans on the
English border, and successfully capturing a hundred head
at a time from the plains—of which they were the terror
—and even from far Moslem tribes.

The trade route from Prizren to Scutari was a rich
plundering ground, and the Mirdite zaptiehs, instituted
to safeguard it, are, so runs the tale, the only gendarmes
regularly paid by the old Turkish Government, as, if their
pay is more than a week or so in arrears, they promptly
" hold up " the road and—in bad cases—cut the telegraph
line. They were in like manner subsidised to " protect "
the plains in part.

The Mirdites by no means always shave the head, as
do most other tribes. In many instances, indeed, they
shave only a very small patch on the temples.

As two of the five bariaks are of different blood, it is
not surprising that the type should vary much. Tall,

grey - eyed men and small, dark ones both occur frequently, and all the intermediates.

Travellers who have described Mirdites as all "dark"
or "fair" have visited only one part. So far as I know,
none of the Mirdites tattoo.

Mirdita's recent history has been tragic. By the side
of Kapetan Marko's house stand the ruins of the house
of the head of the tribe, Prenk Pasha, burnt by the Turks
in 1877. Mirdita had taken no part against the Montenegrins during the beginning of the war of 1876, but was
known to be planning independence. Prenk was in
treaty with the Montenegrins, when Servia and Montenegro made a temporary peace with Turkey. This set
free the Turkish troops, eight battalions marched on Mirdita. The Moslems of Djakova, Ljuma, and Matija, who
all had old scores to pay, attacked at the same time, and
Mirdita was overwhelmed on all sides at once. The
Turkish troops reached Oroshi, and burnt the house of
the young chief, who then escaped. As we looked at
the ruins, I was told how he was treacherously captured
later. This was in 1881. The Albanian league had
resisted the cession of Albanian territory to Montenegro,
ordered by the Powers. The Turkish Government, which
had made peace with the Mirdites, now suspected the
young Prince as a possible champion of Albanian independence. Meeting him one day, at dinner, at the
Austrian Consulate, Dervish Pasha invited him to inspect a Turkish war vessel, then off Medua. Contrary,
it is said, to the advice of his friends, the young Prince
went. The vessel at once got up steam, and the little
pleasure trip became a twenty-eight years' exile, passed,
for many years in Kastamuni, in Asia Minor. Recently,
the Prince was taken into favour at Constantinople, and
made aide-de-camp to the Sultan, but not permitted to
return home.

His coming was now daily nearer, and Mirdita was

aflame with expectation, and torn by doubt of Turkish promises.

From the house of the Kapetan I went to that of the Abbate, the brain of the Mirdita—perhaps the strongest personality in North Albania. When anything of importance is on hand, one of the first questions asked by all, priest, layman, Consul of every nation—is, "What does the Abbate think of it?" And they never know.

Of his church, designed by himself—the largest in all the mountains—his great house furnished throughout in European taste, and his princely hospitality, I need not here tell. They are well known to all who visit Scutari and make a trip in the mountains.

He was not then at home, but his sister, who greeted me kindly as a former acquaintance, and the priest of Oroshi, did the honours of the house. But Oroshi without the Abbate is "Hamlet" without Hamlet, and Prenk Pasha was not yet due.

A Kthela zaptieh, off duty for a time, was on his way home—a dark, gay, boyish thing. I started off for Kthela with him as guide. He was a Kthela man, he said, but was originally of Kilmeni (Seltze). "A long time ago" a family had emigrated and settled in Kthela, and had now expanded into twenty houses, which are intermarriageable with the rest of Kthela. The track, a good one, led along the left bank of the Fani i vogel, over it and up the other side to the church-house of Blinishti, in the bariak of Kushneni.

The little old church is of the usual Mirdite pattern. The tiled roof projects at the end, and is supported on posts to form a large entrance-porch or verandah. A huge oak hard by was thickly covered with a species of mistletoe—not the English one. I asked about it in hopes of learning some superstition, but found it an object of no interest. From Blinishti we went on to Shpal—the church which is the gathering-point for all

Mirdita—and, descending again into the valley of the Fani, crossed it at Peshkes and struck up through wooded slopes for Kthela. A sad massacre of big oaks was going on. A tree is felled, and then the whole trunk is chopped down into one small, irregular plank. The track and the hillside were heaped with chips. A man was hard at work hacking the last felled giant. I vainly urged that a saw was very cheap, and that four or five planks at least could be made from one trunk—much more result for the labour. He and the Kthela men were cross at this, and said this was the proper way. They had always made planks like this, always would, and did not want to be interfered with. They had the right to do as they pleased with their own trees—which was unanswerable.

We rode through wood along the hillside, and, coming out of it at the end, saw all Kthela below us—a sea of forested hills in which scarce a house is visible. One great square-headed mountain, Mal Selatit, rose on the left. At its foot, said our guide, was a fortress of Lek Dukaghin, and beyond it, on the other side, the "city of Skenderbeg," ruins which few strangers have ever seen. His account was vague; he had been there, but it was very dangerous—all Moslems.

The priest of Kthela welcomed us. His house was very primitive, the short broad planks all axe-hewn, and his beehives, at the back, fenced round with ox and horse skulls on posts, "to keep off the evil eye," he said, laughing.

Kthela consists of three bariaks—Kthela, Selati, and Perlati. Kthela is all Catholic, the two others mixed. They border on Luria, and Islamism is spreading.

Kthela is chiefly forest, and lives largely by cattle-lifting. It had not accepted Constitution, asked doubtfully, " What is Constitution ? " and opined that if it were Turkish it was bad.

" Has the prison in Scutari been pulled down yet?"
they asked eagerly. " If it is true that Konstitutzioon
means that all the land is free, it will not be wanted
any more ! "

" But how can the Constitution punish a thief without a prison ? "

" Chop off his hand," said every one promptly.

" That is very cruel," said I.

" Not half so bad as prison. He has stolen with his
right hand. Very well. Chop it off, but do not take
away his freedom." (I have even met priests who upheld
this theory. Knowledge of Turkish prisons makes it not
so extraordinary as it appears.) " If Konstitutzioon
means prisons—down with it."

Our lively guide explained to me, before an applauding
audience, that, so far, Konstitutzioon was a dead failure.
" It promised to give us roads, and railways, and schools,
and to keep order and justice. We have had it two
whole months, and it has done none of these things. We
have given our *besa* till St. Dimitri, and if it has not done
them by then—good-bye Konstitutzioon ! "

I said no Government, however good, could do all
these things in the six weeks left. They shouted me down.

" It could if it chose. A Government can do just as
it likes, or it is not a Government."

I urged the cost—railways, for example.

" Railways, dear lady, cost nothing. They are always
made by foreign companies."

" Schools cost thousands of piastres—the house, the
master, books."

"Schools in all civilised lands cost nothing. They
are all free. The Government pays for them."

" In England," I said, "we have to pay a great deal
for schools."

They retorted that the English Government must be
bad, and they did not want a poor one like that. I said,

firmly, that every other land had to pay for all these things, and Albania must too, or go without. But one of the party knew as a fact that, in Austria and Italy, the Government built most beautiful things and paid for them itself.

In despair, and thinking it was a subject they could understand, I pointed out that it would take more than six weeks to organise gendarmerie to keep order in all Albania. They were indignant, and said they did not want Turkish zaptiehs in their land, were not afraid of them, and would defend their kulas even against artillery.

" But you say you want a good Government and law and order. How can order be kept without zaptiehs or a prison ? "

" By the Konstitutzioon."

I fell back exhausted from the unequal combat, and they triumphed.

" When all is set in order," they said, " when we have " (here followed a list of all required to fit out a first-class Power and a small Utopia), " then, if we are quite satisfied, it would be right for us to pay a little tax. But it would be silly to pay for a thing before we know how we liked it. If Konstitutzioon is not rich enough to do these things, it can go to the devil—the sooner the better."

I was filled with sorrow for this child-people, helpless before the problems of grown-up life. Loyal, capable of much hero-worship, they would follow to the death a Prince in whom they believe ; but of this intangible, invisible Konstitutzioon, they understood, and could understand, nothing.

It is hard to be hurled from somewhere about the fourth century, at latest, into the twentieth, without one breathing-space. I asked myself doubtfully whether Konstitutzioon understood them any better than they did it. Above all, I was anxious that by no futile and ill-timed revolt they should damn themselves in the eyes of Western politicians, to whom the blessed word Constitution seems to be a sort of Morison pill to cure all evils.

Time did not permit further wandering in Kthela. I left it for Robigo, where, said the priest, I should find good quarters at the Franciscan's. The Kthela lad volunteered to guide us again. Passing through Rsheni, where there is a flourishing school—due to the energy of the local priest—we descended to the Fani i vogel, followed it, and crossed it just above its junction with the Fani i madh (which is, I believe, the same river whose source I saw on the Chafa Malit, under a different name). Here there is a piece of debatable land, claimed both by Mirdita and the tribes of the Alessio Mountains, over which there has been so much bloodshed, that for the time being it has been left by both, and the trees have grown tall and fine. Then we pounded along the shingly half-dried bed of the united Fanis till, as evening was closing in, we saw the church of Robigo high on a crag above the river, approached it on the wrong side, found no track in the dim light, and scrambled up on foot.

I was extremely surprised on the top to find a large block of buildings, and not at all surprised to be met by a stern and foreign Franciscan and the word " *clausura*." It was a friary, and he could do no other than refuse me admission. My faithful guides were horrified. As usual with Albanians, they cared no pin for Church rule when it ran counter to Albanian custom. Hospitality to a stranger guest was a sacred duty. To refuse it was an outrage on the Albanian people. They told the foreign Franciscan their opinion of him. They would, I believe, have spoken in like manner to the Pope himself. I was anxious only to go and find other shelter before it was pitch-dark.

The foreign Franciscan, naturally, remained unmoved

by the tale of my many virtues and the quantities of ecclesiasts much higher than himself who were only too glad to know me. But he sent a boy to guide us to possible quarters.

We forded the river in the dark, and stumbled along

Fireplace
Mirdita.
M.E. Durham 1905

to a large house, whose owner received us at once, lamenting only that he had not been warned in time to make preparations. To all he had we were welcome. A ladder in the dark led us to a great cavernous room devoid of all furniture and lighted only by the fire that blazed beneath the huge hood that reached from the raftered roof to within some three feet of the floor. We sat round it with the large family. Our host was very angry at my rejection by the friary. I said in vain that they could not do otherwise. It was an insult, he said, to Albanian hospitality. He made broad remarks on the celibacy of the clergy, heard with great interest of all our wanderings, but only returned to rage that I should have gone so far and have been insulted at Robigo. Nor would he look on it in any other light.

We sat on the floor and supped around the *sofra*. He pointed out his eldest daughter, a nice-looking girl of sixteen. She ought, by now, to be married, he said. He betrothed her as a child. The marriage day had been fixed. Priest and bridegroom were all ready, and then she said she would not have him. She had never seen him before. The priest refused to marry them without her consent. Her parents had tried to force her. The bridegroom had then gallantly offered to release her without demanding blood, saying very sensibly, that he did not want a wife who did not want him, and that she could marry whom she pleased so far as he was concerned — the only case I met in which a reasonable view was taken of a girl's refusal. Marko, who has enlightened views on the subject, suggested that child betrothals must generally cause trouble. But the father maintained, " She must marry according to my pleasure and not for hers." When it was sleep-time they gave me a *yorgan* to lie on. But the rest of the company simply lay down on the boards anywhere, and slept.

Next morning early saw us on the way to Alessio, riding down the left bank of the Fani, and passing, on the way, its junction with the Mati. Our lively zaptieh cheered the route with an instructive tale of the siege of a certain kula we passed, by soldiers from Scutari sent to collect cattle-tax. The tax had been, so the district thought, exorbitantly raised. The district already paid some. The headman was bound to resist. " So the soldiers were sent. As I am a zaptieh, I had to go too.

What did I do? Oh, of course all we zaptiehs fired in the air. We were all on the man's side. We had to go because we were told." He roared with laughter. Aided thus by the zaptiehs, the tax-collecting expedition naturally failed.

By noon the wonder-world of the mountains was left behind us; we rode out on to the plain—into the common-place—and stopped at Miloti, a pretty village, where its charming old priest at once invited us in. We had a festive lunch with the old gentleman, who was grieved to hear about the Robigo adventure, and, to my surprise, thought the friary had acted wrongly. We parted here with our friend of Kthela, no more guiding being required; but our courteous old host insisted on having his horse saddled and riding with us as far as the ford. He waited till we reached the other side, waved farewell, and rode away.

We followed the *kaldrmi* through Shenkol to Alessio, I remembering the track as one does a bad dream. Four years before I had crawled and staggered along it on foot, through mud and water, half starved. One broken-down hut recalled to me vividly how I had thought there that I could go no farther, and knew that I must.

The theory of beating the boundaries is correct. There is nothing like pain for stamping minute details ineradicably in the mind.

Alessio had improved since my last visit, and had a "hotel"—humble, it is true, but the bed was clean and the supper good. Alessio was much excited. Prenk Pasha had arrived that very morning at Medua, been met by a large party, and had gone to Scutari. Events were likely to march, and we must march too.

And to Scutari we hastened next morning.

CHAPTER XII

THE RETURN OF PRENK PASHA

"Hail to the Chief who in triumph advances!"

THE return of Prenk Pasha to his people was the final act in the great drama of the Coming of the Constitution.

The other Christian tribes had light-heartedly rejoiced, filled only with child-like belief that any change must be for the better, and a wild hope that some Power was about to intervene and save them. Mirdita and Kthela alone hung back, silent, cautious. They would not exchange their little lamp of liberty for the patent flarelight of the New Constitution, till they felt satisfied of the truth of its much-advertised advantages. Others sang and fired volleys; the men of the Mirdite mountains remained dumb among their rocks.

"The Mirdites are coming to-morrow," said Rumour— "on Thursday—on Saturday—one day next week." But they gave no sign. Then the Djimiet (Young Turk Committee) in Scutari became anxious and annoyed. It believed that a brain, and a canny one, was responsible. The Young Turk is the son of the Old Turk, and the Djimiet thought to attain its end by assuming a bullying attitude. It sent a letter to the Archbishop of Scutari, bidding him inform the Abbot of the Mirdites that if his tribe did not at once come down to Scutari and accept the Constitution, he must take the consequences. To this the astute Abbot replied, with the courtesy for which he is renowned, that, in the first place, he was not under the Archbishop of Scutari; in the second, he was possessed of purely spiritual power; he therefore could not interfere in temporal affairs; the Mirdites, of course, *had* a Prince, but he, most unfortunately, was in Constantinople, and there was no one to command them. He added that it had never been the custom of the Mirdites to meet in Scutari, but always at the centre point of the tribe, the old Church of Shpal (St. Paul).

The Djimiet realised of a sudden that even Young Turks make mistakes sometimes, communicated at once with Constantinople, and, after nearly thirty years of exile, Prenk Pasha was returned to his native land, almost as fast as it was possible to send him.

The Abbot had conquered. The excitement was great. The Moslems of Scutari were furious—talked of shooting Prenk when he arrived. But the Christians were filled with a great joy. The-Man-that-was-born-to-be-Prince was coming, and all would be well. I learned much of the Divine right of Kings—the mediæval faith that put the fate of a people in one man's hands. Of Prenk Pasha himself, folk could tell me nothing at all. They were uncertain even whether he could still speak Albanian. But of his capacity to rule, to set wrong right, they had no shadow of a doubt. "He is the son of Bib Doda, and the blood of the Dukaghins is in his veins."

The restoration of an exiled Prince to his people in a wild, mediæval land—in the twentieth century—was an event that for dramatic interest could have no rival. It cried to me, and I went.

The gathering of the tribesmen was fixed for September 30, 1908. Prenk Pasha was to be two days on the way.

Marko and I left early, so as to be well ahead, and rode over the parched plain and through the shrunken Drin, which was yet deep enough to flow over the tops of my boots, though I twisted my feet up as high as they would go.

We pulled up at the *han* at Naranchi, on the borders of Mirdita. The *hanjee*, a Scutarene, was all agog with the approaching event. The men of Mnela, the border village of the Dibri bariak, were coming in force to hail and escort their chief.

In another half-hour down they trooped at a double, all of a pack, firing as they came—small, dark men for the most part, wiry and eager—the most notorious robbers and skilled cattle-lifters of the district. Rattle, clatter, over the loose stones, followed their priest—a long, black figure, on a strong, white horse. The wall of a ruined cottage, burnt for blood, served as a look-out post, whence the Mnela men took it in turn to scan the plain anxiously. The rest sat, as is their wont, in a circle, and debated the coming event.

At first sight of the distant cavalcade there was a great cry, and a party rushed off to meet it. The remainder drew up in rude order by the wayside—tense, listening. Distant shots — the replying ones — he is coming, he is coming! In a cloud of white smoke, and the dan-dan-dan of the rifle-shots, Prenk Pasha—befezzed, and in uniform gold-corded—cantered up on a white horse with his escort, drew rein, and threw himself from the saddle. A roar of rifles rang out, as Mnela, in a solid mass, fired over our heads. And then it was obvious that Prenk Pasha was a stranger in the land. He recoiled, deafened from what, to the tribesmen and myself—for I had been under fire on and off for two months—was only a pleasing exhilaration.

Prenk Pasha had arrived. There was a certain irony about the fact that the man who had left as a prisoner— treacherously kidnapped on board a Turkish warship— was now returning to the land of his birth, in Turkish uniform, as aide-de-camp to the Sultan, and attended by two Turkish guardian angels—Young Turks in officers' uniforms.

The halt was short. It was already late. We remounted. The Pasha, with his cousin, Kapetan Marko,
and his escort, pushed on, I following, up the valley of
the Gjadri. We were stopped to receive hospitality at
the house of a headman—the most celebrated cattle-lifter
of them all—where we sat on a scarlet carpet, drank *rakia*,
and ate tepid mutton with our fingers, the Young Turks
kindly pulling off lumps from the main animal for me.

The Pasha showed no desire to prolong this meal.
We remounted, and hustled up the mountain-side
towards Mnela as fast as the shades of night allowed.
The sun had gone down sullen in a purple storm-cloud,
leaving blood-red gashes over the indigo mountains. We
clattered up a zigzag—I following the white horse in
front of me, that showed as a luminous spot in the
gloom—till we saw the sudden red blaze of beacon fire,
beyond the small oak wood that hid the priest's house.

It was an unusually large house; but even so I do
not know how guests, escort, and servants all crowded
into it—but they did.

I dined in state with Prenk Pasha, Kapetan Marko,
the Padre, and the two guardian angels.

The Pasha, like a man in a dream, overwhelmed by a
whirl of half-remembered, half-forgotten bygones, paced
the room uneasily, too much excited to eat. "What
tricks I played here when I was young!" he said, half
dazed, "and now all the old generation are gone! I know
no one—no one." He broke off abruptly, and I thought
of "The Man that was." "You know, Mademoiselle,"
he added, with a laugh, "it is said that they are all
robbers, and I am a robber chief!"

The Young Turks were hungry, and did justice to the
boiled mutton. They were Djimiet young men, and held
golden views of the Constitution. Not having been up
country themselves, they were most anxious to hear how
I had found things. One was fluent in French; we got

on well. I told of the state of things at Djakova and
Luria, and the views of Kosovo vilayet.

He was rather taken aback. The idea of possible
difficulties surprised him.

"The plan was," he said, "to send Hodjas to the
mosques, all through Ramazan, to explain liberty and
equality to the people—all would be arranged. They
were only ignorant."

I suggested that ignorance was one of the most
dangerous of enemies, and reflected that the preaching of
the Hodjas would not mend matters—which was the case.
It was even then Ramazan, the towns swarmed with
Hodjas, and that Ramazan was the worst on record for
years.

"Alors vous trouvez Mademoiselle que notre Constitution n'a pas encore réussi?" he asked naively.

"Succeeded!" said I. "How can a Constitution succeed in a few weeks? You have not begun yet. All the
difficulties now begin. There are the Serbs, the Albanians,
the Bulgarians, the Turks, the Greeks, the Vlahs, who all
are of different temperaments and have quite different
ideas. It is true that they all disliked the old Government, but if they will like the new one—that is quite
another thing. The Albanian question, for example, is
of great difficulty, and needs quite special treatment."

"Oh mon Dieu, mon Dieu," said he, "il faut arranger
quelquechose." He harped a great deal on the Albanians.
England's help was what he reckoned on. If only England would help. He was very young, and, according to
his own account, had not been much in the interior of
his country at all.

The blessed word Constitution seemed to be to him a
sort of talisman, certain to put all right. But it leaked
out later that, in spite of his optimism, he was aware
that there were "flies in the ointment." He became
confidential.

" After you had left, Mademoiselle," he said, " a certain Englishman arrived here. He, like you, wished to go up to Djakova and Prizren. We discussed if we should send him, and decided to send him with a guard of suvarris." He looked at me interrogatively.

" That," said I wickedly—for I knew perfectly well what escorts are for—" was not necessary. Under your Constitution all is peace, is it not? For myself, I have travelled everywhere without arms or escort in those parts without difficulty."

We looked at one another. He knew that I knew—and I knew that he knew, and he said sweetly: " That is true, but see, Mademoiselle, this was a little affair of politics. It appears that this Monsieur was the secretary of a political society, very powerful, which has even worked much for Bulgarians. Therefore we thought it better he should travel with an escort. Vous comprenez, n'est pas ? "

" Perfectly," said I.

" And," he continued triumphantly, " it appears that we succeeded even marvellously. All that he saw impressed him so well that already he has held a conference about our Constitution, full of enthusiasm." We both laughed. All the world's a stage. I wondered if I were watching the last scenes of a farce or the beginning of a great tragedy. The Constitution seemed the link that joined the sublime and the ridiculous.

Prenk Pasha wisely made no remarks.

At Kalivaci, where I pulled up at the *han* at noon next day, the farcical element predominated. Marko and I, not wishing to cumber the Pasha's train, had started early by another trail.

The *hanjee*, flushed and excited, was swinging by his arms from a beam over his gateway.

" Don't come here," he cried ; " I can do nothing for you. Prenk Pasha is coming to-day, and I am quite drunk."

On learning that we should be satisfied with the loan of a cooking-pot, a fire, and some water, he asked us in, and dropped from his beam, and, while Marko blew up the fire, which was in the yard, and warmed up the remains of yesterday's lunch, told us that he had been thirty years in this place, and had twelve packhorses. Had tried to do a little business exporting sumach and hides, and importing sugar and coffee, but had suffered greatly. Whenever the pay of the Mirdite zaptiehs was in arrears (and, as it depends on the Turkish Government, this is often the case), they close the road, and "hold up" all goods upon it till the pay is forthcoming. They were quite honest, he said, and always returned the goods, but the hides were often ruined by a fortnight's detention—not to speak of loss of work through delaying the horses along with them.

"But now Prenk Pasha is coming. We shall have law and order, and all will go well. I'm going to be drunk and happy all day."

He sat and beamed on us, but refused a glass of our *rakia* on the grounds that he was quite drunk enough, and did not mean to be too drunk to greet Prenk Pasha with gunshots when he arrived.

We left with many promises to return some day when he was sober, and dine sumptuously; and, leaving the valley, struck up over hills that, thick with sumach scrub, blazed in a glory of gold and crimson against the intense blue of the mountains beyond; for the sumach, one of Mirdita's chief exports, lives usefully and dies beautifully.

At even we came to the church of Kacinari, high on the hillside. The priest was not yet home, but the cavernous, black-raftered kitchen was full of company. We sat round a great fire that burnt in the middle of the floor; while one tinkled music on a tamboritza, another roasted coffee and turned the fragrant seeds, smoking and black and shiny, on to the carved shovel-shaped tray to cool—and all talked.

Mirdita did not mean to give itself away. Would accept no Moslem rule; brook no interference with its privileges, and was in no mood for conciliation, for the Catholics, so cruelly persecuted last winter and spring (1907-1908) near Djakova and Prizren, were, for the most part, of Mirdite blood. Mirdita had been on the point of descending to protect and avenge them, and would have done so by now had it not been for the universal *besa*, which it could not refuse to swear, all other tribes having accepted it. All their hopes were centred now on Prenk Pasha. As for the Constitution, it was only one more Moslem trick, " a flam of the Devil." European intervention was the only possible cure.

Our host, two more large priests, and one small Franciscan came in soon, all bound for Shpal on the morrow.

September 30th dawned bright and breezy. We started early, the Franciscan heaped up on a wonderfully active donkey, the rest of us on horseback, and all the men of Kacinari trailing snake-like after us over hill and dale. Our journey was neatly timed. We arrived at the trysting-place just before the Pasha. The wood round the little church, the heart of Mirdita, was full of tethered horses; the bare hillside beyond, crowded with Mirdites, grouped according to their bariaks. The men and boys of Prenk Pasha's house stood foremost, anxious and eager for the first glimpse of their Head. And the man upon whom all hopes hung came at the head of his escort, upon his white horse, and rode around the great gathering. A mighty cry arose. Some thousand bullets ripped with a tearing swish between the hills as he passed.

The impossible had happened; the Prince had returned to his people. He dismounted with the air

of one that knows not if he be asleep or awake.   It is
hard to be called on suddenly to play the part of a
demi-god.

We thronged into the wood, where, under a great
tree, was spread a carpet.   He took his seat upon a
chair, his crimson fez making a brilliant blot on the
greenleaf background.   Then all his male relatives—
many born since he was exiled—were presented to him.
I thought of the Forest of Arden, where they "fleeted the

Kisha Shpalit   Church of S' Paul Mirdita

time pleasantly as in the Golden Age"—as each in turn
strode up, "an hero beauteous among all the throng"
dropped on one knee, and did homage, kissing his
chieftain's hand with simple dignity.   The tribesmen
stood around in a great circle, the sunflecks dancing
on their white clothes, and glinting on gunbarrel and
cartridge-belt.

There came a pause.   Nature, exhausted by emotion,
needed food; moreover, it was midday.   I shared a cold
sheep's liver with the two Young Turks, who, though it
was Ramazan, made each a hearty lunch, as was noted by
the tribesmen with contempt, for a Mirdite holds that to

break a fast is the one unpardonable sin. The red wine
flowed, and the cold mutton was hurled about in lumps.
A few minutes emptied the bottles and bared the
bones.

We awaited the coming of the Abbate. Mirdita without the Abbate is "Hamlet" without the central figure.
Nor had we long to wait. His gold-banded cap shone
over the heads of the crowd, that parted and let him
through on his fat white horse, gay with a gold saddle-
cloth, followed by the rest of the priests of Mirdita.

We went out on to the bare hillside. There was
no room among the trees for the great concourse now
assembled. The men of the five bariaks—Oroshi, Fandi,
Spachi, Kusneni, and Dibri—and the neighbour tribe
of Kthela squatted or knelt in a huge and dense
circle.

It struck me suddenly that among some two thousand
five hundred armed men I was the solitary petticoat.
The Young Turks and I were the only anachronisms—
blots on the old-world picture. The Abbate stepped into
the middle, and spoke with a great voice that rang over
the land. His words were weighty—"The Constitution
was the will of the Sultan. Mirdita would remain loyal
to him—but would retain, as before, her privileges, and
be self-governed according to the Canon of Lek Dukaghin
—from this day forth those laws would be truly enforced.
Blood-vengeance was to cease. Peace was to be sworn
until Ash Wednesday, 1909, by which time all bloods
were to be pacified; and hereafter any ·man that kills
another shall be banished, not only from Mirdita, but
from all Albania. Robbery between the tribes was
to be stopped, and the law enforced (for one thing
stolen two should be returned), even were it necessary
to summon three battalions from Scutari to help to
enforce it."

Prenk Pasha briefly confirmed the Abbate's speech;

Kapetan Marko stepped forward and emptied his revolver over us ; the circling crowd fired in return, and broke up at once into the five bariaks, which withdrew—each with its priests—to discuss the momentous announcement.

It was a very momentous announcement. I could only admire the skill and policy of the Abbate, who, after working for fifteen long years with all the means in his power to cleanse the land of the curse of blood in vain, had seized this supreme moment in the tribes' existence —the return of the man whom they were born to obey—to make a bold effort to crown his labour and wipe out the custom finally and for ever. If he succeeded, this day was the end of the old life, its sins and sorrows.

The Mirdites are a silent people. The meetings of other tribes are a continuous roar, as each shouts the other down. But there was no clamour from the five groups that discussed in earnest undertones the question of " to be or not to be." How was a man to keep his honour clean if he might not shoot? vexed many an honest soul. It is better to die, said they, than to live dishonoured. It seemed doubtful, very doubtful, if the tribe, as a whole, would accept the terms that had taken but a few moments to explain. Finally, hereditary loyalty to the Chief triumphed over private passions—each priest came forward and announced that his flock was agreed. Peace was proclaimed till Ash Wednesday, 1909, and by then ways and means were to be determined.

The five bariaks spread again in a great circle. The Abbate had triumphed. He stood erect in the centre, ordering with uplifted arm the final volleys, as the Pasha rode round acclaimed by all.

The great meeting was over, the white groups melted away, like snow on the mountains. The Pasha, the Abbate, and all the chief actors in the scene filed in long procession down to the valley of the Fani i vogel, on their way to the Abbate's Palace at Oroshi. Soon none were left on the historic spot, but the dead asleep in the lonely graveyard. A chill wind arose, and the autumn leaves fell in showers. For better or for worse, a page had been turned in Albania's history. The summer had gone, the year was dying. I had seen the Land of the Living Past.

EPILOGUE

"For the surest way to prevent Seditions is to take away the Matter of them. For if Fuell be prepared it is hard to tell whence the Spark shall come that shall set it on Fire. The Matter of Seditions is of Two kindes—Much Poverty and Much Discontent."

EVENTS moved fast. Already the Moslems suspected that Constitution was an attack on their religion. Throughout Ramazan they ran through the Christian quarters at night, yelling, beating on doors, breaking lamps. The Young Turk Committee when appealed to was powerless. The old troops had all left. Their pay, by the way, was "borrowed" from the Christians, who "lent" it lest their shops should be looted. The new recruits had but just come in, and were all undrilled. Police force there was none sufficient. A crowd of Moslems demanded the closing of the club the Christians had just opened. The Young Turks admitted the club's right to exist, but ordered its closure, unable, in truth, to protect it.

Austria annexed Bosnia. This still further incensed the Moslems both against the Catholics (who are nominally under Austrian protection) and against the Young Turks for submitting to it.

Three times rumours came in that war had begun. "Let it come," said every one, "no matter where or with whom." War might smash up the new régime. On one point Christian and Moslem agreed; Albania had never yet entirely accepted Turkish rule, and would not be cheated out of its rights by Young Turks. "It would be a second Turkish conquest."

It was hoped at first that Constitution really meant some reform. When the Christians found things worse than before, their hopes faded. One special "reform" hoped for was that among those to be arrested and made to disgorge their plunder, would be Ezzad Bey, called the "tyrant of Tirana," of whom in the neighbourhood of Tirana I heard much complaint. He was "abroad for his health." Folk said he would not dare return. When the revolution had been effected, however, he returned and announced that he was on the Young Turk side, and was put on the Committee of Union and Progress. This shook folks' faith as to the beneficial nature of the progress to be made.

The elections drew near. The electoral district of Scutari includes nearly all the Christian tribes, and, at a moderate computation, there are two Christians to one Moslem. When this transpired, the authorities proceeded to disqualify Christians in numbers. The mountain men then sent deputies to the Archbishop. He called a large meeting of town and mountain Christians, which debated two days. He then telegraphed to the Grand Vezir and the Djimiets at Constantinople, Saloniki, and Monastir, asking only for a fair count. He received no reply at all. But a telegram was sent to the Vali, bidding him proceed with the election. The Archbishop asked to see the telegram, and was refused. He called to speak with the Vali, and was not admitted.

Next day a ballot-box was sent to the Cathedral grounds, and the Christians were told to vote. They replied that as the result was a foregone conclusion, and the electorate had not been chosen according to the rules of the Constitution, they would not. Also all notices about the election had been given out in Turkish—understood by very few, and not in the language of the people, as set forth by the rules. Two Moslems were elected. I asked why further protest had not been made, and was told: "This is the first election, and will be the last. Why trouble?"

Others lamented bitterly, saying, "But a few weeks ago we were so happy. We thought at last justice would be done. Fools that we were. Cursed be he that putteth his faith in a Turk. The wolf can change his hair, but not his habits."

National development and fair play had been hoped for. But when Dervish Hima, a well-known Albanian literary man, returned to Scutari after a long absence in Europe, he was arrested for speaking of the hopes of Albania and thrown into prison. There was no Albanian nation, said the new Government; all were Ottomans.

No Albanian will call himself an Ottoman. Dervish Hima made such an admirable defence that the court could not convict him. He was sent to Saloniki for re-trial, and finally, after much delay, acquitted. But the affair made a very bad impression.

About this time the Greeks pointed out that, according to the broken Berlin Treaty, certain lands round Janina should be Greek. The Turks then called on the Albanian nation, whose existence they had before denied, to defend their lands.

Meanwhile the unlucky fifteen Shala and Shoshi men, arrested in the first week of Constitution, had been over two months untried in prison. Appeals to the Djimiet, pointing out they had broken no law, elicited only the reply, "No time to attend to it."

Finally the mountain men, furious, threatened to descend on the town and force their release. They were then set free. But it was too late to restore the shattered faith of the tribes.

"Why," I was asked on all sides, "do the English people, who have a hundred times declared the Turk unfit to rule, believe he has changed his whole nature in twenty-four hours? Why, after holding out hopes to the Balkan peoples, do they now rejoice to nail us once more under the Turk? Why should we suffer because it suits British politics that the Turk should remain?"

"Give us a protectorate such as Crete has, under which we can become autonomous," said Albania eagerly. (Crete was then reckoned free and safe.)

"The Constitution is but a temporary affair that will not ultimately upset our plans," said Bulgaria sweetly.

"We shall support it till we are quite ready to move, and not a moment longer," said Greece decidedly.

"Its existence would be the ruin of all our national hopes," said Servia and Montenegro sadly.

"England has betrayed us!" cried all the Balkan peoples aghast: "where are those Liberal friends in whom we believed, and who urged each of us in turn 'to go in and win'?"

"We have the whole German army behind us, and shall take what we please. *You* (England) can do nothing!" cried Austria jubilant.

It was not until I came to London in December (1908) that I met people who really believed in "Konstitutzioon."

In the Balkan Peninsula, as elsewhere, the fittest survive in the struggle for existence. The next few years should be interesting.

I cannot write

FINIS

for the END is not yet.

INDEX

Printed by Ballantyne, Hanson & Co.
Edinburgh & London

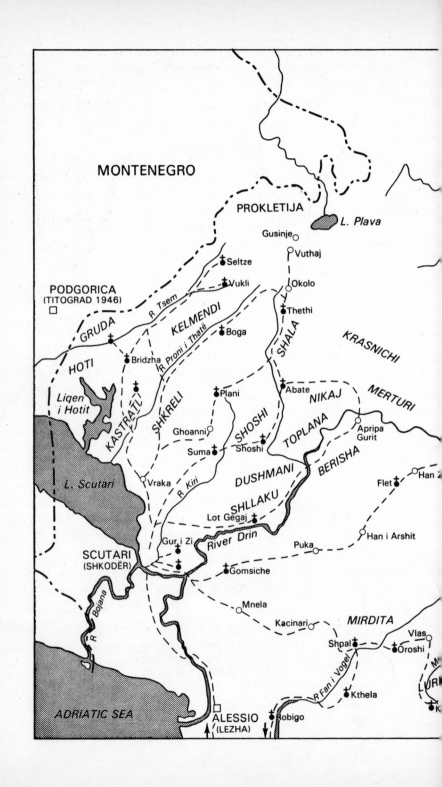

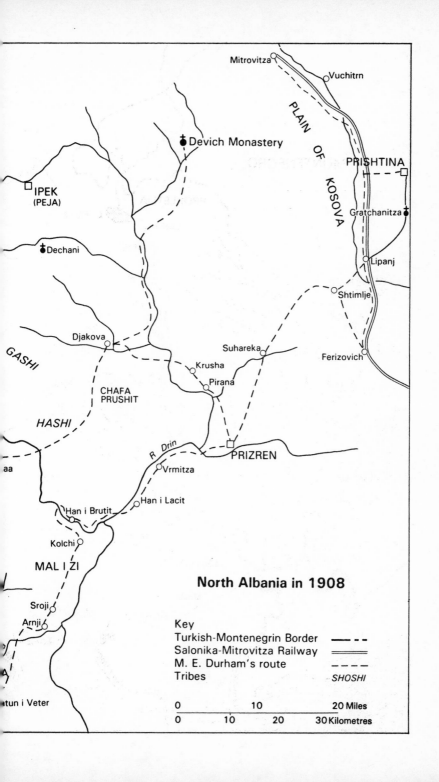

Mitrovitza

Vuchitrn

PLAIN OF KOSOVA

Devich Monastery

PRISHTINA

IPEK (PEJA)

Gratchanitza

Dechani

Lipanj

Djakova

Shtimlje

GASHI

Suhareka

Ferizovich

Krusha

CHAFA PRUSHIT

Pirana

HASHI

R. Drin

PRIZREN

aa

Vrmitza

Han i Lacit

Han i Brutit

Kolchi

MAL I ZI

North Albania in 1908

Sroji

Arnji

Key

Turkish-Montenegrin Border — - -

Salonika-Mitrovitza Railway =====

M. E. Durham's route — — —

Tribes   *SHOSHI*

tun i Veter

0		10		20 Miles

| 0 | | 10 | | 20 | | 30 Kilometres |